# Abu Salabikh Excavations
## Volume 3

# CATALOGUE OF
# EARLY DYNASTIC POTTERY

By Jane Moon

BRITISH SCHOOL OF ARCHAEOLOGY IN IRAQ
1987

# ABU SALABIKH EXCAVATIONS

General Editor: J.N. Postgate

Volumes published

Printed in England by
Stephen Austin and Sons Ltd, Hertford

ISBN 0 903472 11 2

# CONTENTS

*To the memory of*
*Major A. G. Moon, 1893-1985*

# INTRODUCTION

This catalogue deals with Early Dynastic pots excavated at Abu Salabikh between 1975 and 1983. Pottery of other periods is being dealt with separately, though some slightly earlier forms of conical bowl and one or two other vessels are included here for comparison. No reference is made to material from the 1963 and 1965 excavations by the Oriental Institute of the University of Chicago. Work at Abu Salabikh is still continuing and we hope it will go on for some time, but it was decided to make available now the ceramic evidence which has been collected so far, leaving that from subsequent seasons for later.

Over several years of studying Abu Salabikh pottery I have reached the conclusion that whole pots and sherds represent two largely distinct forms of information, offering different potential and requiring different treatment. As the sherd material is taking much longer to prepare for publication, only 'whole' pots are treated here, though the term is interpreted quite loosely, meaning roughly enough of a vessel to quote the original character of its complete form. General information from the sherds which is already available is included in the introductory remarks on each type.

I have tried to mention every 'whole pot' found up to the end of the 1983 season, with certain exceptions. Conical bowls, which occur as Mackay put it 'in embarassing quantities' (1925 p. 36) would require a volume of their own if each was to be included, so a representative selection has been made. Hand-made unbaked miniature vessels found in the Ash Tip are to be published with the other objects from this interesting context, in a separate volume. A few vessels require further processing and were not available for study at the time of writing; a list of these appears in Appendix A. No doubt further omissions will emerge in the course of time. Some of the pots which do appear here have been published before, but are repeated for the sake of completeness, and in some cases it has been possible to make changes to the drawings and measurements, mostly very minor. Where real discrepancies exist between previous publications and this one, this should be taken as the correct version. The form of the catalogue entries is explained in Appendix C.

*Provenances, dates, dating, and typology.*
The dates given as 'I', 'II', 'III', 'IIIA', 'IIIB' refer of course to the commonly used sub-divisions of the Early Dynastic period. While these have acknowledged shortcomings, the Abu Salabikh corpus alone does not justify the invention of a new system nor much elaboration of the old. No single corpus does. This exercise can only profitably be performed by reference to genuinely comparable assemblages. Of the older excavations on Sumerian sites only those in the Lower Diyala valley were conducted so as to produce such material, and these sites are too distant from Abu Salabikh to form an ideal starting point. This is not to suggest that comparisons with Ur, Kish, etc. should not be made, just that a thoroughgoing re-shuffle of our terminology is premature. The fixed points for applying the divisions of the Early Dynastic period to Abu Salabikh are given in Appendix B. Ultimately, the dates given represent what I think they ought to be, based primarily on context, and when this is dubious, on shape and style, taking into account parallels from Abu Salabikh and elswhere. The less satisfactory the context, the more open the dating is to argument. No pot from a good context should be *later* than stated; anything can be earlier than its findspot.

In order to study ancient pottery it is necessary to sort it, if only to provide a means of reference for other scholars. It is always worth keeping in mind that the divisions thus created are artificial and for our own convenience, not generic to the pottery itself. The types below are divided into large groups according to common salient characteristics e.g. single handles, round bases. Almost anyone else would probably prefer to arrange them differently, which is why the sections have been kept as broad as possible. Even so, anomalies and ambiguities are inevitable. Within the broad groups the vessels are arranged by body shape, again with anomalies, and again they could be re-shuffled in many ways.

Some of our dating, as mentioned, is open to future revision, so grouping by date has been avoided. It is the more satisfying when convincing chronological groups form themselves from the shape typology sometimes, as though one were watching Early Dynastic ceramic studies emerge from infancy and approach adolescence.

*Acknowledgements*
From 1975 to 1977 Carolyn Postgate was in charge of the Abu Salabikh pottery, helped in the first and third seasons by Roger Moorey and in the second and third by myself. Martha Patrick and Lucy Crowther did some of the drawing for the first two seasons, Robert Britton was professional draughtsman for the third. I assumed overall responsibility for the pottery in 1981, helped for both seasons of that year by Siriol Mynors, who was also in sole charge during 1978. In 1983 I benefited from general assistance by Tricia Fox and some professional drawing by Barbi Garfi. The form of the resulting volume and its shortcomings are mine, but it owes its very existence to the incredibly hard work and unlimited patience contributed by these people, usually under the most trying conditions.

The research needed to convert the pottery notes and field drawings into a book was carried out between 1983 and 1985 while in receipt of generous grants from the British School of Archaeology in Iraq. To Nicholas Postgate I owe permission to study and publish pottery from Abu Salabikh, and a lot of help and encouragement at all stages of doing so. Dr. Bahijah Khalil, Director of the Iraq Museum, has been generous with permission to study material housed in the Iraq Museum, despite unfavourable circumstances.

# CONICAL BOWLS

The conical bowl or 'Blumentopf' persists throughout the Early Dynastic levels at Abu Salabikh, growing smaller and shallower towards the end, as at every site where it is recorded in sufficient quantities to notice. This phenomenon has been much remarked upon, and it is hoped that the publication of the sherd corpus will incorporate more sophisticated statisticical information on conical bowl sizes, and include measurements for all profiles found. Some preliminary ones are given in Moon 1985 fig. 3.

The excavation has not produced any evidence either in favour of nor against the use of these mass-produced bowls as ration-bowls or for any specific purpose. It seems much more likely that such a common and cheap vessel was as versatile as its modern Iraqi counterpart, a shallow tin bowl of roughly similar proportions, which functions basically as a drinking-cup, but can double as almost anything else: lid, soap-dish or ashtray. Drinking-vessels are kept separate in practice, but do not have a special form.

Special functions are sometimes recognizable among the ancient vessels: a pair of conical bowls from Level II of the Area E sounding had holes in the side, maybe to fasten them together (nos. 93·and 94).

Some base fragments show clearly that the bowl had been used to store bitumen. Others have holes knocked through (like no. 66) to serve as funnels.

The manufacture of conical bowls does not seem to have merited much care: they usually have no surface finish and are often rough and lopsided. The manufacture of the pre-ED forms found on the West Mound, including the curious bevelled-rim variety (nos. 95-96) is discussed in Postgate and Moon 1982 (p. 110-113).

All conical bowls have string-cut base

1. **6G66:196**
   Ash Tip (Batch 433)
   Half base extant, less of rest.
   Pink clay.
   Buff surface.
   Grit temper.
   H. 5.3
   Rim di. c. 18.0
   Ba. di. (reconstruc.) 5.0

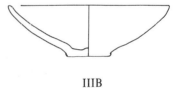

IIIB

2. **6G75:267** (AbS 2127)
   Grave 195 (Batch 3645)
   Intact but for small chip.
   Pink clay.
   Rather fine grit temper.
   H. 5.5
   Rim di. 15.8-16.1
   Ba. di. 4.8

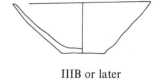

IIIB or later

3. **4J88:54** (AbS 2213)
   Grave 197 (Batch 4209)
   Intact but cracked and salted.
   Surface buff inside,
   red and buff outside.
   Grit temper.
   H. 8.2
   Rim di. 17.4
   Ba. di. 4.6

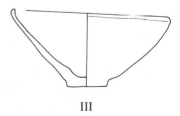

III

4. **6F05:158**
   Grave 182 (Batch 6015)
   Slightly chipped.
   Orange clay.
   Cream slip.
   Fine grit temper.
   H. 5.6
   Rim di. 13.6
   Ba. di. 4.1
   Blackened out on one side.

IIIA late

5. **6G47:112** (AbS 1604)
   Grave 126 (Batch 2551)
   Much of rim and body missing.
   Pink core.
   Perhaps cream slip.
   Grit and veg. temper.
   H. 5.0
   Rim di. c. 13.0
   Ba. di. 4.0

IIIA late

6. **6G76:602**
   Grave 146 (Batch 2633)
   About half extant.
   Red clay.
   White slip.
   Temper unknown.
   H. 5.5
   Rim di. 12.0
   Ba. di. 4.2

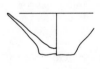

IIIB

7. SIMILAR: **6G37:117** (AbS 861)
                Grave 32 (No. 15)
                Condition and ware unknown.
                H. 5.0, rim di. 11.5, ba. di. 3.7    IIIB

8.              **6G63:296** (AbS 1278)
                Grave 79 (No. 5)
                Intact.
                Greenish clay, temper unknown.
                H. 5.4, rim di. 11.9, ba. di. 4.3    III

9. **2G46:74**
   Surface, probably from ED I wall (Batch 5520)
   Much of rim missing.
   Pink clay.
   Perfunctory cream slip.
   Fine grit and veg. temper.
   H. 4.5
   Rim di. (reconstruc.) 11.0
   Ba. di. 3.8
   [Postgate and Moon 1982:fig. 3. no. 12]

I

10. SIMILAR: **6G66:20** (AbS 415)
                 Ash Tip (Batch 406)
                 Intact.
                 Ware unknown (surface buff)
                 H. 6.4, rim di. 13.4, ba. di. 4.5
                 Bitumen staining.    IIIB

11.              **6G45:43** (AbS 1624)
                 Grave 143 (Batch 2915)
                 Intact.
                 Pink clay, grit temper.
                 H. 5.2, rim di. 11.9, ba. di. 4.8    IIIA-B

12. **6G85:43**
Grave 165 (Batch 1805)
Most of rim and much of body missing.
Red clay.
Cream slip out.
Sandy temper with occasional large grits.
H. 5.7
Rim di. c. 13.0-14.0
Ba. di. 4.2

IIIA

13. SIMILAR: **5I10:74** (AbS 404)
        Room 1 fill (Batch 1018)
        Complete.
        Ware unknown (surface cream)
        H. 7.7, rim di. 16.7, ba. di. unknown.    IIIA

14. **6G64:204** (AbS 387)
Room 46 fill (Batch 20)
Part of side missing.
Ware unknown (surface cream)
H. 7.5
Rim di. 14.4
Ba. di. 5.1
Bitumen staining.

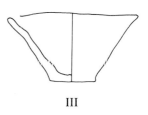

III

15. **6F05:23**
Grave 168 (Batch 6000)
Quarter of rim and some of body missing.
Red clay.
Paler surface out.
Sparse sandy temper.
H. 5.5
Rim di. c. 12.0
Ba. di. 4.0-4.4

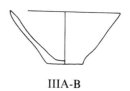

IIIA-B

16. SIMILAR: **5I21:258** (AbS 886)
        Pit in Room 6 east (Batch 1115)
        Small piece missing from body.
        Creamy yellow clay, spongey grit and veg. temper.
        H. 6.0, rim di. 11.6-12.6, ba. di. 4.0-4.2    III

17. **6G85:32**
Grave 165 (Batch 1805)
Half rim and some of body missing.
Pink clay.
Buff slip out.
Sandy temper.
H. 6.2
Rim di. 14.5
Ba. di. 4.5

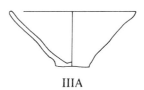

IIIA

18. **6G85:48**
Grave 165 (Batch 1805)
Intact.
Pink clay.
Cream slip.
Sandy temper.
H. 6.4
Rim di. 13.5
Ba. di. 4.0
Uneven.
Greyish discolouration on outer surface.

IIIA

19. **6G74:354**
    Grave 170 (Batch 687)
    Half of rim and body missing.
    Pink clay.
    Cream slip.
    Sparse temper of fine sand.
    H. 7.4
    Rim di. 14.4
    Ba. di. 5.2-5.8

IIIA late

20. **6F06:20**
    Grave 181 (Batch 6205)
    Base complete, and about half rest.
    Orange clay.
    Temper of veg. and a little grit.
    H. 7.2
    Rim di. 14.0
    Ba. di. 3.6-4.2

III

21. SIMILAR: **6G64:130** (AbS 388)
    Room 46 fill (Batch 20)
    Piece missing from rim.
    Ware unknown (surface cream)
    H. 6.7, rim di. 13.9, ba. di. 4.7
    Bitumen staining.    III

22.              **6G36:132** (AbS 1603)
    Room 119 fill (Batch 2417)
    Condition and ware unknown (except grit-tempered)
    H. 7.0, rim di. 12.6-14.0, ba. di. 4.0-4.5   III

23.              **6G36:45** (AbS 1602)
    Grave 117 (Batch 2414)
    Complete.
    Ware unknown (except cream slip)
    H. 7.0, rim di. 13.3-14.5, ba. di. 5.2   III

24. **6F05:148**
    Grave 183 (Batch 6012)
    Intact.
    Buff clay.
    Grit temper.
    H. 7.8
    Rim di. 13.2-13.9
    Ba. di. 4.6-5.0
    Blackened patch on one side.

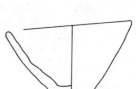

IIIA (mid?)

25. **6G84:9**
    Room 80 floors (Batch 1703)
    About half extant.
    Red clay.
    Buff slip.
    Sandy temper.
    H. 5.8
    Rim di. 11.6
    Ba. di. 4.5

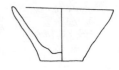

IIIA

26. **2G46:71**
    West Mound, near surface (Batch 5500)
    A third of rim and upper body missing.
    Pink clay.
    Buff slip out.
    Hard fine grit temper.
    H. 6.4
    Rim di. c. 13.0
    Ba. di. 5.0
    [Postgate and Moon 1982:fig. 3 no. 13]

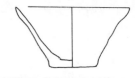

I

27. **6G75:200**
Grave 162 (Batch 3629)
Complete.
Soft red clay.
Veg. temper.
H. 7.6
Rim di. 13.8-14.2
Ba. di. 4.6-5.2

IIIA-B

28. **5I11:131**
Room 2 floor (Batch 1243)
Much of rim and body missing.
Brown clay (burnt?)
Fire-blackened surface.
Grit temper.
H. 8.1
Rim di. (reconstruc.) 16.5
Ba. di. 4.3-4.4

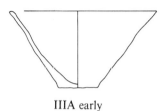

IIIA early

29. **6G65:321**
Ash pit, above Level 1a (no Batch number)
A quarter of rim and body missing.
Red clay.
Sandy temper.
H. 6.4
Rim di. 13.4-13.6
Ba. di. 4.2-4.6

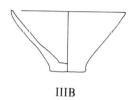

IIIB

30. SIMILAR: **6G37:104** (AbS 867)
Grave 38 (No. 40)
Large pieces missing from body.
Ware unknown.
H. 7.8, rim di. 12.4-13.4, ba. di. 4.4-4.8   IIIA

31. 　　　　**6G47:113** (AbS 1605)
Grave 126 (Batch 2551)
Piece missing from rim.
Pink clay, cream slip, fine grit temper.
H. 7.0, rim di. 13.8-14.2, ba. di. 3.6-4.0 IIIA late

32. **6G75:192**
Fill of Room 58 above Grave 162 (Batch 3627)
Half of upper part missing.
Soft red clay.
Veg. temper.
H. 6.9
Rim di. 14.0
Ba. di. 4.9

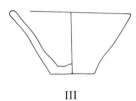

III

33. **6G84:37**
Large pit in Room 80 (Batch 1711)
Complete.
Loose red clay.
Grit and veg. temper.
H. 6.8
Rim di. 13.2
Ba. di. 4.8

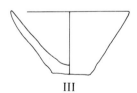

III

34. **6G84:41**
Grave 179 (Batch 1712)
Nearly half missing, but base intact.
Soft brownish clay.
Patchy white surface.
Sand and veg. temper.
H. 7.4
Rim di. 13.7
Ba. di. 4.2

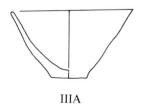

IIIA

35. **6G84:96**
    Grave 187 (Batch 1724)
    Nearly complete.
    Orange clay.
    Vestiges of buff slip.
    Grit and veg. temper.
    H. 7.4
    Rim di. 14.4-15.4
    Ba. di. 4.0-4.2

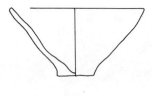

IIIA

36. **6G64:203** (AbS 383)
    Room 46 fill (Batch 20)
    Much of body missing.
    Ware unknown (cream surface)
    H. 7.8
    Rim di. 14.5
    Ba. di. 4.8
    Bitumen-stained.

III

37. SIMILAR: **6G64:128** (AbS 389)
            Room 46 fill (Batch 20)
            Intact.
            Ware unknown (cream surface)
            H. 8.0, rim di. 13.6, ba. di. 4.2    III

38. **6F05:176**
    Grave 183 (Batch 6012)
    Half rim missing.
    Orange clay.
    Vague buff slip.
    Grit and white grit temper.
    H. 7.0
    Rim di. 14.0
    Ba. di. 3.9-4.2

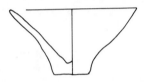

IIIA (mid?)

39. **6F05:175**
    Grave 183 (Batch 6012)
    Much of rim missing.
    Red clay.
    Cream slip out.
    Grit and black grit temper.
    H. 7.6
    Rim di. (reconstruc.) 14.0
    Ba. di. 5.2

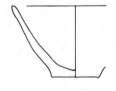

IIIA (mid?)

40. **5I98:134**
    Grave 205 (Batch 7420)
    Quarter of rim missing, gaps in body.
    White clay.
    Grit and veg. temper.
    H. 9.0
    Rim di. 13.7-15.0
    Ba. di. 5.0

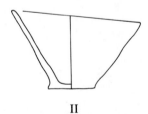

II

41. **4J97:294**
    Room 50, phase 4 floors
    (Batch 4473)
    Chip in rim and body.
    Pink clay.
    Sandy temper.
    H. 8.0
    Rim di. 14.1-14.5
    Ba. di. 3.7-3.8

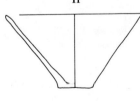

II

42. **5I98:154**
   Grave 205 (Batch 7420)
   Rim slightly chipped.
   Red clay.
   Sandy temper.
   H. 9.4
   Rim di. 15.5-16.4
   Ba. di. 4.5

II

43. SIMILAR: **6G38:109** (AbS 922)
   Grave 52 (No. 4)
   Intact.
   Red clay, fine grit temper.
   H. 9.5, rim di. 14.5-15.5, ba. di. 4.0-4.3   II

44. **6G62:70**
   Room 65, west wall (Batch 2214)
   Slightly chipped.
   Green clay.
   Grit temper.
   H. 9.2
   Rim di. 13.8
   Ba. di. 4.2-4.9

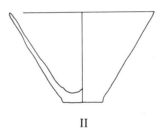

II or early IIIA

45. **5I89:25**
   Room 195 fill (Batch 7504)
   Half rim and body missing.
   Greenish clay.
   Sandy grit temper.
   H. 9.6
   Rim di. (reconstruc.) 16.0
   Ba. di. 4.3

II

46. SIMILAR: **6G37:80** (AbS 868)
   Grave 38 (No. 34)
   Base and part of side only.
   Red clay, fine sandy temper.
   H. 3.8, rim di. (reconstruc.) 16.8, ba. di. 4.3        II

47. **6G62:119**
   Room 65 west wall (Batch 2214)
   Half of rim and body missing.
   Red clay.
   Sandy temper.
   H. 8.8
   Rim di. 15.0
   Ba. di. 3.5-4.1

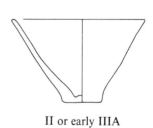

II or early IIIA

48. **5IS:278**
   Grave 193 (Batch 5385)
   Rim slightly chipped.
   Red clay.
   Buff slip out.
   Fine grit temper.
   H. 9.2
   Rim di. 15.4
   Ba. di. 5.0-5.2

II

49. SIMILAR: **6G37:69** (AbS 904)
   Grave 38 (No. 36)
   Scant profile.
   Red clay, vague buff slip, sand and fine veg. temper.
   H. 9.8, rim di. (reconstruc.) 15.4, ba. di. 4.7-4.9
   Fire-blackened out.    II

50. SIMILAR: **6G37:73** (AbS 869)
  Grave 38 (No. 37)
  About a third of rim and body missing.
  Red clay, grey core, buff slip,
  temper of sand and fine veg.
  H. 9.0, rim di. 15.6, ba. di. 4.8-5.1   II

51. **4J97:227**
  Grave 208 (Batch 4449)
  Half rim and body missing.
  Pink clay.
  Sandy temper.
  H. 8.2
  Rim di. 12.6
  Ba. di. 4.6
  One side smoked out.

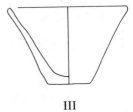

III

52. SIMILAR: **5I10:70** (AbS 883)
  Room 2 fill (Batch 1015)
  Piece missing from rim.
  Pink clay, vague buff slip, fine grit and veg. temper.
  H. 6.5, rim di. 11.0, ba. di. 3.2-3.4
  Very neatly made.   IIIA

53. **4J97:318**
  Room 50 phase 2 floors (Batch 4451)
  Nearly half rim and body missing.
  Pink clay.
  Sandy temper.
  H. 6.4
  Rim di. 9.9
  Ba. di. 3.2-3.3

III

54. **3G81:230**
  Uruk floor running under
  plano-convex brick wall (Batch 5602)
  Very little of rim and body.
  Red clay.
  Buff slip.
  Grog and grit temper.
  H. 6.7
  Rim di. c. 10.0
  Ba. di. 3.8
  [Postgate and Moon 1982:fig. 3 no. 10]

Uruk

55. **5I98:85**
  Grave 205 (Batch 7420)
  Rim slightly chipped.
  Pink clay.
  Sandy grit temper.
  H. 9.6
  Rim di. 16.4-17.0
  Ba. di. 5.0
  Scratches inside.

II

56. **4J97:313**
  Room 50, inside storage jar
  no. 443 (Batch 4475)
  Intact.
  Pink surface.
  Grit temper.
  H. 8.5
  Rim di. 14.0-14.5
  Ba. di. 3.8

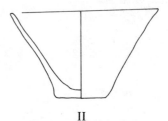

II/III

57. SIMILAR: **6G64:206** (AbS 385)
        Grave 2 (No. 24)
        Two large pieces missing from rim.
        Ware unknown (except surface cream)
        H. 8.5, rim di. 14.8, ba. di. 4.1
        Bitumen staining.    IIIA early

58. **6G75:232**
    Grave 162 (Batch 3631)
    Complete.
    Pinkish clay.
    Sandy temper.
    H. 8.4
    Rim di. 14.6-15.3
    Ba. di. 4.0-4.6

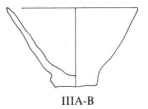

IIIA-B

59. **6G84:42**
    Grave 179 (Batch 1713)
    Quarter of rim and body missing.
    Soft brownish orange clay.
    Patchy buff slip.
    Temper of grit and fine veg.
    H. 7.2
    Rim di. 12.4-12.6
    Ba. di. 3.9-4.3
    Burnt under base and on outside.

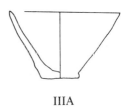

IIIA

60. SIMILAR: **6G64:202** (AbS 384)
        Room 46 fill (Batch 21)
        Rim chipped.
        Ware unknown (surface cream)
        II. 7.2, rim di. 13.1, ba. di. 4.1
        Bitumen staining.    III

61. **6G37:140** (AbS 1092)
    Grave 109 (Batch 523)
    Complete.
    Red clay.
    Temper unknown.
    H. 8.5
    Rim di. 14.3
    Ba. di. 4.4
    Contained small jar no. 468

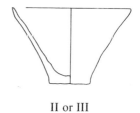

II or III

62. **5IS:276**
    Grave 193 (Batch 5385)
    Half rim and some of body missing.
    Red clay.
    Paler surface.
    Sparse sandy temper.
    H. 10.8
    Rim di. 16.7
    Ba. di. 4.5

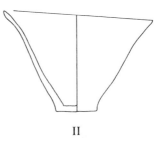

II

63. **6G75:233**
    Grave 162 (Batch 3631)
    Virtually complete.
    Pinkish clay.
    Buff slip.
    Fine grit and veg. temper.
    H. 8.2
    Rim di. 14.0-14.6
    Ba. di. 4.7-5.0

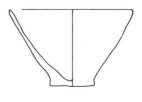

IIIA-B

64. SIMILAR: **6G64:220** (AbS 382)
      Grave 1 (No. 7)
      Intact.
      Ware unknown (surface buff)
      H. 8.8, rim di. 13.2, ba. di. 3.8
      Contained fish-bone 6G64:28
      [Postgate and Moorey 1976:fig. 8 no. 12]      IIIA early

65.          **6G64:132** (AbS 391)
      Grave 2 (No. 3)
      Intact.
      Ware unknown (surface cream)
      H. 9.1, rim di. 14.2-14.3, ba. di. 3.9-4.2
      Bitumen staining.    IIIA early

66.          **5I21:110** (AbS 689)
      Grave 26 (No. 10)
      Condition and ware unknown.
      H. 8.2, rim di. 15.6, ba. di. 4.7
      Base pierced through centre,
      presumably for use as filter.    IIIA late

67. **5I98:32**
      Room 193 floors (Batch 7412)
      Base intact, rest very fragmentary.
      Pink clay.
      Grit temper.
      H. 10.0
      Rim di. (reconstruc.) 16.0
      Ba. di. 4.6

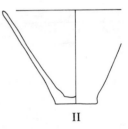

II

68. **6F05:207**
      Grave 183 (Batch 6009)
      Much of rim and some of body missing.
      Soft orange clay.
      Pink surface.
      Temper of veg. and a little grit.
      H. 8.2
      Rim di. (reconstruc.) 12.0
      Ba. di. 4.2

IIIA (mid?)

69. **4J97:311**
      Room 50, inside storage jar
      no. 443 (Batch 4475)
      Much of rim and body missing.
      Pink clay.
      Sandy grit temper.
      H. 8.0
      Rim di. (reconstruc.) 13.0
      Ba. di. 4.5

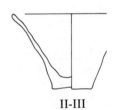

II-III

70. **6G64:205** (AbS 386)
      Grave 2 (No. 25)
      Tiny chip from rim.
      Ware unknown (surface cream)
      H. 9.7
      Rim di. 14.0
      Ba. di. 4.1
      Base is bitumen-stained.

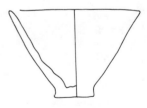

IIIA early

71. SIMILAR: **6G64:131** (AbS 390)
         Grave 2 (No. 23)
         Large piece missing from side.
         Ware unknown (surface cream)
         H. 8.3, rim di. 14.6, ba. di. 4.4
         Bitumen staining.    IIIA early

72. **5IS:283**
    Grave 193 (Batch 5385)
    Over half rim missing.
    Pink clay.
    Sandy temper.
    H. 10.6
    Rim di. (reconstruc.) 14.8
    Ba. di. 4.4

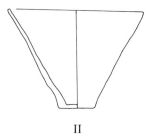

II

73. SIMILAR: **5I31:64**
    Grave 81 (No. 9)
    Some pieces missing.
    Buff clay, temper unknown.
    H. 10.1, rim di. 15.3-15.6, ba. di. 3.3-3.5
    [Postgate 1977:fig. 5 no. 1]   II

74. **3G81:114**
    Uruk floor running under plano-
    convex brick wall (Batch 5602)
    Complete.
    Green clay.
    Veg. temper, also some grog and large
    white grits causing pitted surface.
    H. 11.2
    Rim di. 14.0-15.5
    Ba. di. 5.8-6.0
    [Postgate and Moon 1982:fig. 3 no. 5]

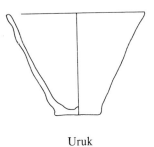

Uruk

75. SIMILAR: **2GS:84** (AbS 1480)
    2G22 sub-surface (Batch 5048)
    Complete.
    Brown clay, grit temper.
    H. 11.3, rim di. 15.4-16.6, ba. di. 5.2-5.5
    Dent near base.
    [Postgate 1983:fig. 17]   I

76.          **2GS:243**
    2G44 sub-surface (Batch 5077)
    Most of rim and much of body missing.
    Red clay, temper unknown.
    H. 8.6, rim di. (reconstruc.) 14.0, ba. di. 4.3-4.5
    [Postgate 1983:fig. 19]   I

77. **5I98:188**
    Grave 203 (Batch 7405)
    Very little of rim.
    Red clay.
    Sandy grit temper.
    H. 9.0
    Rim di. (reconstruc.) 13.0
    Ba. di. 4.6-5.0

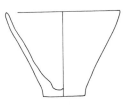

II

78. **5I88:56**
    Room 190 fill (Batch 7108)
    Half of rim and body missing.
    Red clay.
    Sandy grit temper including mica.
    H. 10.2
    Rim di. (reconstruc.) 13.0
    Ba. di. 4.6

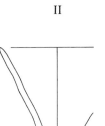

II

79. **5IS:221**
    Grave 193 (Batch 5380)
    Much of rim and body missing.
    Pink clay.
    Buff slip.
    Grit temper.
    H. 10.0
    Rim di. (reconstruc.) c. 15.0
    Ba. di. 4.0-4.2

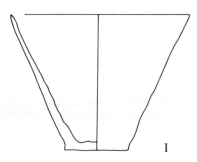

II

80. SIMILAR: **2GS:147**
    2G35 sub-surface (Batch 5098)
    Most of rim and some of body missing.
    Dark green clay, temper unknown.
    H. 10.2, rim di. (reconstruc.) 13.0, ba. di. 3.4-3.5
    [Postgate 1983:fig. 18]   I

81. **2G36:177**
    West Mound Level II pit (Batch 5446)
    A little of rim missing.
    Pink clay.
    Grit and white grit temper.
    H. 14.6
    Rim di. (max.) 19.0
    Ba. di. 6.6-7.2
    [Postgate and Moon:1982 fig. 3 no. 8]

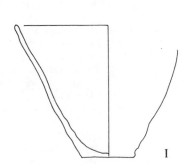

I

82. **2G36:37** (AbS 2076)
    West Mound Level II pit (Batch 5446)
    More than half rim missing.
    Pink clay.
    Cream slip.
    Fine mixed temper.
    H. 14.0
    Rim di. c. 18.0-20.0
    Ba. di. 5.5-6.0

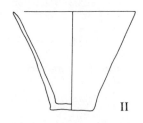

I

83. SIMILAR: **2G36:48** (AbS 2072)
    Large Pit, West Mound Level II (Batch 5408)
    About a quarter of rim and upper body missing.
    Buff to pink clay, cream slip, sand and grit temper.
    H. 14.5, rim di. (oval) c. 18.0-20.0, ba. di. 6.4
    [Postgate and Moon 1982:fig. 3 no. 11]   I

84. **5I88:21**
    Room 190 east, fill (Batch 7108)
    Chip from rim.
    Pink clay.
    Cream surface out.
    Temper mainly of grit and white
    grit, but a little veg. too.
    H. 10.6
    Rim di. 14.2-14.5
    Ba. di. 4.5

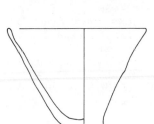

II

85. **0US:10** (AbS 1842)
    Grave 160 (Batch 4056)
    Small piece of rim and body missing.
    Red clay.
    Buff surface in places.
    Sparse temper of fine sand and fine veg.
    H. 10.8
    Rim di. 14.6-16.2
    Ba. di. 5.5
    Found inverted over spouted jar no. 695

I early

86. **5IS:275**
Grave 193 (Batch 5383)
Much of rim and body missing.
Red clay.
Yellowy surface out.
Grit temper.
H. 11.4
Rim di. (reconstruc.) 12.0
Ba. di. 5.0

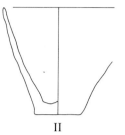

II

87. **5I98:105**
Grave 205 (Batch 7420)
Chip from rim.
Pink clay.
Paler surface.
Sandy grit temper.
H. 9.5
Rim di. 13.2-14.2
Ba. di. 4.6-5.0
Scratches inside.

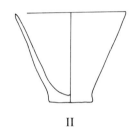

II

88. SIMILAR: **2GS:172** (AbS 1481)
2G46 surface (Batch 5113)
Complete.
Reddish clay, grit temper.
H. 10.6, rim di. 14.7-15.6, ba. di. 4.6-5.1    I

89. **3G81:228**
Sub-surface Uruk level (Batch 5601)
Some of body and much of rim missing.
Greeny-buff clay.
Grog temper.
H. 10.9
Rim di. c. 14.0
Ba. di. 4.5-5.0

Uruk

90. **2G36:166**
Floors associated with FI 81/23 (Batch 5411)
Much of rim and upper body missing.
Pink clay.
Buff slip.
Grit temper.
H. 13.9
Rim di. perhaps around 17.0
Ba. di. 6.2

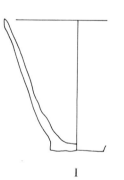

I

91. **3G81:102**
Uruk floor running under plano-
convex brick wall (Batch 5602)
Some of rim and body missing.
Pink clay.
Buff slip.
Grog and veg. temper.
H. 12.5
Rim di. 16.2
Ba. di. 5.4

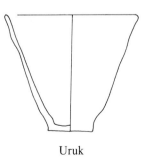

Uruk

92. **6G64:617** (AbS 624)
    Level III floor below base of
    Grave 27 (No. 22)
    Small piece missing.
    Ware unknown.
    H. 16.0
    Rim di. 15.6
    Ba. di. 5.9

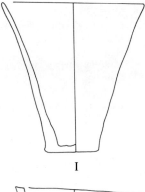

I

93. **6G54:298**
    Sounding Level II (Batch 144)
    Half only.
    Cream clay.
    Temper unknown.
    H. 9.5
    Rim di. 14.0
    Ba. di. 5.3
    Hole in side, perhaps unintentional.

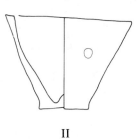

II

94. VIRTUALLY IDENTICAL: **6G54:299**
    Sounding Level II (Batch 144)
    Half only.
    Cream clay, temper unknown.
    H. 8.2, rim di. 14.3, ba. di. 5.0
    Two holes in side – adhering fragments sug-
    gest attachment or repair after firing. II

95. **3G81:243**
    Sub-surface Uruk level (Batch 5601)
    Much of rim and body missing.
    Buff clay.
    Temper of grit and a little veg.
    H. 16.0
    Rim di. 21.0
    Ba. di. 5.6-7.0
    Grooves on inside, too sharp
    to have been made by hand.
    [Postgate 1983:fig. 19]

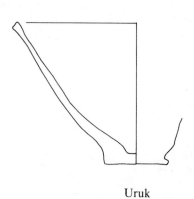

Uruk

96. **3G81:244**
    Uruk floor running under
    plano-convex brick wall (Batch 5602)
    Fragmentary.
    Red clay.
    Sandy temper – surface had groggy
    pock-marks but no grog in section.
    H. c. 15.0
    Rim di. c. 26.0
    Ba. di. 6.8-7.2

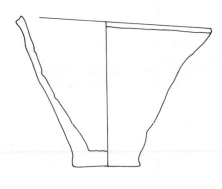

Uruk

# SOLID-FOOTED GOBLETS

Even on the West and North-East Mounds of Abu Salabikh complete solid-footed goblets are rare, as the rims are very fine and fragile and do not survive well. However, the sherd evidence leaves little doubt of their popularity there during the ED I period (there were nearly a thousand base fragments from the large Level II pit in 2G36). Like wall cones, pieces of solid-footed goblet base occur on the Main Mound in secondary contexts, often in mud-brick. However, as they also occur in the deep soundings in 5I31 and 6G64 we may assume that they are not merely the result of bricks or earth being brought from one of the earlier mounds, and do in fact represent ED I settlement on the Main Mound, one of the few indications we are likely to get, as these levels lie too deep for extensive investigation.

Like conical bowls, solid-footed goblets are found in most places where there is extensive early ED occupation, right up to the Hamrin valley, where, however, they are less common, especially on small sites (see for instance Fujii 1981 fig. 19 no. 11). Like conical bowls, they are carelessly made, the foot usually elongated by twisting it by hand once the cup is taken off the wheel. This means there is actually some variation in the exact form of the foot and base. Delougaz suggested that shorter feet might be earlier, but did not have enough evidence (1952 p. 57). There is not enough yet from Abu Salabikh either.

The popularity of these goblets is difficult to fathom: a drinking vessel that cannot be put down until the drink is finished has severe limitations, unless its use was confined to Russian-style toasting. Perhaps the cups were somehow hung up by the feet when not in use.

All solid-footed goblets have string-cut base.

97. **1T:29** (AbS 1458)
    North-East Mound, Room 1
    (Batch 4014)
    Much of rim missing.
    Ware unknown.
    H. 16.8
    Rim di. (reconstruc.) 8.6
    Ba. di. 3.6
    [Postgate 1978:fig. 3 no. 4,
    1983:fig. 16a]

I

98. **1T:30** (AbS 1459)
    North-East Mound, Room 1
    (Batch 4014)
    Much of rim missing.
    Ware unknown.
    H. 17.0
    Rim di. (reconstruc.) 8.4
    Ba. di. c. 4.0
    Contained bone 1T:31
    [Postgate 1978:fig. 3 no. 5,
    1983:fig. 16b]

I

99. **No number**
    Large pit, West Mound
    Level II (Batch 5403)
    Rim and part of body missing.
    Buff clay.
    Fine sparse grit and veg. temper.
    Pres. H. 14.8
    Ba. di. 3.0

I early

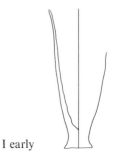

100. **No number**
     Large pit, West Mound
     Level II (Batch 5403)
     Buff clay.
     Fine sparse grit and veg. temper.
     Pres. H. 14.4
     Ba. di. 3.4

I early

101. **0US:12** (AbS 1844)
     Grave 160 (Batch 4056)
     Part of rim missing.
     Reddish clay.
     Fine grit temper and
     perhaps some fine veg.
     H. 20.6
     Rim di. 7.7-8.8
     Ba. di. 2.5-3.5

I early

102. **0US:15** (AbS 1846)
     Grave 160 (Batch 4056)
     Almost complete.
     Dull red clay.
     Cream slip.
     Fine grit and veg. temper.
     H. 20.8
     Rim di. 8.0-8.2
     Ba. di. 2.3-2.5

I early

103. **0US:13** (AbS 1845)
     Grave 160 (Batch 4056)
     Piece missing from rim.
     Reddish clay.
     Temper unknown.
     H. 20.1
     Rim di. 8.5-9.0
     Ba. di. 2.5-3.0
     [Postgate 1983:fig. 16c]

I early

104. **2G36:55**
    Large pit, West Mound
    Level II (Batch 5409)
    Much of rim missing.
    Pink clay.
    Fairly heavy grit temper.
    Pres. H. 17.6
    Ba. di. 3.4-3.5

I early

105. **2G36:111**
    Large pit, West Mound
    Level II (Batch 5416)
    Much of rim and a
    little of body missing.
    Pink clay.
    Fine sandy temper.
    H. 18.2
    Rim di. c. 9.0
    Ba. di. 3.6
    [Postgate and Moon 1982:fig. 3 no. 2]    I early

I early

106. SIMILAR:    **2G36:82**
        Large pit, West Mound Level II (Batch 5408)
        Much of rim missing, pink clay, hard grit temper.
        H. 17.3, rim di. c. 9.6, ba. di. 3.0-3.4
        [Postgate and Moon 1982:fig. 3 no. 3]

107. **2G36:70**
    Large pit, West Mound
    Level II (Batch 5410)
    Half rim missing.
    Pink clay.
    Perfunctory cream slip.
    Hard fine grit temper.
    H. 15.6
    Rim di. c. 8.0-10.0
    Ba. di. 3.0-3.8

I early

# FUNNELS AND SIEVES

The preparation of food and drink from basic raw ingredients requires more filtering and straining operations than modern cookery, and we may assume that the few such clay utensils found were just part of the necessary equipment, including sieves of hair, cloth and so on.

A funnel consisting of a deep bowl pierced through its string-cut base is a type which continues throughout Early Dynastic times with no apparent change. Nearly all examples from Abu Salabikh (nos. 108-114) are overfired, a phenomenon we have noticed also when visiting other sites. This is presumably to ensure that any liquid poured in goes straight through the hole in the bottom and does not start to soak through the fabric and eventually spill.

The holes in the bottom are not always easy to spot, as they can be very worn and difficult to distinguish from accidental damage (no. 113 was such a case, and with no. 110 the question is still not settled). Either the holes were made after firing, therefore ground through the hard base, or the use of the utensil included pushing some resisting substance repeatedly against the bottom causing abrasion to the edges of the hole. There were no definite cases of similar bowls without holes, such as reported by Delougaz for the whole Early Dynastic period alongside the funnel type (1952 Pls. 148, 149).

The two examples of ED I strainers (nos. 116 and 117), with one large hole and small holes in just one side, are presumably from slotted spoons and were once equipped with long perishable handles fixed into the central hole.

The shallow sieve bowls of ED IIIA are confined to graves and form part of the four-piece set repertoire (see Appendix D). Fragments of them, which are easy to recognize, are definitely rare among sherds at Abu Salabikh, in contrast to their ubiquity at other periods all over Mesopotamia.

The 'rhyton' (no. 115) has an exact parallel at Ur (Woolley 1934 Pl. 252 no. 17).

108. **6G45:17** (AbS 1623)
Grave 136 (Batch 2902)
Overfired green clay.
Rather coarse grit temper.
H. 9.0
Rim di. 8.6-9.0
Ba. di. 4.8
String-cut base.

III

109. **0US:4** (AbS 2025)
North-East Mound surface (no Batch Number)
Intact but for chips from rim.
Pink clay.
Green slip.
Grit temper.
H. 8.8
Rim di. 11.0
Ba. di. 4.4
String-cut base.

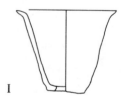

I

110. **6G63:338**
Grave 79 (No. 19)
About half extant.
Overfired green clay.
Grit temper.
H. 7.6
Rim di. 10.1
Ba. di. c. 3.9
String-cut base.

III

111. SIMILAR: **No Number**
Grave 79 (No. 18)
Condition and ware unknown.
H. 7.4, rim di. 8.8, ba. di. 2.8   III

112. **5I79:11**
   Mixed deposit outside town wall (Batch 7336)
   Fragmentary: profile only.
   Green clay.
   Grit temper.
   H. 9.2
   Rim di. (reconstruc.) 10.4
   Ba. di. 4.5
   String-cut base.

ED I to Ur III!

113. **2G46:73**
   West Mound, cut into ED I walls (Batch 5516)
   Much of rim and upper body missing.
   Hard overfired green clay.
   Fine veg. temper.
   H. 9.4
   Rim di. (reconstruc.) 10.4
   Ba. di. 4.4-4.6
   String-cut base, very thin near hole.
   [Postgate and Moon 1982:fig. 4 no. 4]

I

114. **6G47:120** (AbS 1606)
   Grave 124 (Batch 2550)
   Part of rim missing.
   Greeny buff clay.
   Temper of veg. and a little grit.
   H. 8.9
   Rim di. 9.5
   Ba. di. 5.2
   String-cut base: hole made by pushing
   through from underneath, leaving
   two flaps of clay inside and
   rendering base very wobbly.

IIIB

115. **1T:25** (AbS 1450)
   North-East Mound Room 1 (Batch 4008)
   A few gaps.
   Reddish clay.
   Cream slip.
   Temper unknown.
   H. 21.5
   Rim di. c. 15.0
   [Postgate 1978:fig. 3 no. 6]
   A stone vessel of perhaps the same
   shape (2GS:164) was found on the West Mound
   [Postgate 1983:93 and fig. 335
   (not 336 as given)]

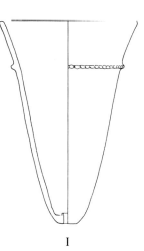

I

116. **2GS:70** (AbS 1453)
   2G22 surface (Batch 5048)
   Slight chip from rim.
   Ware unknown.
   H. 5.0
   Rim di. 11.6
   Central hole made before
   firing, small ones after.
   [Postgate 1983:83, fig. 282 and Pl. VIIa]

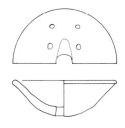

I

117. **2G36:94**
     Large Pit, West Mound
     Level II (Batch 5408)
     Half rim and some of body missing.
     Green clay.
     Soft, fine mixed temper.
     H. 3.4
     Rim di. c. 9.0

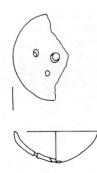

I early

118. **6G45:42** (AbS 1627)
     Grave 143, disturbed fill (Batch 2915)
     Rim chipped.
     Light pink clay.
     Cream slip.
     Fine grit temper.
     H. 7.3
     Rim di. 13.0-14.0

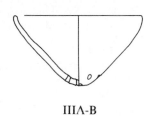

IIIΛ-B

119. **5I21:313** (AbS 1284)
     Grave 96 (No. 7, resting in mouth of
     jar no. 536 below)
     Complete.
     Reddish clay.
     Temper unknown.
     H. 6.7
     Rim di. 11.7
     Ba. di. 2.6-2.8
     6 holes set around 7th central hole.

IIIA late

120. SIMILAR: **5I21:160** (AbS 778)
                 Grave 28 (No. 17)
                 Complete but for sieve part.
                 Dense red clay, cream slip out, varying
                 to pale pink in, sparse sandy temper.
                 Pres. H. 7.0, rim di. 13.1   IIIA late

121.             **6G37:134** (AbS 1019)
                 Grave 38 (No.33)
                 Rim and base fragments only.
                 Ware unknown.
                 9.6 x 7.6   II or III

122.             **4I09:194**
                 Grave 95 (No. 3)
                 Less than half extant.
                 Brown clay, buff surface, grit temper.
                 H. c. 5.4, rim di. c. 11.0
                 Six holes; warped.    IIIB

123. **6G64:612** (AbS 620)
     Grave 1 (No. 60)
     Rim slightly chipped.
     Ware unknown.
     H. 9.5
     Rim di. 17.2
     Ba. di. 2.5
     [Postgate and Moorey 1976:fig. 8 no. 17 and Pl. XXVc]

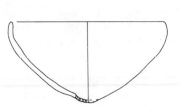

IIIA early

124. **6G54:82** (AbS 658)
Grave 48 (No. 8)
Complete but for tiny chips.
Pink clay.
Cream slip.
Grit temper.
H. 9.0
Rim di. 14.5
Ba. di. 2.5
Made first as a bowl, then pulled out to a funnel.
Filter piece made separately and stuck in.
Surface has pink staining, perhaps post-depositional.
Well-made.

IIIA late

125. **6F05:162** (AbS 2008)
Grave 182 (Batch 6015)
Intact (cracked)
Dark red clay.
Cream slip.
Rather sparse grit temper.
H. 6.4
Rim di. 14.0-14.8

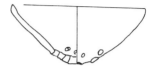

IIIA late

126. **6G64:660** (AbS 944)
Grave 2 upper fill (Batch 13)
Quarter extant: full profile.
Pink clay.
Buff slip out.
Fine grit temper.
H. 5.0
Rim di. 10.5
Fragmentary but apparently central hole in base surrounded by
four others, then probably ten holes near top of vessel.
[Accidentally omitted from Postgate 1985]

IIIA early

127. SAME TYPE: **5I21:365** (AbS 1456)
Grave 42 (No. 8)
Fragments of filter only.
Pink clay, buff surface, no apparent temper.
Central hole surrounded by others.    IIIA late

# TINY OPEN VESSELS

Usually found in graves as part of four-piece sets (Appendix D), these little vessels are normally wheel-made despite their diminutive size. They almost never occur among the sherds, and must have had a very specialised function. The specimen from Grave 1 (no. 134) is carefully finished, but the rest are roughly made and often do not stand well. So far all examples are from ED III contexts.

The square bases on nos. 131 and 137-139 are rather intriguing. There is a parallel from Telloh in the Musée du Louvre (AO 12861) and a possibly related form from Khafajah (Delougaz 1952 A.243.900).

128. **5I21:159** (AbS 531)
    Grave 28 (No. 19)
    Intact.
    Buff to pink surface.
    Grit temper.
    H. 6.1
    Rim di. 3.8
    Ba. di. 3.8
    String-cut base.

IIIA late

129. **5I21:121** (AbS 591)
    Grave 26 (No. 37)
    Intact.
    Red surface.
    Fine grit temper.
    H. 6.5
    Rim di. 3.0
    Ba. di. 3.1
    String-cut base.
    Contents sampled as 5I21:270

IIIA late

130. **5I21:227** (AbS 613)
    Grave 42 (No. 6)
    Intact.
    Red to buff surface.
    Grit temper.
    H. 6.5
    Rim di. 3.1
    Ba. di. 3.4
    Shaved down near base outside.

IIIA late

131. **6G54:83** (AbS 657)
    Grave 48 (No. 7)
    About a quarter of rim
    and body missing.
    Pink clay.
    Buff surface out.
    Coarse veg. temper.
    H. 6.8
    Rim di. 3.3
    Ba. di. 2.0
    Hand made.

IIIA late

132. **6G75:112** (AbS 1939)
    Room 58, north-west corner
    (Batch 3612)
    Intact.
    Red clay.
    Sparse sandy temper.
    H. 9.6
    Rim di. 5.4-5.6
    Ba. di. 3.5-4.2
    String-cut base.

IIIA

133. SIMILAR: **4I09:24** (AbS 1097)
　　　　　　　Grave 95 (No. 11)
　　　　　　　Intact.
　　　　　　　Brownish surface, perhaps fine grit temper.
　　　　　　　H. 9.5, rim di. 5.1, ba. di. 3.5
　　　　　　　String-cut base.
　　　　　　　Found inside round-based jar no. 414 below. IIIB

134. **6G64:611** (AbS 581)
　　　Grave 1 (No. 61)
　　　Complete but for small chips.
　　　Pink clay.
　　　Cream surface.
　　　Fine sand and veg. temper.
　　　H. 9.0
　　　Rim di. 5.6
　　　Ba. di. 5.0
　　　Shaved down with knife on lower body and under base.
　　　[Postgate and Moorey 1976:fig. 8 no. 16, and Pl. XXVC]

IIIA early

135. **5I21:325** (AbS 1283)
　　　Grave 96 (No. 5)
　　　Intact.
　　　Reddish clay.
　　　Temper unknown.
　　　H. 6.5
　　　Rim di. 4.9
　　　Ba. di. 3.0
　　　String-cut base.

IIIA late

136. **6F05:233** (AbS 2040)
　　　Grave 182 (Batch 6015)
　　　Complete but for chip from rim.
　　　Orange clay.
　　　Grit temper.
　　　H. 6.0
　　　Rim di. 6.1-6.5
　　　Ba. di. 3.6-4.0
　　　String-cut base.

IIIA late

137. **6G65:231** (AbS 748)
　　　Grave 54 (No. 3)
　　　Intact but for surface chips.
　　　Red clay.
　　　Fine sparse grit temper.
　　　H. 6.5
　　　Rim di. 8.1
　　　Ba. di. 3.8
　　　String-cut base.

III

138. **6G84:55** (AbS 1945)
　　　Pit in Room 80 (Batch 1710)
　　　Intact.
　　　Burnt greyish brown clay.
　　　Temper indeterminate.
　　　H. 5.1
　　　Rim di. 3.6
　　　Ba. di. 2.3 x 2.5
　　　Base pinched into square.
　　　Hand-made.

III

139. SIMILAR: **6G76:742** (AbS 1946)
　　　　　　　Pit into Ash Tip (Batch 2655)
　　　　　　　Rim missing, badly eroded.
　　　　　　　Burnt red clay, sparse sandy temper.
　　　　　　　Pres. H. 5.3, ba. di. c. 1.5
　　　　　　　Base pinched into square.
　　　　　　　Presumably hand-made.　IIIB or later (or residual)

# MOULDED BOWLS

A specialised function may be guessed at for these decorated bowls, unusual for the predominantly plain Early Dynastic assemblage. They are moulded in a single piece, including the pierced lugs. There is no evidence that any of the bowls found had more than one lug, which may have been to attach a handle to form a ladle or perhaps to fasten the bowl down if it was used as a lid. Despite the similarity of the designs none of the bowls shown here are actually from the same mould.

Very few fragments were found apart from those illustrated, and dating is rather dubious. Most of the pieces here seem to derive from the area of a large public building on Area A, but the actual contexts are a little dubious and a different date is certainly possible. Parallels are generally late or post-ED (e.g. Delougaz 1952 B.041.710). The palm-branch design seems to go with the general form – see also Kish, Mackay 1929 Pl. XLV no. 4.

All hand-made before pressing into mould.

140. **4J98:9**
     Room 24 fill
     (Batch 1600 + 1617)
     Piece of rim and body only.
     Brown clay.
     Grit temper.
     Pres. H. c. 3.4
     Rim di. c. 10.0

III

141. **4J98:96**
     Room 24 fill (Batch 1617)
     Part of rim and body only.
     Reddish clay.
     Fine grit temper.
     Pres. H. c. 3.7
     Rim di. c. 12.0

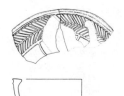

III

142. **4J97:135 + 214** (AbS 2218)
     Pit from surface
     (Batch 4430 + 4449)
     Complete but salt-encrusted.
     Buff clay.
     Fine grit temper.
     H. 3.4
     Rim di. 10.8-11.1

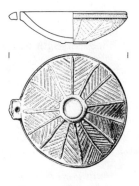

III

143. **4J98:8**
     Surface (Batch 1600)
     Rim fragment only.
     Buff clay.
     Greenish slip.
     Fine grit temper.
     Pres. H. 2.8
     Rim di. c. 9.0

III

144. **4J98:7**
     Surface (Batch 1600)
     Rim fragment only.
     Red clay.
     Fine grit temper.
     H. 3.5
     Rim di. c. 12.0                                               III

145. **6G37:131** (AbS 1023)
     Room 103 fill (Batch 508)
     Fragment only (there could
     have been a lug).
     Red clay.
     Cream slip out.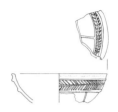
     Hard sparse grit temper.
     Pres. H. 3.1
     Rim di. c. 10.5
                                                                   III

146. NOT ILLUSTRATED: **4I09:64** (AbS 1154)
                       Grave 83 (No. 5)
                       Parts of rim and body missing.
                       Very fine buff clay, temper unknown.
                       Rim di. (x) x 7.4, ba. di. 6.0 x 2.7
                       [For photo see Postgate 1985 Pl. XXVII e-f]        III

147.                   **6G76:679** (AbS 1771)
                       Ash Tip (Batch 2637 + 2638)
                       About half extant.
                       Pink clay, temper unknown.
                       H. 4.6, rim di. 9.5, ba. di. 2.8
                       Design includes concentric circles      IIIB or later (or residual)

# LIDS

Very few lids have been identified as such among the Abu Salabikh pottery and even those here are only so-called because we cannot think of another use for them. It is not even certain which way up they were used. It is hardly possible that lids were really rare household items in a country where dust and sand settle on all unprotected surfaces within an hour or so, even indoors on a still day. Any food or drink left uncovered is soon spoilt, if not from sand then from objects or creatures dropping from the roof-mats and of course by flies in the warm weather. Obviously covers of perishable material such as cloth or woven straw were probably employed, and it is also likely that ordinary utensils (such as conical bowls) doubled as lids, just as as they do nowadays in traditional Iraqi kitchens.

Two lids very similar to nos. 149 and 150 were found in ED III context at the North Temple at Nippur (McCown et al 1978 Pl. 46 nos. 5 and 8), and the type with a knob on top, like no. 151, is found in the Lower Diyala (Delougaz 1952 Pl. 70 e-i), 'characteristic of ED II......though a few specimens were found in ED I context' (ibid. p. 81).

148. **5I11:135** (AbS 1108)
    Room 2 floor (Batch 1243)
    Probably complete ('unfinished'
    edges make it difficult to say)
    Coarse reddish clay.
    Surface cream and pink in patches.
    Heavy grit temper.
    Pres. H. 2.4
    Width 10.2
    Some grey discolouration inside.

IIIA early

149. **0US:2**
    North-East Mound surface
    (no Batch number)
    Rim worn very thin, perhaps broken.
    Red clay.
    Temper unknown.
    H. 5.0
    Rim di. 4.9
    Max. width 11.3

I

150. **0US:3**
    North-East Mound surface
    (no Batch number)
    Intact.
    Pink clay.
    White slip in places.
    Temper unknown.
    H. 4.3
    Rim di. 4.5
    Max. width 10.6-11.0

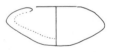

I

151. **2GS:85** (AbS 1461)
    2G13 surface (Batch 5056)
    Small hole in base (probably
    deliberate); end of handle missing.
    Ware unknown.
    Pres. H. 7.0
    Max. width 10.2
    [Postgate 1983 Pl. VIIb]

I

# LARGE BOWLS

Large open bowls, usually with a ring-base, are normally found in graves at Abu Salabikh, predominantly graves of late ED IIIA. Large bowls form a component of the four-piece sets found in graves of this date (see Appendix D). They do not seem to be a feature of the Lower Diyala assemblage, but then neither are the other members of the sets. The apparent absence of the large ring-based bowl elsewhere is more difficult to account for. The nearest neighbour comes from the 'maquette architécturale' at Mari, being of the same general type as nos. 167 and 168, albeit with flat base (Parrot 1967 fig. 314 no. 3219). There are a number of flat or round-based bowls at Kish, including an exact parallel for no. 152 (Mackay 1929 Pl. LII no. 17).

Sherd evidence, as well as that of nos. 165 and 166, shows that the apparent preference for funerary contexts may be an illusion created by the relatively frail nature of these large vessels. Many fragments are found in ED II and III parts of the site of the kinds of rim used for these bowls. The two ED I specimens shown here are quite distinct from later forms (nos. 161 and 169).

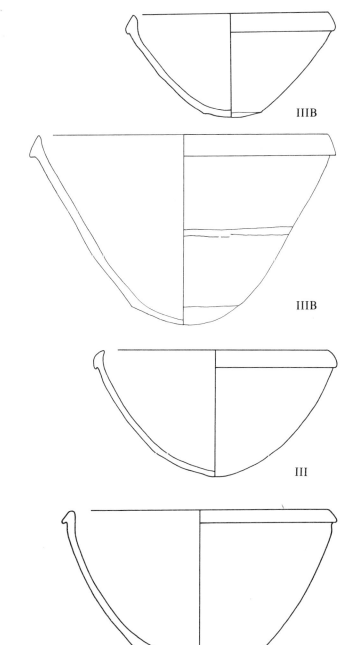

152. **6G66:44** (AbS 405)
     Grave 14 (No. 2)
     Complete.
     Ware unknown (cream surface)
     H. 11.0
     Rim di. 21.6

     IIIB

153. **5I11:35**
     Grave 22 (No. 2)
     Nearly complete.
     Pink to buff clay.
     Cream surface.
     Temper unknown.
     H. 20.2
     Rim di. 31.2-32.0
     Inside scraped down near base.

     IIIB

154. **6G56:67** (AbS 1280)
     Grave 97 (No. 5)
     Complete but for chips.
     Dense red clay.
     Vague buff slip out.
     Patchy buff and pink in.
     Fine sparse grit temper.
     H. 14.1
     Rim di. 25.2

     III

155. **5I21:118** (AbS 747)
     Grave 26 (No. 35)
     Complete.
     Dense pink clay.
     Thin cream slip.
     Sparse grit temper.
     H. 17.2
     Rim di. 30.5
     Ba. di. 13.0
     Base of same clay as pot.
     [Postgate and Moorey
     1976:Pl. XXVc]

     IIIA late

156. **6G63:55**
(AbS 1102)
Grave 73
(No. 29)
Rim complete,
rest fragmentary.
Dense red clay.
Sparse temper of
hard fine grit,
including mica.
H. 20.8
Rim di. 34.4
Ba. di. 17.0
Ring-base made
separately in
veg.-tempered clay.

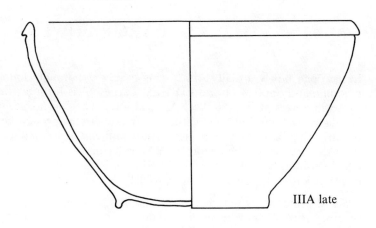

IIIA late

157. VERY SIMILAR:   **5I21:311** (AbS 1281)
Grave 96 (No. 3)
Intact but for chips.
Red clay, perfunctory cream slip, temper unknown.
H. 15.6, rim di. 23.6, ba. di. 11.0
Base added in veg.-tempered clay. IIIA late

158. **6G85:31** (AbS 1853)
Grave 165 (Batch 1805)
Pieces of body missing.
Pink clay.
Cream slip.
Sandy temper.
H. 15.4
Rim di. 30.2
Ba. di. 12.5
Base made separately in
buff clay with veg. temper.

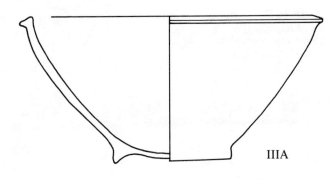

IIIA

159. SIMILAR:   **5I21:224** (AbS 1030)
Grave 42 (No. 7)
Fragmentary.
Ware unknown.
H. c. 18.5, rim and ba. di. unknown.    IIIA late

160. **6G85:72**
Grave 171
(Batch 1809)
Part of rim
and body missing,
and some of base.
Badly salted.
Red clay.
Little apparent temper:
perhaps some sand.
H. 18.6
Rim di. c. 35.8
Ba. di. 13.0-14.0
Base of same clay as bowl.

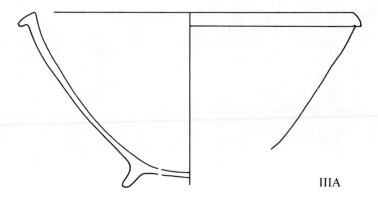

IIIA

161. **2G36:161**
West Mound
Level II floors -
possibly con-
taminated
(Batch 5413)
Base and half of
rim and body missing.
Orange clay.
Buff slip.
Hard grit and
white grit temper.
Pres. H. 17.4
Rim di. c. 41.0-42.0
Scraped inside.
[Postgate and Moon 1982:fig. 4 no. 13]

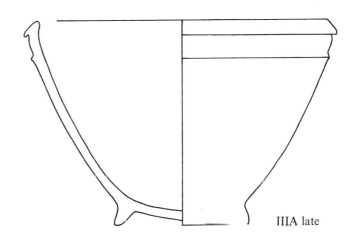

162. **6G47:100** (AbS 1600)
Grave 118 (Batch 2515)
Part of rim and much
of body missing.
Pink core.
Cream slip.
Temper unknown.
H. 21.7
Rim di. 32.0
Ba. di. 14.5

IIIA late

163. **6F05:161** (AbS 2017)
Grave 182
(Batch 6015)
Complete.
Orange clay.
Cream slip.
Grit temper.
H. 19.0
Rim di. 35.0-35.5
Ba. di. 16.4
Base added in veg.
-tempered clay.

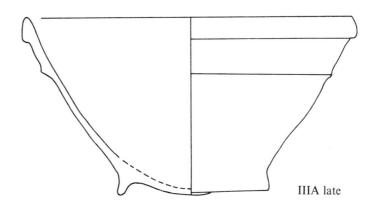

IIIA late

164. NEARLY IDENTICAL: **6G54:85** (AbS 660)
Grave 48 (No. 5)
Virtually complete.
Pale pink clay, cream slip, soft
temper of fine sand and fine veg.
H. 17.7, rim di. 27.6, ba. di. 12.8
Base and rib added in veg.-tempered clay.     IIIA late

165. **6G55:178**
     Fill east of
     Room 47
     (Batch 314)
     Part of rim
     and body only.
     Pink clay.
     White slip.
     White grit temper.
     Pres. H. 15.0
     Rim di. c. 32.0

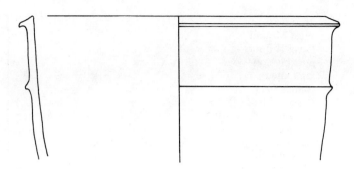

III

166. **6G75:488**
     Floor of Room 58 (Batch 4501)
     Non-joining fragments.
     Pink clay.
     Fine sparse sandy grit temper.
     Pres. H. upper part 14.4
     Pres. H. lower part 5.0
     Rim di. (reconstruc.) 12.5
     Ba. di. 14.8

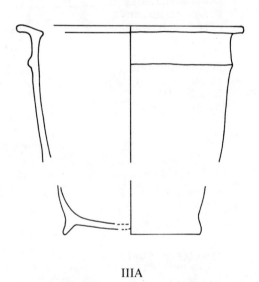

IIIA

167. **5I21:148** (AbS 783)
     Grave 28 (No. 16)
     Base damaged, some chips.
     Dense red clay.
     Buff slip.
     Sparse grit temper.
     H. 18.4
     Rim di. 28.0-31.0
     Ba. di. 14.0
     Base and ribs added in
     extremely coarse veg.
     -tempered clay.

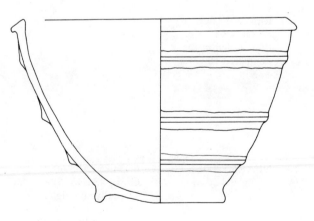

IIIA late

168. SIMILAR: **6G64:592** (AbS 651)
Grave 1 (No. 58)
Complete.
Ware unknown.
H. 22.7, rim di. 39.0, ba. di. 16.0
Ring-base and ribs added,
presumably in veg.-tempered clay.
[Postgate and Moorey 1976:fig. 8. no. 19 and Pl. XXVc]
IIIA early

169. **6G54:374**                          Sounding Level III (Batch 185)
Rim sherd only.                    Pres. H. 13.0
Pink clay.                         Rim di. c. 43.0
Grog and veg. temper.              Perhaps coil built.
Bitumen-coated out.

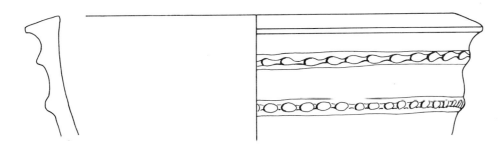

I

# BURNISHED BOWLS

Burnished bowls with flat bases are an early ED type, as noted by Delougaz (1952 p. 58). The specimens he illustrates are all grey and considered by him to be imitations of stone bowls, which is certainly feasible for the smaller examples illustrated here. The larger bowls, none of which have a grey surface, are not so convincing, notwithstanding the fact that stone bowls do come in a variety of colours. Many fragments were found in excavation on the West Mound, and occasional pieces occur on the Main Mound, such as No. 170. The bowls come in a broad size-range, some with the burnish applied more thoroughly to the inside, like No. 172, some with more attention paid to the outside, like Nos. 170 and 173. The former would be more practical if the effect was primarily for waterproofing, the latter suggests a decorative purpose.

170. **6G64:646** (AbS 712)
   Cut in Rooms 39 and 44
   (Batch 44 + 45)
   Profile only.
   Grey-brown clay.
   Sparse temper of sand and a little veg.
   H. 5.8
   Rim di. (reconstruc.) 13.0
   Ba. di. (reconstruc.) c. 5.4
   Perfunctory vertical burnish in,
   same out but producing hard shine.

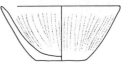

Residual I?

171. **5I31:60** (AbS 1211)
   Grave 81 (No. 6)
   Part of rim missing.
   Brown clay.
   Grey surface.
   Fine grit temper, perhaps not deliberate.
   H. 5.0
   Rim di. 11.3
   Ba. di. 4.7
   Burnished vertically out, diagonally in.

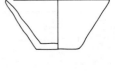

II

172. **6G54:303** (AbS 1204)
   Sounding Level III
   floor (Batch 170)
   Many gaps.
   Dense red clay.
   Cream slip with
   buff patches out.
   Temper of sand, much
   fine veg., and mica.
   H. 13.0
   Rim di. 33.0
   Ba. di. 12.0
   Vague burnish out, better in;
   vertical except just inside rim, where horizontal.
   Vessel-walls of uneven thickness.
   [Postgate 1977:fig. 5 no. 9]

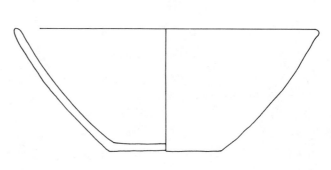

I

173. SIMILAR: **6G54:361**
   Sounding Level III floor (Batch 170)
   Rim sherds only.
   Red clay, buff core, pink surface, grit temper.
   Pres. H. 7.8, rim di. 30.4
   Vertical burnish out.   I

174. **2G46:69**
    Part of upper body only.
    Red clay.
    Buff slip.
    Hard mixed temper.

Surface, probably floors assoc-
iated with FI 81/21 (Batch 5514)
Pres. H. 14.0
Rim di. c. 37.0

Burnished vertically out and probably in (now salted).
[Postgate and Moon 1982:fig. 4 no. 9]

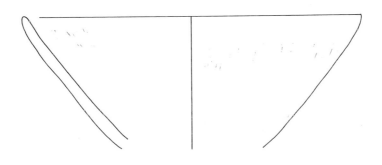

I early

# MISCELLANEOUS OPEN FORMS

A number of open forms occur which cannot be classified except as 'unusual' in as much as there is so far only one example of each from the site and no wealth of convincing parallels. Nos. 187-188 are an exception to this generalisation: there are two of them, and occasional similar types do turn up, though not all are thoroughly convincing (Uch Tepe, Gibson 1981 Pl. 63:12; Mari, Lebeau 1985 nos. 2-27, dated to ED I). Another example from Mari is very close as far as shape is concerned, but in black ware (Parrot 1956 Pl. LXX no. 54).

The spouted bowl No. 192 is known to be an Akkadian type (e.g. Delougaz 1952 C.053.312), but the rest of the forms illustrated in this section are fairly motley and miscellaneous. It is perhaps no coincidence that a fair proportion of them must be dated to ED II, that irritating grey patch in our ceramic chronology.

175. **6G63:160** (AbS 1155)
Pit in south wall
of Room 61 (Batch 926)
Some pieces missing.
Pink clay.
Vague cream to buff slip.
Sand and veg. temper.
H. 9.0
Rim di. 18.0-20.0
Ba. di. 5.0-6.0
String-cut base

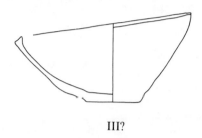

III?

176. **4J97:330**
Room 50, inside storage
jar no. 443)
(Batch 4472)
Non-joining fragments.
Pink clay.
Sandy grit temper incl. mica.
Pres. H. probably around 12.0
Rim di. c. 22.0
Ba. di. c. 11.0
String-cut base.
[Postgate 1984:fig. 7 no. 5]

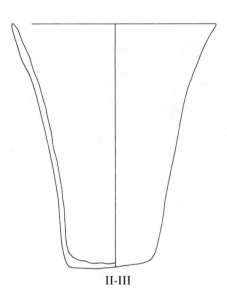

II-III

177. **5IS:191** (AbS 2036)
Grave 185 (Batch 5372)
More than half rim missing.
Red clay.
Yellow slip.
Fine temper of grit and veg.
H. 26.0
Rim di. 22.4
Ba. di. 8.8
Base scraped, not string-cut.

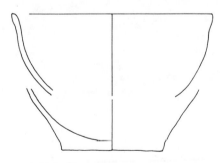

II

178. **6G75:228** (AbS 2074)
    Grave 162 (N) fill (Batch 3627)
    About half of rim and body missing.
    Pink clay.
    Buff slip.
    Fine mixed temper.
    H. 19.8
    Rim di. c. 15.0
    Ba. di. 5.6
    Base added in coarse straw-tempered clay.

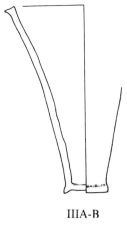

IIIA-B

179. **1T:47** (AbS 1773)
    North-East Mound surface (Batch 4025)
    About half extant.
    Greenish clay.
    Temper unknown.
    H. 2.5
    Pres. length 7.4
    Max. pres. di. 9.5

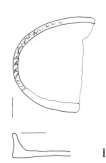

I

180. **6G75:474**
    Grave 162 (S) fill (Batch 3644)
    Less than half extant.
    Red clay.
    Sandy temper.
    H. 6.4
    Rim di. (reconstruc.) 8.0
    Ba. di. 4.5
    Some black staining on
    surface, but also over breaks.

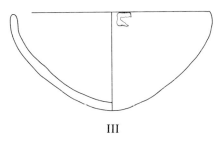

IIIA-B

181. **6G54:192** (AbS 1088)
    Grave 60 (No. 9)
    About two thirds extant.
    Dense red clay.
    Cream slip out.
    Hard fine sandy temper.
    H. 10.5
    Rim di. 22.0
    Square stub at rim, presumably
    for lug, and traces of another
    approximately opposite.

III

182. **4I09:8** (AbS 1098)
    Grave 95 (No. 9)
    Complete but for chips.
    Red clay.
    Temper unknown.
    H. 5.5
    Rim di. 11.8
    Ba. di. 5.5
    String-cut base.
    Contained bones 4I09:52
    [Postgate 1985:fig. 140 (wrong scale)]

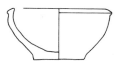

IIIB

183. **6G54:280** (AbS 1171)
     Sounding Level II pit (Batch 144)
     Part of rim and body missing.
     Red clay.
     Fine cream slip.
     Temper unknown.
     H. 6.4
     Rim di. 6.0

II

184. **5I21:303**
     Grave 63 (No. 1)
     Base missing.
     Buff clay.
     Green slip.
     Fine grit temper.
     Pres. H. 6.6
     Rim di. 8.5

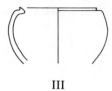

III

185. **6G75:318** (AbS 2131)
     Grave 162 (S) (Batch 3623)
     Intact.
     Pink clay.
     Cream slip.
     Grit temper.
     H. 8.9
     Rim di. 8.4-8.6
     Max. width 11.7
     Base cracked inside.

IIIA-B

186. **2G36:150** (AbS 2073)
     Large Pit in West Mound
     Level II (Batch 5408)
     Nearly half extant.
     Red clay.
     Cream slip out.
     Temper of fine black and white grit.
     H. 5.2
     Rim di. 6.0
     Ba. di. 3.4

I early

187. **6G37:219** (AbS 1199)
     Grave 89 (No. 7)
     Intact.
     Red clay.
     Temper unknown.
     H. 6.5
     Rim di. 8.4
     Ba. di. 3.1
     String-cut base.

IIIB

188. **6G37:347** (AbS 1380)
     Room 102 fill (Batch 560)
     Intact.
     Buff clay.
     Temper unknown.
     H. 7.9
     Rim di. 10.2
     Ba. di. 4.6
     String-cut base.

III

189. **6FS:20** (AbS 1941)
Grave 173 (Batch 5212)
About half extant.
Red clay.
Very sparse grit temper.
H. 5.0
Rim di. 9.8
Ba. di. 3.7
Outside smoke-blackened.
Pinched ring-base.
This is *not* the broken top of a small stemmed
dish: the base has been deliberately formed.

IIIB

190. **5IS:155** (AbS 1973)
Grave 185 (Batch 5372)
Complete.
Greyish clay.
Green surface.
Coarse temper of
veg. and some grit.
H. 11.6
Rim di. 18.0
Ba. di. 13.2-13.4
String-cut base.

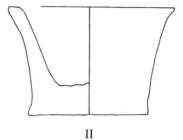

II

191. **6G86:283**
Surface (Batch 1975)
Part of side only.
Red clay.
Sandy grit temper.
Pres. H. 11.4
Rim di. (reconstruc.) 14.0

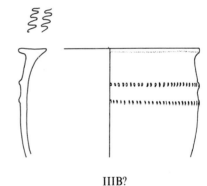

IIIB?

192. **6G36:290** (AbS 1927)
Late pit cutting
street area and
walls of Eastern
Houses (Batch 2480)
Much of rim and body
missing; base frag.
does not join.
Reddish clay.
Cream slip out and inside neck.
Temper unknown.
Pres. H. 13.0
Rim di. c. 25.0
Base flat, but probably
had added ring-base.

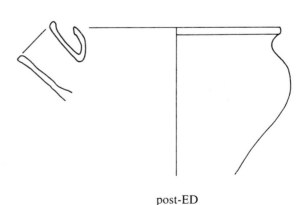

post-ED

# COARSE VESSELS

Hand-made coarse-ware is probably the most under-represented general type in our records of Abu Salabikh pottery, and perhaps in Early Dynastic pottery generally. Although shapes like those illustrated below are rare in the literature, the surface of every Early Dynastic site is littered with coarse, vegetable-tempered fragments, their original form often quite unrecognizable as they are not very hard-fired and abrade easily. A number of examples from Uch Tepe are illustrated by Thuesen (Gibson 1981 Pl. 74 nos. 9 and 10, Pl. 75). The rims of deep bowls such as nos. 207-209 are distinctive, also pieces of the support 'flaps' from ones like nos. 203-206. No particular date within the Early Dynastic period can be pinned to any one shape.

Large shallow bowls like nos. 193-201 were presumably multi-functional. Bowls with internal division like no. 202 look as though a more particular use was intended. Such vessels are used in Iraq today to hold water and seed for domestic birds.

Bowls with clay 'flaps' connecting the rim to a central compartment (nos. 203-206) are especially well-represented among sherds, and presumably intended as a support for something else. Variations in shape can be seen from examples from the Lower Diyala sites (Delougaz 1952 C.011.201, D.201.201).

Nos. 210-212 must be stands too, in fact a miniature version of a larger type once again often found in pieces but rarely complete. An example from an Akkadian grave at Uch Tepe demonstrates the full-size version (Gibson 1981 Pl. 97:3). Similar types are found elswhere (for instance at Mari, Parrot 1956 fig. 106 no. 810, fig. 107 no. 1570, illustrated upside-down). The shallow top dish with pouring lip is designed to pour off any liquid entering it without letting it accumulate, so the stand must have been to support something that dripped, the liquid being concentrated by the lip for pouring into a third vessel. Porous pots which allow a certain amount of the contents to leak slowly through and drip are commonly used for cooling water in the Near East. The action of evaporation on the wet outer surface keeps the inside cool. Dripping water jars are a constant irritation, as for maximum effect they need shade and draught, and are therefore often placed in gateways or doorways, just where puddles are most inconvenient. Placing a container directly underneath the jar is not entirely satisfactory as it is difficult to see when it needs emptying. A stand such as no. 211 would have been ideal.

Deep bowls with ring-base such as nos. 207-209 are invariably collapsed when found *in situ*, with the rim fallen in and the sides caved in, breaking along the lines of the coils from which they were built. The breaks are usually abraded, making physical reconstruction impractical and allowing scope for imagination when drawing. The ring-bases, by contrast, are always well-preserved and seem to be harder-fired. Whether they were made and baked separately before the rest of the pot was built on, or whether the firing method somehow caused the base to get more heat we cannot say. The characteristic rims of these large pots can be seen on the surface of most ED sites: one or two from the Lower Diyala region were preserved (Delougaz 1952 D.654.310, D.743.310).

All hand made unless otherwise stated.

193. **4J98:92**
     Surface (Batch 1600)
     Condition and ware unknown.
     H. 6.9
     Rim di. (reconstruc.) c. 26.8
     Ba. di. (reconstruc.) c. 21.0

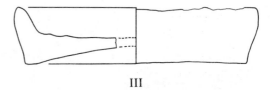

III

194. **6HS:226**
     6H31 sub-surface
     (Batch 7020)
     Fragment only.
     Green clay.
     Grit and veg. temper.
     H. 5.4
     Rim di. c. 26.0-27.0
     Ba. di. c. 26.0-27.0

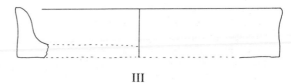

III

195. **6HS:261**
6H82 sub-surface (Batch 7054)
About a quarter extant.
Overfired green clay.
Veg. temper.
H. 6.6
Rim di. (reconstruc.) 28.0
Ba. di. c. 28.0

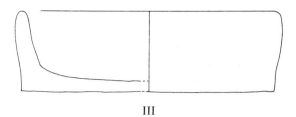

III

196. **6HS:227**
6H10 surface
(Batch 7016)
Just over half extant.
Red clay.
Cream surface.
Grit and veg. temper.
H. 7.0
Rim di. 31.0
Ba. di. 31.0

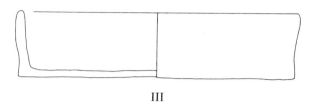

III

197. **6HS:350** (AbS 2210)
6H83 sub-surface, inverted
over spouted jar 6HS:351
(not yet processed, but
c.f. no. 706) (Batch 7042)
Complete and intact.
Pink clay,
Grog and veg. temper.
H. 8.6
Rim di. 30.4
Ba. di. 27.5

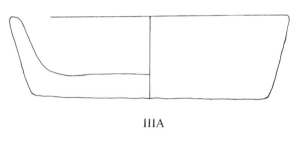

IIIA

198. **5IS:121** (= FI 81/16)
Small piece of rim and side missing.
Red clay.
Greenish surface.
Grog and veg. temper.
Probably coil-built.

5I87 sub-surface
(Batch 5213)
H. 11.0
Rim di. c. 47.0
Ba. di. c. 47.0
Found upside-down.

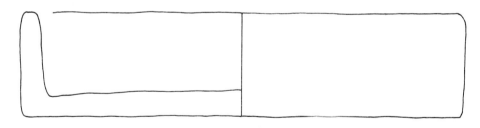

II

199. SIMILAR: **6G55:41** (AbS 395)
Cut in Room 47 (Batch 326)
Condition and ware unknown (cream slip).
H. 10.1, rim di. 30.0
[Postgate and Moorey 1976:fig. 8 no. 14]   III

200. **5IS:77**
    5I97 sub-surface,
    in street
    (Batch 5334)
    Fragment only.
    Coarse green clay.
    Veg. temper.
    H. 7.2
    Probably oval, not round.

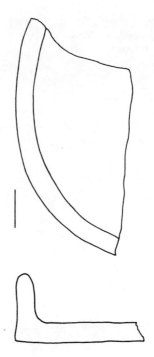

II

201. **6G64:1066**
    Room 46 floor, NW corner.
    (Batch 2787)
    Part of base and one
    side only.
    Red clay.
    Cream surface.
    Temper unknown (except 'coarse')
    H. 7.5

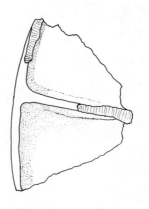

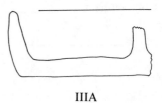

IIIA

202. **2GS:105**
    2G21 sub-surface (Batch 5030)
    Condition unknown.
    Coarse red clay.
    Brown surface.
    Temper unknown.
    H. 8.2
    Rim di. 28.6
    [Postgate 1978:fig. 3
    no. 7, and 1983:fig. 87]

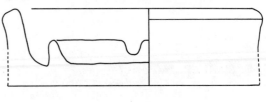

I

203. **6G47:115**
    Grave 126 (Batch 2551)
    Very fragmentary, perhaps not
    intentional part of deposit.
    Yellowish clay.
    Temper unknown.
    H. 9.6
    Rim di. 34.2
    Ba. di. 33.2

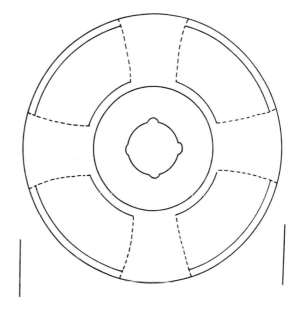

PROBABLY SIMILAR:

204. **4IS:1** (AbS 1943)
    4I17 surface
    (no Batch number)
    About two thirds preserved, but
    'flaps' broken off.
    Overfired green clay, grit temper.
    H. 5.2, rim di. 29.0, ba. di. 30.1
    Perhaps coil-built. III

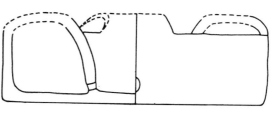

IIIA late

205. **6G55:30** (AbS 708)
    Pit in Room 47
    (Batch 322)
    Fragment only.
    Ware unknown.
    H. 11.0
    Holes as in no. 203 III

206. **5I10:43** (AbS 894)
    Pit in Room 11
    (Batch 1009)
    Centre part only.
    Ware unknown.
    H. 17.4
    Probably three 'flaps' and holes originally. III

207. **6G84:7**
    Room 80 floors
    (Batch 1709)
    Lower part intact,
    upper part missing.
    Non-joining
    rim-fragment.
    Red clay.
    Coarse grog temper.
    Pres. H. c. 38.0
    Ba. di. 24.0
    Perhaps coil-built.
    *This illustration at 1:8*

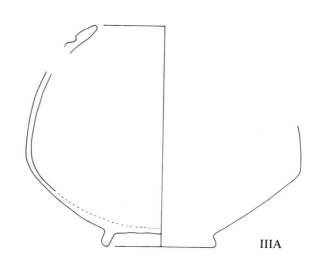

IIIA

208. **6HS:344**
     6H81 sub-surface
     (Batch 7060)
     Base and sides base
     preserved, but
     latter collapsed,
     distorting original shape.
     Pink clay, black core.
     Temper of grog and
     veg.- some still
     preserved unburnt!
     Pres. H. 40.0
     Ba. di. 24.0
     Max. width 64.0
     Coil-built.
     Left *in situ*.
     *This illustration at 1:8*

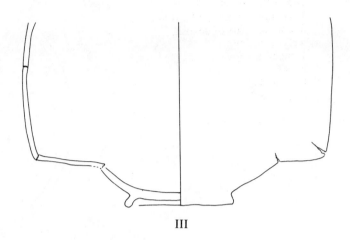

III

209. **6HS:221**                          6H62 sub-surface
     Lower body and base only.            (Batch 7031)
     Orange clay, pink core.              Pres. H. 38.0
     Greeny surface.                      Max. width c. 92.0
     Grit temper.                         Ba. di. c. 26.0
     Left *in situ*                       *This illustration at 1:8*
     Shape of body difficult to determine accurately.

III

210. **5I10:130** (AbS 506)
     Grave 19 (No. 3)
     Intact.
     Ware unknown.
     H. 9.4
     Rim di. 8.4
     Ba. di. 12.1
     Made partly by hand,
     partly on the wheel.
     [Postgate and Moorey
     1976:fig. 8 no. 13]

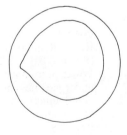

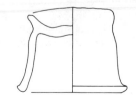

IIIB

211. **6FS:26** (AbS 1942)
      Grave 173 (Batch 5212)
      Intact but for tiny chip on top.
      Red clay.
      Traces of buff slip.
      Sandy temper.
      H. 8.8
      Rim di. (excluding lip) 7.4
      Ba. di. 9.2
      Cylindrical body closed over at top
      with separate piece of clay which is
      pinched up to form a shallow dish.
      Lip is lower than rim so anything
      poured in comes straight out.
      Round-based jar no. 145 fits well on top.

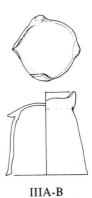

IIIA-B

212. **6G45:54** (AbS 1772)
      Grave 143 (Batch 2919)
      Pouring lip chipped, one lug
      missing, otherwise intact.
      Reddish clay, grey core.
      Grit and coarse veg. temper.
      H. 9.6
      Rim di. 9.5
      Ba. di. 9.4
      Made from wheel-thrown deep cup
      with rest added on by hand.

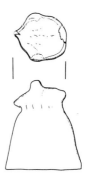

IIIB

# STEMMED DISHES

A commentary on stemmed dishes found during the first three seasons of excavation at Abu Salabikh was published in *Iraq* 43 (Moon 1981), and though many more have been found since then there has not been any wealth of new types, and nothing to suggest substantial modification of what was said then, though one or two remarks can be added.

Plain stemmed dishes (nos. 213-231), as far as one can suggest from the small sample, favour an ED II or ED IIIB date: they were not so popular in-between. The favourite ED IIIA style, starting at least as early as Grave 1, is a well-proportioned stand with comparatively wide dish and base, notched edges to the rim, and typically with a single row of incised triangles round the base (nos. 236-246). In late ED IIIA the stems start to get longer and thinner and the rim-notching coarser and more careless. The more baroque forms of decoration start to become popular, including moulded figures and 'doorways' carved out of the stem (nos. 251-256). Both styles last into ED IIIB.

Newcomers to the Abu Salabikh repertoire are the 'gerillte' rim of no. 241, previously found at Kish and Ur (Mackay 1925 Pl. XII nos. 18 and 20; Moon 1982 figs. 10-13), and fragments of stemmed dishes made in grey clay and stamped, perhaps for white inlay (nos. 264-265).

The distribution map for stemmed dishes (Moon 1982 fig. 1) can now be be altered to include Warka and Jokha among sites where they are found (Finkbeiner 1985 Abb. 15 no. 30; Rumayidh 1981 fig. 15, 20b).

213. **6G36:235**
　　　Grave 116 (Batch 2487)
　　　Part of stem and a little
　　　of base missing.
　　　Dense red clay.
　　　Yellowish slip out.
　　　Sparse veg. temper.
　　　Pres. H. dish c. 5.0
　　　Pres. H. rest c. 15.0
　　　Rim di. c. 22.0
　　　Ba. di. 19.0

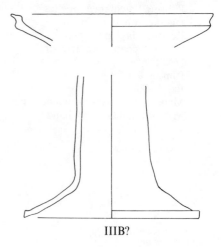

IIIB?

214. SIMILAR:　**6G64:674** (AbS 1394)
　　　　　　　Grave 88 (No. 8)
　　　　　　　Much of dish missing.
　　　　　　　Buff clay, cream slip, temper unknown.
　　　　　　　H. 27.5, rim di. c. 24.0, ba. di. 21.4
　　　　　　　[Postgate 1977:fig. 5 no. 12]
　　　　　　　[Moon 1981:no. 67]　II-IIIA

215.　　　　　**6G63:294 + 5** (AbS 1391)
　　　　　　　Grave 79 (No. 3 + 4)
　　　　　　　About half of dish missing.
　　　　　　　Reddish clay, cream slip, temper unknown.
　　　　　　　H. 14.1, rim di. 13.5, ba. di. 11.5-12.1
　　　　　　　[Moon 1981:no. 72]　III

216.　　　　　**6G55:17** (AbS 392)
　　　　　　　Grave 4 (No. 5)
　　　　　　　Pieces missing overall.
　　　　　　　Ware unknown (except surface pinkish buff)
　　　　　　　H. 13.8, rim di. 15.2, ba. di. 14.8
　　　　　　　[Moon 1981:no. 76]　III

217. **6G76:604** (AbŚ 1754)
Grave 146 (Batch 2633)
Part of rim missing.
Pinkish clay.
Cream slip.
Fine grit and veg. temper.
H. 8.4
Rim di. 10.5
Ba. di. 8.5

III

IDENTICAL, NOT
ILLUSTRATED:

218.          **4I09:201** (AbS 1409) (Grave 93, no. 6)   IIIB
219.          **4I09:118** (AbS 1402) (Grave 93, no. 12)   IIIB
220.          **4I09:181 + 204** (AbS 1403) (Grave 93, no. 10)   IIIB
221.          **4I09:203** (AbS 1405) (Grave 93, no. 11)   IIIB
222.          **4I09:200** (AbS 1407) (Grave 93, no. 5)   IIIB
223.          **4I09:206** (AbS 1410) (Grave 93, no. 9)   IIIB
224.          **4I09:105** (Grave 93, no. 13)   IIIB
              [Moon 1981:nos. 55-61. No. 55 is wrongly numbered AbS 1401 and
              the clay colour described as buff: it is red.]
225.          **4I09:119** (Grave 93, no. 14)   IIIB
226.          **4I09:174** (AbS 1408) (Grave 93, no. 4)   IIIB
227.          **4I09:201** (AbS 1409) (Grave 93, no. 6)   IIIB
228.          **4I09:202** (AbS 1406) (Grave 93, no. 7)   IIIB
229.          **4I09:205** (AbS 1404) (Grave 93, no. 8)   IIIB

230. SIMILAR:   **6G62:1** (AbS 1400)
               Grave 61 (No. 8)
               Parts of rim and base missing.
               Buff clay, cream slip, temper unknown.
               II. 18.0, rim di. 22.5, ba. di. 17.4
               Contained small jar 6G62:5 (no. 476 below)
               [Moon 1981:no. 71]   III

231.           **6G37:976** (AbS 936)
               Grave 38 (No. 22)
               About half dish missing.
               Ware unknown.
               H. 12.0, rim di. 13.0, ba. di. 11.0
               [Postgate and Moorey 1976:fig. 7 no. 5 and Pl. XXVa]
               [Moon 1981:no. 80]   II?

232. **6G37:466 + 471 +**
    **489 + 495** (AbS 1482)
    Grave 38 (No. 11)
    Almost complete.
    Red clay.
    Pink to cream surface.
    Grit and veg. temper.
    H. 23.9
    Rim di. 22.0-23.7
    Ba. di. 18.3

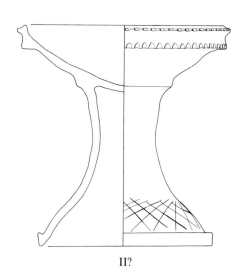

II?

233. SIMILAR:   **6G55:182**
               Grave 49 (No. 6)
               Dish missing.
               Ware unknown.
               Pres. H. 26.0, ba. di. c. 25.0
               [Moon 1981:no. 78, given as un-numbered]   IIIB

234. **6G75:280** (AbS 2129)
      Grave 198 (Batch 3658)
      Two thirds of rim and dish
      missing, and edge of base rim.
      Red clay.
      Black core.
      Sandy temper with a little straw,
      especially in base rim and added
      support rib for dish.
      H. 41.5
      Rim di. (reconstruc.) 32.0
      Ba. di. 28.8

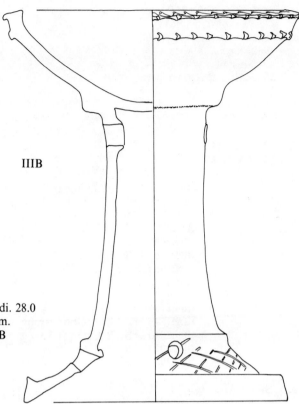

IIIB

235. SIMILAR:   **5I11:73** (AbS 1036)
      Grave 50 (No. 3)
      Centre of dish missing.
      Red clay, paler surface,
      temper unknown.
      H. 40.7, rim di. 26.8, ba. di. 28.0
      Two long openings in stem.
      [Moon 1981:no. 62]   IIIB

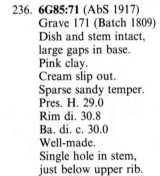

236. **6G85:71** (AbS 1917)
      Grave 171 (Batch 1809)
      Dish and stem intact,
      large gaps in base.
      Pink clay.
      Cream slip out.
      Sparse sandy temper.
      Pres. H. 29.0
      Rim di. 30.8
      Ba. di. c. 30.0
      Well-made.
      Single hole in stem,
      just below upper rib.

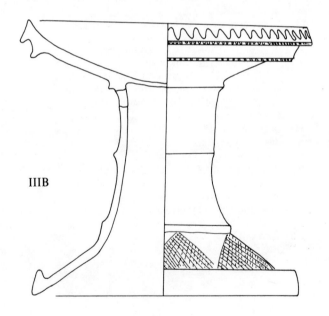

IIIB

237. VERY SIMILAR:   **5I21:204** (AbS 811)
      Grave 35 (No. 2)
      Condition and ware unknown.
      H. 29.7, rim di. 30.0, ba. di. 28.4
      [Moon 1981:no. 66]   IIIA early

238. SIMILAR: **6G74:26**
          Cut in Rooms 54/55 (Batch 606)
          Dish missing.
          Pink clay, cream surface, temper unknown.
          Pres. H. 23.2, ba. di. c. 24.0
          [Moon 1981:no. 50]   III

239.         **6G64:31** (AbS 393)
          Grave 1 (no. 6)
          Complete.
          Ware unknown (except surface pinkish buff)
          H. 31.6, rim di. 32.6, ba. di. 30.4
          Base decoration is triangles with multiple
          outline, not hatched ones.
          [Postgate and Moorey 1976:fig. 7 no. 5 and Pl. XXVa]
          [Moon 1981:no. 69]   IIIA

240.         **6G63:413** (AbS 1389)
          Grave 100 (Batch 977)
          Complete but for chip from stem.
          Red clay, temper unknown.
          H. 27.0, rim di. 27.7, ba. di. 25.9
          Base decoration is triangles with
          multiple outline, not hatched ones.
          [Moon 1981:no. 77]   IIIA

241. **6G74:209**
     Grave 45 (No. 5)
     Much of base and part
     of rim missing.
     Pink clay.
     Cream slip.
     Temper of grit and
     maybe fine veg.
     H. c. 27.0
     Rim di. 27.5
     Ba. di. (reconstruc.) 26.5
     'Gerillte' rim.

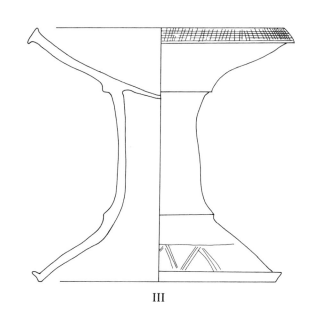

III

242. SIMILAR
     DECORATION: **6G63:157**
          Pit in south wall of Room 61 (Batch 926)
          Centre of dish missing.
          Red clay, temper unknown.
          H. 33.2, rim di. 25.8, ba. di. 25.6
          Contained rodent bones 6G63:237]
          [Moon 1981:no. 51]   IIIB?

243.         **5I21:225**
          Grave 42 (No. 4)
          Most of dish missing.
          Red clay, temper unknown.
          Pres. H. 22.2, ba. di. 24.0
          [Moon 1981:no. 65]   IIIA late

244. **6G84:45**
   Grave 179 (Batch 1712)
   Nearly half of dish missing.
   Pink clay.
   Yellowish slip.
   Sandy temper.
   H. 14.9
   Rim di. 19.5
   Ba. di. 15.2-16.0

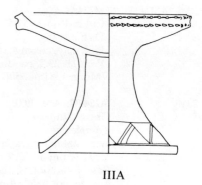

IIIA

245. SIMILAR:   **5I21:131 + 163** (AbS 582)
   Grave 26 (No. 34)
   Condition and ware unknown.
   II. 24.6, rim di. 24.3, ba. di. 21.9
   [Postgate and Moorey 1976 Pl. XXVa]
   [Moon 1981:no. 64]   IIIA late

246.              **6G64:374** (AbS 673)
   Grave 1 (No. 52)
   One or two pieces missing.
   Ware unknown.
   H. 24.5, rim di. 28.5, ba. di. 23.3
   [Postgate and Moorey 1976 Pl. XXVa]
   [Moon 1981:no. 68]   IIIA early

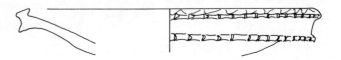

247. **6F05:9 + 25**
   Grave 168 (Batch 6000)
   Dish is missing centre
   and does not join stem.
   Dense red clay.
   Yellowish slip out.
   Fine grit and veg. temper.
   Pres. H. dish c. 5.0
   Pres. H. rest c. 29.2
   Rim di. 30.8
   Ba. di. 33.4

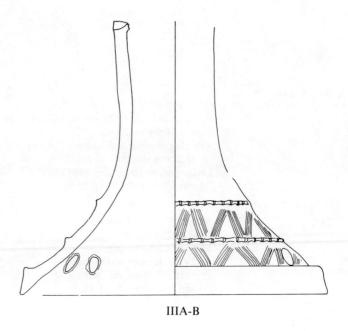

IIIA-B

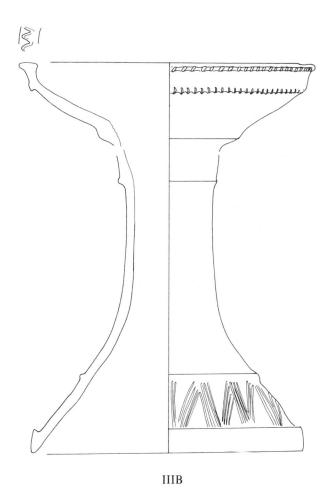

IIIB

248. **4J97:78**
Grave 200 (Batch 2206)
Fragmentary: rim
does not join.
Red clay, grey core.
Temper of sand,
grog and veg.
H. probably 41.2
Rim di. 33.0
Ba. di. 30.0

249. SIMILAR:   **6G63:225** (AbS 1170)
Grave 73 (No. 41)
Piece missing from rim.
Red clay, temper unknown.
H. 32.8, rim di. 34.0, ba. di. c. 27.7
[Moon 1981:no. 75] IIIA late

250.   **6G75:332**
Grave 162 (S)
(Batch 3673)
Dish missing.
Green clay, grog and veg. temper.
Pres. H. 36.2, ba. di. 31.4   IIIA-B

251. **6F05:74** (AbS 1976)
     Grave 176 (Batch 6008)
     Centre of dish missing,
     and some chips.
     Dense pink clay.
     Cream slip.
     Grit and veg. temper.
     H. 47.8
     Rim di. 33.7
     Ba. di. 31.2-31.5

252. SIMILAR:  **5I21:265** (AbS 899)
              Grave 28 (No. 20)
              Fragmentary: most
              of stem missing.
              Buff clay, paler surface,
              temper unknown.
              Rim di. 29.4, ba. di. 30.0
              Two long openings in stem.
              [Moon 1981:no. 63]  IIIA late

253. **6G47:104** (AbS 1753)
     Grave 124 (Batch 2552)
     Part of stem missing.
     Pink clay.
     Cream slip.
     Temper unknown.
     H. 42.0
     Rim di. 55.5
     Ba. di. 34.0

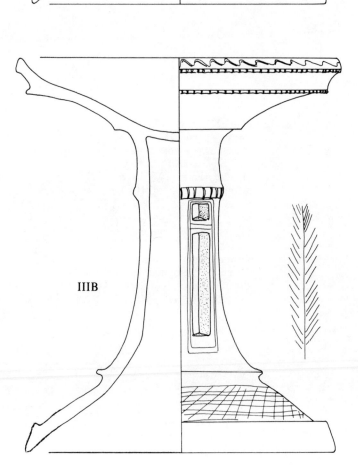

IIIB

IIIB

254. **6F05:131** (AbS 2056)
Grave 182 (Batch 6015)
Nearly half dish
missing, and
parts of stem.
Orange clay.
Yellowish slip.
Grit temper.
H. 46.3
Rim di. 37.6
Ba. di. 34.4

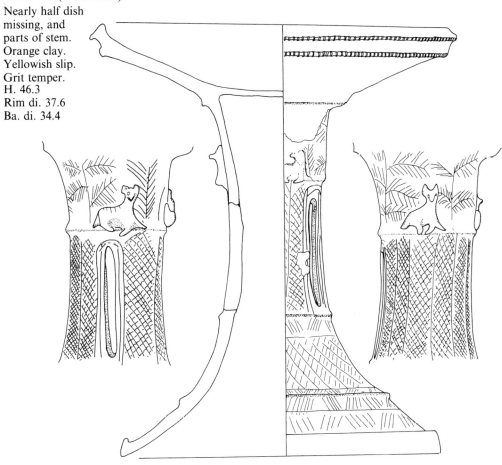

IIIA late

255. **6G75:145** (AbS 2057)
Grave 162 (Batch 3618)
Part of stem and
base of dish only.
Pink clay.
Cream slip.
Sandy temper with obvious
large mica inclusions.
Pres. H. 16.0
Clay figures made separately and
stuck into clay pocket on side of
stem. Probably fired at the same time.
[Postgate 1982:fig. 43]

256. SIMILAR:  **6G38:89** (AbS 947)
Grave 51 (No. 4)
Dish missing.
Ware unknown.
Pres. H. 41.0, ba. di. 37.0
[Postgate and Moorey 1976 Pl. XXVd]
[Moon 1981:no. 81] IIIB

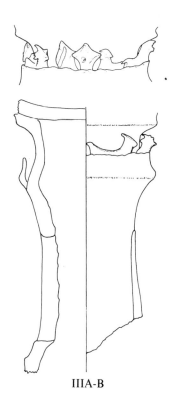

IIIA-B

257. **6G75:460**
     Grave 162 (Batch 3690)
     Dish and base missing.
     Pink clay.
     Cream surface out.
     Grit temper.
     Pres. H. 37.2
     Max. pres. di. top 17.2
     Max. pres. di. base c. 26.0

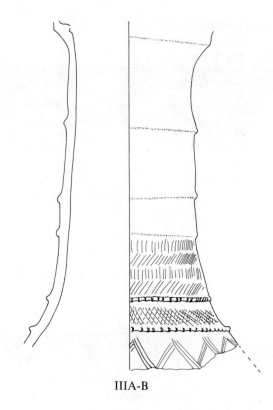

IIIA-B

258. **4J97:220**
     Pit dug from surface
     into Grave 206 (Batch 4449)
     Part of stem and base only.
     Red clay.
     Paler surface.
     Sparse grit temper.
     Pres. H. 20.4
     Max. pres. width 26.0

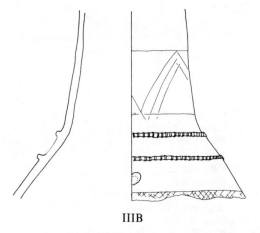

IIIB

259. SIMILAR:   **6G63:104**
                Room 61 fill (Batch 920)
                Stem only.
                Buff clay, paler surface, temper unknown.
                Pres. H. 21.7
                [Moon 1981:no. 49] III

260.            **6G63:442**
                Surface (Batch 901)
                Part of base only.
                Pink clay, whiteish surface out, temper unknown.
                Pres. H. 3.5
                [Moon 1981:no. 53] III?

261. **6G75:187**
     Floors outside SE wall
     of Room 54 (Batch 3624)
     Section of stem only.
     Buff clay.
     Fine grit and veg. temper.
     Pres. H. 19.4
     Max. pres. width c. 12.0

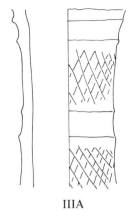

IIIA

262. SIMILAR:   **6G36:261**
                Pit in or just north of Room 118 (Batch 2486)
                Part of stem only.
                Reddish brown clay, cream slip, sandy temper.
                H. 15.2, max. pres. width 10.2   III

263.            **6G64:113** (AbS 394)
                Grave 2 (No. 4)
                Stem and half dish only.
                Ware unknown (except surface reddish).
                Pres. H. 25.0, rim di 31.0
                [Moon 1981:no. 70]   IIIA early

264. **6G86:274**
     Ash Tip (Batch 1973)
     Rim sherd only.
     Burnt greyish buff clay.
     Perhaps sand temper
     Pres. H. c. 4.8

IIIA-B

265. **6G75:131**
     Grave 162 upper fill (Batch 3614)
     Sherd only.
     Grey clay (probably burnt).
     Fine even grit and veg. temper.
     Pres. H. 2.9
     Rim di. between 28.0 and 30.0
     Design stamped or rouletted, not with same
     instrument as no. 264, though very similar.

IIIB

266. **6G37:132** (AbS 881)
     Grave 38 (No. 23)
     Pink clay.
     Cream slip.
     Grit temper.
     Pres. H. 2.0
     Rim di. c. 7.0

IIIB?

267. **6G64:644** (AbS 714)
     Ash Pit cutting Rooms 39/44 (Batch 43)
     Fragment only.
     Pink clay.
     Cream slip.
     Grit temper.
     Pres. H. 2.4
     Rim di. 10.0
     Patch of unslipped surface near base
     of dish shows where stem was attached.
     Scratchy attempt at incision.

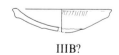

IIIB?

NOT ILLUSTRATED:

268. **6G85:39** (AbS 1855)
     Grave 165 (Batch 1805)
     Stem and part of dish and base: no rims preserved.
     Red clay, cream slip, temper of sand and some veg.
     Pres. H. 33.5. di. of stem 11.0
     Two ribs under dish added in veg.-tempered clay, one
     on lower stem.
     Two diametrically opposed holes at top of stem.
     Four regularly spaced holes just below lowest rib.
     Incised hatched triangles at top of base.    IIIA

269. **6G63:439** (Room 61 fill, Batch 920)
     Decoration on lower stem. [Moon 1981:no. 48
     (wrongly numbered 339)]    III

270. **6G63:440** (surface, Batch 900)
     Decoration on lower stem. [Moon 1981:no. 52]    III

271. **4I08:25** (AbS 1215) (Grave 84, no. 1)
     Hatched decoration on base. [Moon 1981:no. 54]    IIIB

272. **6G52:1** (AbS 504) (Grave 17, no. 1)
     Long opening and stylised tree. [Moon 1981:no. 73]    IIIA

273. **6G66:140** (AbS 810) (Grave 5, no. 2)
     Outline trangles on base. [Moon 1981:no. 74]    IIIB

274. **6G37:107** (AbS 1017) (Grave 32, no. 8)
     Crude. Stem decorated.
     [Postgate and Moorey 1976:fig. 7 no. 6]
     [Moon 1981:no. 79]    IIIB

# STANDS

A 'stand' is defined here as a vessel, usually cylindrical, probably used to support another pot, though we are not always entirely sure of the function.

Large, decorated hollow stands such as nos. 275 and 276 rarely survive intact, but the high percentage of fragments of them found among sherds shows they must have been relatively common. The surface of the West Mound was particularly rich in such pieces, and hollow stands must have been especially popular in ED I times. No profiles have been found in ED III levels, and it is just possible that all the sherds of hollow stands we find in them are in fact derived. That their use continues into ED II at least is confirmed by no. 276. No apparent changes in style have been observed, the cut-out triangles of no. 275 and the incised inverted Vs of no. 276 both apparently remaining popular for a long time. Cut-out circles and squares have also been noted.

For the late Early Dynastic parts of the site there is nothing to quarrel with Delougaz' remark that 'there can be little doubt ... that ... such utensils were intended for ritual rather than domestic use. Indeed they are often depicted in ritual scenes' (1952 p. 56). However, the situation on the West Mound suggests either that these rituals were themselves of a domestic nature, i.e. every household shrine had its own hollow stand, or that another use is indicated too. No evidence of burning has been noted to help the theory that hollow stands were used as braziers. Projections to the inside near the base (as survive on no. 275) are usual, and must have supported a saucer or something similarly shallow.

The long slender ribbed stands from Room 50 (nos. 277-279) are among the few pottery artefacts from southern Babylonia that recall ED II parallels in the Diyala region (Delougaz 1952 Pl. 68 a-c, from ED II levels at Tell Agrab and the Square Temple at Tell Asmar). The style is not identical, but they clearly have a related purpose. The surviving top of no. 279 looks as though a bowl or something was attached to it once, as with nos. 291-293. Pieces of wide bases of stands like nos. 280-282 are often found among sherds, particularly from the late Early Dynastic parts of the site, but we do not yet know what the whole vessel looks like. Indeed it is often difficult to decide whether small pieces come from stands or large bowls. It would be satisfying to find some clues as to the real use of the holes in these and other forms of stand.

Plain, short tubular potstands, very common at other periods, are generally rare at Abu Salabikh, though there are a number of fragments from post-ED contexts such as drains (like nos. 287-288) and the late rubbish beyond the town wall in 5I79. The people of Early Dynastic Babylonia obviously usually found some other way of stopping their pots falling over on uneven mud floors. Tall, plain potstands found in ED II and III contexts elsewhere have not so far been identified at Abu Salabikh. Tiny pottery rings such as no. 283 occur all over Mesopotamia from at least the 'Ubaid to the Akkadian period (for instance at Kish, Mackay 1929 Pl. XLIV no. 1). Their actual purpose is unknown, and fragments are often overlooked because the thin edge can be rough and appear to be broken. They are often overfired and contain a lot of grit, suggesting their function involved getting very hot. Kiln-separators would be an obvious guess, but these are not in fact necessary with unglazed pots. Perhaps the rings simply played some role in baking.

The two earlier 'stands' from the West Mound (nos. 289-290) are included here as potstands as a demonstration of other possibilites for supporting pots. Artefacts similar to these have been found in Jamdat Nasr contexts elsewhere (Moon 1982 p. 118).

Nos. 291-293 are a kind of potstand to which the pot is permanently attached. Few examples have been recognized so far at Abu Salabikh and it is not possible to suggest a usual date for them. We noticed several on the surface of al-Hiba, and there is one from Khafajah (Delougaz 1952 C.026.410, shown upside-down).

Sieve-stands like nos. 294-305 only occur in combination with four-part sets (see Appendix D), and are therefore more or less confined to graves of late ED IIIA. They vary much more in shape and size than other members of the sets. Unless stated, it is not known which way up any of them were used. Sherds of what would seem to be a very much larger version of the same shape are often found, so far none sufficiently complete to say much about the original shape (e.g. Postgate 1985 Grave 2 no. 18).

275. **2GS:242**
     2G31 sub-surface (Batch 5029)
     Fragmentary.
     Overfired green clay.
     Temper unknown.
     Pres. H. 21.7
     Ba. di. 20.0
     [Postgate 1978:fig. 3 no. 3,
     1983:fig. 291]

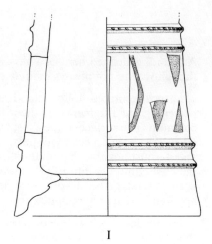

I

276. **6G54:98** (AbS 1042)
     Sounding Level II floors (Batch 125)
     Rim and base lost.
     Ware unknown.
     Pres. 28.0
     Max. pres. width. 27.5
     Scraped vertically in.
     [Postgate 1977:fig. 5 no. 11]

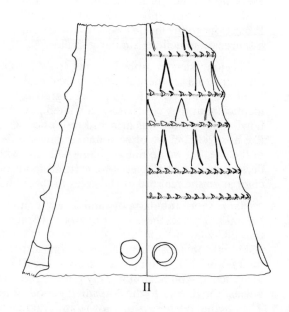

II

277. **4J97:297**
     Room 50 phase 4 floors (Batch 4473)
     Part of stem only.
     Pink clay.
     Cream slip out.
     Sandy temper.
     Pres. H. 18.5
     Max. pres. width c. 21.0
     [Postgate 1984 Pl. VIa]

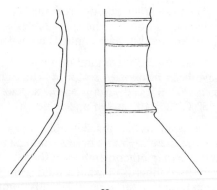

II

278. **4J97:296**
Room 50, phase 4 floors (Batch 4473)
Part of stem and one end only.
Pink clay.
Paler surface.
Dense sandy grit temper.
Pres. H. 21.8
Mouth di. (reconstruc.) 23.0
[Postgate 1984 Pl. VIa]

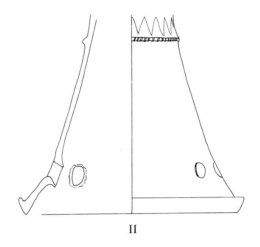

II

279. **4J97:268**
Room 50 phase 4 floors (Batch 4473)
Most of stem present, both ends missing.
Pink clay.
Perfunctory cream slip out.
Grit temper.
Pres. H. 32.8
Max. pres. width 21.8
[Postgate 1984 Pl. VIa]
Rough edge at top: probably
joined to dish of some kind.

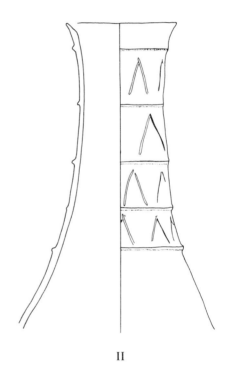

II

280. **6G75:297**
Grave 194 (Batch 3640)
Fragment only.
Pink clay.
Cream slip.
Grit temper.
Pres. H. 8.8
Ba. di. c. 18.0

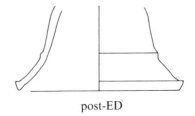

post-ED

281. **5IS:240**
FI 81/7 in 5I77
(Batch 5381)
Fragmentary.
Red clay.
Cream slip out.
Sandy temper.
Pres. H. 13.2
Ba. di. 40.4
Probably four
opposed pairs of holes.

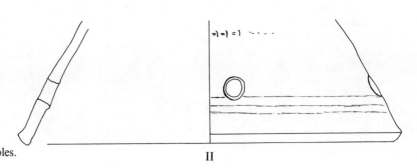

II

282. **6G85:90**
Fill of room E. of corridor joining
Rooms 54 and 82 (Batch 1815)
Base frag. only.
Orange clay.
Cream slip.
Temper of sand and fine grit.
Pres. H. 13.4
Ba. di. c. 28.0
Two surviving holes in body.

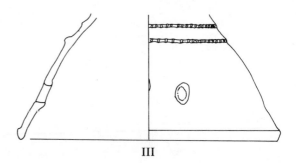

III

283. **6G77:89**
Ash Tip (Batch 3906)
Fragment only.
Browny buff clay.
Grit temper.
H. 1.1
Top di. 7.2
Bottom di. c. 10.0

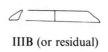

IIIB (or residual)

284. **6G54:151** (AbS 1078)
Grave 48 (No. 16)
Complete but for chips.
Red clay.
Vague cream slip out.
No apparent temper.
H. 6.3
Rim di. 10.0
Ba. di. 13.0

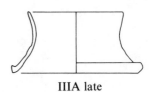

IIIA late

285. **5I21:267** (AbS 1022)
Grave 31 (No. 13)
Condition and ware unknown.
H. 6.9
Top di. 9.3
Bottom di. 13.8

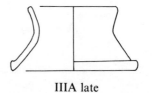

IIIA late

286. **6G36:153**
Cut in Room 118 (Batch 2440)
About one quarter preserved.
Orange clay.
White slip.
Temper of grit including
a little fine white grit.
H. 6.8
Rim di. 13.0-18.0
Ba. di. 18.4

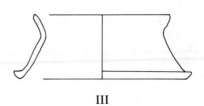

III

287. **6G75:105**
    Drain packing (Batch 3608)
    Red clay.
    Cream slip.
    Grog and veg. temper.
    H. 6.5
    Rim di. c. 18.0
    Ba. di. 20.0

post ED

288. NEARLY IDENTICAL: **No number**
    Drain packing in 6G65 (Batch 252)
    Condition and ware unknown.
    H. 7.5, rim di. 19.6, ba. di. 20.8    Post ED

289. **2G36:83**
    Large Pit, West Mound Level II (Batch 5410)
    About a quarter preserved:
    centre and edge of rim missing.
    Pink clay.
    Buff slip out.
    Hard grit and veg. temper.
    Pres. H. 8.0
    Ba. di. c. 11.0
    String-cut base.

residual Jamdat Nasr?

290. **2G36:191**
    Foundation for West Mound
    Level II building (Batch 5441)
    About a quarter preserved,
    centre missing.
    Green clay.
    Rough grog and veg. temper.
    H. 4.4
    Rim di. c. 19.0
    Ba. di. c. 19.0
    Inside edge may have been notched.
    [Postgate and Moon 1982:fig. 4 no. 3]

residual Jamdat Nasr?

291. **5I78:15**
    Rubble fill between
    boundary walls (Batch 7209)
    One end only.
    Red clay.
    Sandy grit temper.
    Pres. H. 9.4
    Rim di. 10.0
    Rim rough as though once attached to
    something, perhaps like no. 292 (below).

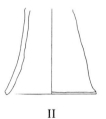

II

292. SIMILAR:    **6G55:175**
    Grave 49 (No. 5)
    Base and dish broken off.
    Ware unknown.
    Pres. H. 24.0, top di. 12.6    IIIB

293. **6G65:318**
    Room 49 Level IA/B
    floors (Batch 206 + 241)
    Two non-joining sherds,
    presumed same vessel.
    Greyish clay.
    Temper unknown.
    H. 5.0
    Top di. 5.0
    Bottom di. 12.4
    Probably fixed to long tubular
    stand like no. 291 above.

IIIA

294. **6G55:171**
     Grave 49 (No. 4)
     Fragmentary.
     Red clay.
     Grit temper.
     H. 7.0
     Rim di. 5.4
     Ba. di. 6.4

IIIB

295. **5I21:272**
     Grave 42 (No. 11)
     Both rims broken.
     Fine pink clay.
     Paler surface.
     Temper unknown.
     H. 9.6
     Rim di. 7.0
     Ba. di. c. 9.0
     Well-finished.

IIIA late

296. SIMILAR:   **5I21:161** (AbS 575)
                 Grave 28 (No. 18)
                 Condition and ware unknown.
                 H. 10.8, rim di. 8.6, ba. di. 12.8    IIIA late

297. **6F05:163** (AbS 2006)
     Grave 182 (Batch 6015)
     Intact but for chips.
     Dark red clay.
     Fine sparse temper of sand
     and a little white grit.
     H. 12.0
     Rim di. 7.5
     Ba. di. 12.5-13.0
     Found on its side, but narrow end nearest
     sieve bowl it presumably supported.

IIIA late

298. **5I21:324** (AbS 1282)
     Grave 96 (No. 4)
     Buff clay.
     Cream slip.
     Temper unknown.
     H. 12.9
     Rim di. 9.4
     Ba. di. 10.0
     Found this way up.

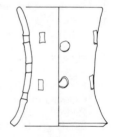

IIIA late

299. SIMILAR:   **6G63:151**
                 Grave 73 (No. 42)
                 Fragmentary.
                 Red clay, patchy red and cream surface, grit temper.
                 Pres. H. 11.0, rim di. 10.8, ba. di. 11.2    IIIA late

300. **6G85:40** (AbS 1856)
     Grave 165 (Batch 1805)
     Intact.
     Pinky-orange clay.
     Buff slip.
     Sandy temper.
     H. 13.2
     Rim di. 8.1-8.5
     Ba. di. 10.5-10.8
     Found lying on side.

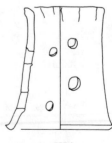

IIIA

301. SIMILAR:   **6G54:84** (AbS 659)
                 Grave 48 (No. 6)
                 Complete, ware unknown.
                 H. 13.8, rim di. 10.1, ba. di. 11.7    IIIA late

302. **6G85:73**
Grave 171 (Batch 1809)
Fragmentary.
Red clay.
Temper of much sand.
H. 18.1
Rim di. c. 8.0
Ba. di. c. 14.0

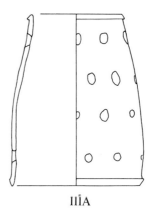

IIÎA

303. **6G75:427** (AbS 2214)
Grave 162 (S) fill (Batch 3644)
Much of base ring missing,
also a little of rim and body.
Pink clay.
Bùff slip.
Temper of grit
including white grit.
H. 20.4
Rim di. 14.3-14.7
Ba. di. (reconstruc.) 14.8

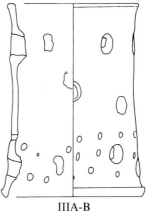

IIIA-B

304. **5I21:120** (AbS 656)
Grave 26 (No. 36)
Small piece of top rim missing.
Ware unknown.
H. 17.8
Rim di. 9.7
Ba. di. 10.9
Found this way up.

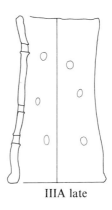

IIIA late

305. **6G64:613** (AbS 550)
Grave 1 ( No. 59)
One or two chips.
Soft red clay.
Sand and veg. temper.
H. 25.0
Rim di. 11.5
Ba. di. 16.5
[Postgate and Moorey 1976:
fig. 8 no. 18 and Pl. XXVc]

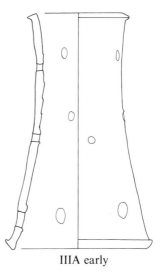

IIIA early

# BOTTLES

Bottles are defined here as jars with restricted necks, treated separately from other round-based closed forms, as they offer scope for particular comments and comparisons worth making separately.

Pieces of small bottles occur throughout the ED levels at Abu Salabikh, though not with heavy frequency, but only two ED I specimens are preserved enough to illustrate (nos. 308 and 309). Some of the ED II examples (nos. 317-319) have good parallels (e.g. Delougaz 1952 B.545.540 for no. 317), which is all too rarely the case with ED II types. The distinguishing chronological feature is the narrow base of the neck, and the rim is also fairly distinctive with a depression just inside. This is difficult to demonstrate without close-up photographs, but an exaggerated form can be seen on the ED II pilgrim-flasks from Khafajah (ibid. B.806.570). Only one small bottle with double-angled sides has so far appeared at Abu Salabikh (no. 312) though they seem common enough elsewhere, mostly ED III or later (e.g. Mackay 1925 Pl. XVI nos. 28-30, some red-slipped and burnished). The sharp-shouldered bottles (nos. 321-322) on the other hand do not seem to have relations on other sites.

The large bottles, nos. 323-327, can be found all over Mesopotamia from ED IIIA onwards. The ones with scored neck or neck and shoulder like nos. 325 and 326 look somehow alien to the Early Dynastic assemblage, but are well-paralleled (for instance in the Lower Diyala, Delougaz 1952 B.666.540b; at Kish, Mackay 1929 Pl. LIII no. 53; at Ur, Woolley 1934 Pl. 257 no. 106). No. 326 with its very fine, gritty orange fabric is especially curious and quite unlike Abu Salabikh ceramics generally, though occasionally sherds of this kind of ware do occur. Bottles like these are among the few types that stretch right up the Euphrates at this period (for instance to Mari, Parrot 1956 fig. 106 no. 693 (grey)), and one might hazard that the idea of making such bottles, if not the bottles themselves, came with Syrian craftsmen.

The unusually-shaped no. 328 with its curious heavy pierced lugs has a parallel at Khafajah (Delougaz 1952 B.564.371), and, as with the large bottles, related forms stretch far to the north-west (to Chuera, Kühne 1976 Pl. 21 no. 3). This type shares features with the 'pilgrim flasks' of the Diyala region, but is not really the same. Only two pieces of possible pilgrim flask have been recorded at Abu Salabikh, although future study of the sherds may reveal one or two more. These flasks, with pierced lugs on the side of the neck occur in ED III and 'protoimperial' levels at Khafajah and Tell Asmar (Delougaz 1952 B.816.521), but what little survives of the Abu Salabikh specimens is not convincingly like them. Certainly they do not resemble the high-shouldered lugless type found in ED II graves at Khafajah (ibid. B.806.570, B.807.570). The 'superficial impression' that there were many pieces of pilgrim flask in Level II of the Area E sounding (Postgate 1977 p. 294) would seem to be based on no. 328, which in fact came from a Level I floor of the sounding. No. 329, from a foundation trench dug for an ED II wall into ED I levels seems more likely (though not inevitably) to belong to the disturbed deposit than to have been introduced by the builders (Postgate 1984 p. 108).

306. **6G37:145** (AbS 1109)
    Room 104 fill (Batch 525)
    Complete.
    Red clay.
    Temper unknown.
    H. 8.4
    Rim di. 3.7
    Ba. di. 3.4
    String-cut base.

II or III

307. **4I09:106**
    Grave 93 (No. 15)
    Rim and some
    of body missing.
    Red clay.
    Grit and shell temper.
    Pres. H. 9.2
    Ba. di. 4.5
    String-cut base.

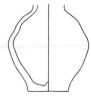

IIIB

308. **1T:6** (AbS 1454)
North-East Mound,
perhaps Grave 111 (Batch 4000)
Rim and neck missing.
Red clay.
Buff slip out.
Heavy temper of fine grit.
H. 8.5
Ba. di. 3.4

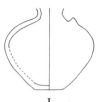

I

309. **1T:3** (AbS 1452)
Grave 111 (Batch 4000)
Complete but for chipped rim.
Red clay.
Heavy grit temper
including mica.
H. 9.6
Rim di. 5.5
Ba. di. 2.2

I

310. **6HS:296** (AbS 2212)
6H92 sub-surface, inside
drain 6HS:293 (Batch 7086)
Nearly complete, but rim
abraded and surface salted.
Pink clay.
Yellowy surface.
Sandy temper.
H. 9.0
Rim di. 3.6
Max. width 9.6

III

311. **4I08:28** (AbS 1214)
Grave 84 (No. 4)
Virtually complete.
Buff clay.
Cream slip.
Temper unknown.
H. 10.2
Rim di. 6.2

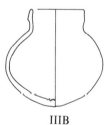

IIIB

312. **6G75:103** (AbS 1947)
Probably Grave 184 (Batch 3601)
Part of side missing, rim abraded.
Friable red clay.
Perhaps originally cream slip out.
Sandy temper.
H. 9.5
Rim di. (reconstruc.) c. 4.0
Max. width 10.4

IIIB?

313. **6G63:256**
Pit in Room 61 (Batch 914)
Rim missing.
Red clay.
Grit temper.
Pres. H. 9.4
Ba. di. 5.0

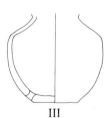

III

314. **6G37:432** (AbS 1384)
Grave 80 (No. 17)
Intact.
Pale pink clay.
Cream slip.
Grit temper.
H. 11.4
Rim di. 4.3
[Postgate 1977:fig. 5 no. 6]

II

315. **6G37:106** (AbS 762)
Grave 38 (No. 30)
Large gap in side.
Red clay.
Cream slip out.
Sandy temper.
H. 9.0
Rim di. 5.5

II

316. **5I98:186**
Grave 203 (Batch 7405)
Gaps in shoulder
and body, rim chipped.
Pink clay.
Dense fine grit temper.
H. 15.0
Rim di. 8.2
Ba. di. 5.4
Lower body shaped by shaving down on outside.
[Postgate 1984:fig. 7 no. 2]

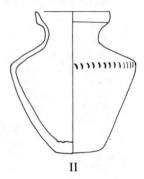

II

317. **5I98:101** (AbS 2231)
Grave 205 (Batch 7420)
Intact.
Pink surface.
Sandy grit temper including mica.
H. 12.2
Rim di. 4.4
Max. width 12.6
[Postgate 1984:fig. 7 no. 1]

II

318. **5I31:61** (AbS 1212)
Grave 81 (No. 7)
Rim slightly chipped.
Fine grey clay.
Temper unknown.
H. 6.9
Rim di. 3.8
Surface well-smoothed
but not actually burnished.
Contained fish bone 5I31:81
[Postgate 1977:fig. 5 no. 2]

II

319. **8GS:23** (AbS 1451)
Grave 110 (no Batch no.)
Intact.
Pink clay.
Vague cream slip.
Grit temper.
H. 10.4
Rim di. 5.3

II

320. **4J98:29** (AbS 1208)
Room 26 fill (Batch 1610)
Rim missing.
Buff clay.
Traces of cream slip.
Temper unknown.
H. 11.0
Max. width 17.4
Found inside ribbed spouted jar no. 706

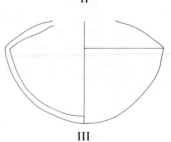

III

321. **6G38:29** (AbS 1004)
     Room 110 fill (Batch 806)
     Rim and much of body missing.
     Red clay.
     Cream surface.
     Temper unknown.
     Pres. H. 7.2
     Max. width 15.5
     [Postgate and Moorey 1976:fig. 8 no. 11]
     Contained jewellery hoard [ibid.:158, 166]

II

322. **6G37:163**
     Grave 33 (No. 3)
     Shoulder and body fragments,
     and very abraded rim extant.
     Red clay.
     Fine sand and mica temper.
     Rim di. 3.6
     Angle of body not
     so steep as no. 321

III

323. **6G45:18** (AbS 1616)
     Grave 136 (Batch 2902)
     Intact.
     Pink clay.
     Patchy pink and buff surface.
     Grit and mica temper.
     H. 18.3
     Rim di. 4.5
     Max. width 12.6

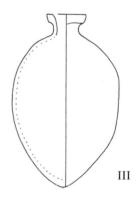

III

324. **6G75:459** (AbS 2209)
     Grave 162 (S) fill (Batch 3684)
     Quarter of lower
     body and side missing.
     Pink clay.
     Cream slip.
     Grit temper.
     H. 18.8
     Rim di. 5.2
     Max. width 14.4

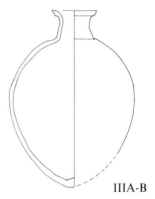

IIIA-B

325. **6G37:180** (AbS 1173)
     Grave 89 (No. 13)
     Intact.
     Buff clay.
     Cream slip.
     Temper unknown.
     H. 23.2
     Rim di. 7.1
     Traces of possible jar seal-
     ing (reddish concretion) on neck.
     Base had remnants of
     rush circle adhering.

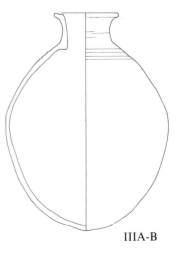

IIIA-B

326. **6F05:169**
     Grave 183 (Batch
     6007 + 6012 + 6018)
     Fragmentary upper parts of two
     identical bottles, with the lower
     (non-joining) part of one, probably A.
     Dull orange clay.
     Temper of much grit
     including white grit.
     A: Pres. H. c. 23.2
     Rim di. 6.8
     B: Pres. H. 4.5
     Rim di. c. 6.0
     Both vessels have reserve-slip
     on upper body, B. has it on
     neck too, exaggerated to grooving.

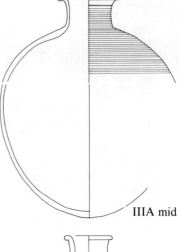

IIIA mid

327. **5I21:236** (AbS 901)
     Grave 42 (No. 9)
     Condition and ware unknown.
     Pres. H. 16.5
     Rim di. 5.1

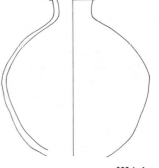

IIIA late

328. **6G54:375**
     Room 41 floors (Batch 123)
     Neck and small part of body only.
     Buff clay.
     Yellow slip.
     Temper of grit and a
     very little fine veg.
     Pres. H. 6.0
     Rim (rectangular) 2.3 x 3.5
     Two heavy square flat lugs attached
     to neck and shoulder, pierced horizontally.

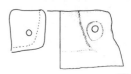

IIIA

329. **5I78:56**
     Foundation trench for
     boundary wall (Batch 7218)
     Side of neck only, including lug.
     Pink clay.
     Perfunctory cream slip.
     Heavy grit temper.
     Pres. H. 4.8
     Rim di. c. 6.0

I

330. **6G63:361** (AbS 1277)
     Grave 100 (Batch 973)
     A little of rim and base missing.
     Buff clay.
     Cream slip.
     Very sandy temper.
     Pres. H. 12.9
     Rim di. 6.0
     Ba. di. 7.0
     Two applied lugs,
     horizontally pierced.
     Ring base added
     in veg.-tempered clay.

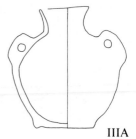

IIIA

# JARS WITH FOUR RIM-TABS

Round pots with four rim-tabs and often with scraped decoration on the shoulder are diagnostically ED I, and at Abu Salabikh are usually only found on the West and North-East Mounds except for a very few sherds from surface or soundings on the Main Mound. The early ED I date is supported by the depth to which fragments were found in the Tell Asmar sounding, overlapping with 'protoliterate' style painting (Delougaz 1952 Pl. 64 nos. 24 and 43).

These pots contain a certain amount of grit temper but not the heavy quantities often found in cooking-pots. The spherical shape and the frequency with which rim sherds are smoke-blackened, especially around the lugs, suggest however that they were involved in some heating process. It is difficult to imagine what form of cookery would blacken just the rim, but it was obviously not an innovation as we encountered the same phenomenon with 'Ubaid cooking vessels from Tell Madhhur. The lugs are made separately then stuck to the rim, from which they occasionally came unstuck, to judge from sherd finds, no doubt causing cursing and burnt fingers in the kitchen.

All early ED I

331. **No number**
    Large pit, West Mound
    Level II (Batch 5403)
    Rim fragment only.
    Buff clay.
    Sparse fine quartz and veg., much black grit.
    Pres. H. 2.1
    Rim di. 7.0
    Top of rim and single preserved tab smoke-blackened.

332. **2G46:123**
    Floors against West Mound
    Level II enclosure
    wall (Batch 5228 + 5531)
    Base, much of body
    and part of rim missing.
    Pink clay.
    Cream slip.
    Grit and veg. temper.
    Pres. H. 21.6
    Rim di. 10.4
    Rim-tabs unevenly placed.

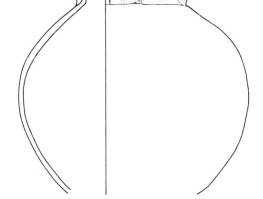

333. **2G36:44**
    Large pit, West Mound
    Level II (Batch 5403)
    One rim fragment with two tabs
    and a little of body, one non-
    joining fragment with another tab.
    Pink clay.
    Buff slip.
    Grit temper.
    Pres. H. 8.8
    Rim di. 13.6
    Shoulder scored horizontally
    to produce similar effect
    to reserve-slip but deeper.

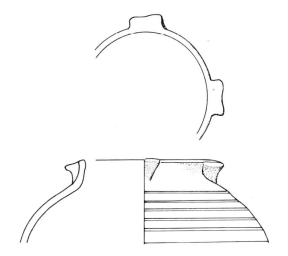

334. **2G36:194**
West Mound Level II, floors cut
by large pit (Batch 5422 + 5444)
Fragmentary, but most of rim extant.
Red clay.
Cream slip.
Sandy temper with much mica.
Pres. H. 18.0
Rim di. c. 10
Shoulder bears horizontal stria-
tions like deep reserve-slip.
Edges of tabs are smoke-blackened.

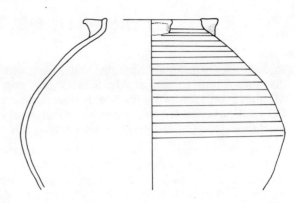

335. VERY SIMILAR: **2G46:116**
West Mound Level II floors against north
face of enclosure wall (Batch 5531)
Base and some of body missing.
Pink clay, buff slip out, fine grit temper.
Pres. H. 21.0, rim di. c. 15.0
Bitumen-lined.
[Postgate and Moon 1982:fig. 6 no. 4]

336. **No number**
Large pit, West Mound
Level II (Batch 5403)
Rim fragment only, one extant lug.
Buff clay.
Sparse fine veg. and
quartz, much black grit.
Pres. H. 5.6
Rim di. 11.0
Scored slip on shoulder.

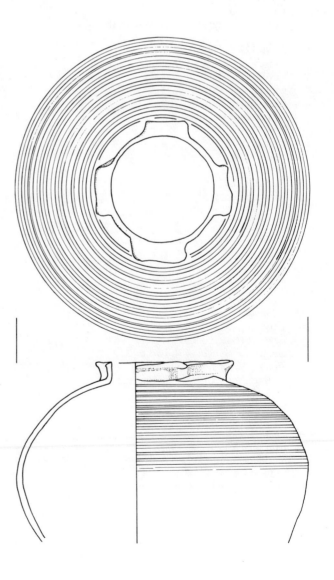

337. **2G46:137**
Floors against
West Mound Level II
enclosure wall
(Batch 5528)
Base and parts
of body missing.
Pink clay.
Cream slip.
Hard grit and
veg. temper.
Pres. H. 19.2
Rim di. 11.0
Shoulder scraped
horizontally, producing
blunt combed effect.

# ROUND-BASED JARS

This large section contains a wide range of pots, some with little in common except their round base. In spite of their overall diversity it has not been feasible to split them up, as the shapes form a continuum and divisions are difficult to impose. Most provoke no particular comments: they are just the typical small or medium-size jars which turn up on all Early Dynastic sites, but usually without really distinctive exact parallels. The majority come from graves: other contexts are not kind to round-based types, but all the same one would expect a few more of the smaller types to have survived if they really were common household items.

ED I is represented in this section only by two globular jars from the Area E sounding (nos. 344-345). A few ED II types occur, probably proportionate to the number of ED II graves found, given that these tend to specialise in conical bowls and spouted jars rather than a variety of shapes. No. 346 is fairly distinctive, and no. 420, but nos. 417-419 are not really usefully different from very similar later styles like no. 420. The ED II jars all have plain rims, but then so do many of the ED III ones. Round-based jars do not, on present evidence, offer much as dating criteria. The longer bodies and base tending towards a point, such as nos. 403-408, are all late ED III.

Nos. 338-345 might be described as cooking pots on account of their globular shape. A few pieces of 'cooking ware' turn up in most baskets of pottery excavated at Abu Salabikh. The fragments leave no doubt that they belonged to a globular, round-based jar with a swollen rim and no neck. The 'cooking ware' is bright pink or orange, the temper consists of much ground quartz, and the outside surfaces of the sherds are usually burnished and often smoke-blackened. This is the universal cooking-pot, near-spherical and heavily tempered in order to withstand direct heat. So far no complete profiles of this type have been found. Nos. 338-345, though of the same shape, were not made from cooking ware. (In spite of the irritating lack of ware descriptions for some, it is highly unlikely that the distinctive cooking-ware was not noted if it occurred).

The small jars with paint stripes on neck and shoulder, and sometimes grooving on the neck too (nos. 361, 363, 364, 366, and 380) stand out among the drab plain types of similar shape, and are another of the closed forms that seem more at home further west, nearer to real painted traditions (at Mari, Parrot 1956, fig. 107 nos. 1548 and 1549). No. 366 is particularly unusual for Abu Salabikh with its hard burnished fabric, more akin to the 'céramique métallique' of the Euphrates valley (Lebeau 1985 Pl. XVI). Others, such as no. 380, are of normal Abu Salabikh pink to buff clay with cream slip. Perhaps plain jars with ridges on the shoulder are also meant to be faint imitations of the same style, like nos. 386 and 389.

Sometimes a single example of a fine and usually badly-eroded small jar is found in a grave, such as nos. 358 and 403, often next to the skull, a position occupied in earlier graves by a bottle (for instance in Grave 81).

The holes near the bottom of some round-base types, apparently a late ED III feature (nos. 412-415, 423, 330-332), were perhaps to filter a liquid with a sediment. It is also sometimes suggested that holes were to allow air to circulate round a non-liquid substance such as grain to prevent mould, but there are much more efficient containers for materials which need good ventilation, such as sacks.

It is tempting to try and guess at a special function for the long-necked vessels (nos. 438-442). They cannot stand up without support, but seem much too big for one-shot drinking cups. They would have hung quite well from something, for instance a saddle, and the thickened rim of all except no. 441 would facilitate suspension. This easily-recognizable shape is occasionally found elsewhere in northern Babylonia (at Kish, Mackay 1929 Pl. XLIV no. 1891B), but is more popular in the far south: there were quite a few in the Royal Cemetery (Woolley 1934 Pl. 254 no. 61).

338. **6G86:91** (AbS 1938)
Grave 175 (Batch 1924)
Complete but surface chipped.
Dark red clay.
Pinkish slip out.
Paler in.
Very sparse temper of fine grit.
H. 10.0
Rim di. 7.2
Max. width 12.8

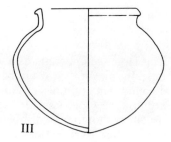

III

339. **5I21:125** (AbS 757)
Grave 26 (No. 28)
Many small gaps in body.
Ware unknown.
H. 13.5
Rim di. 11.8

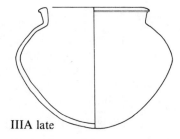

IIIA late

340. **4I09:7** (AbS 1113)
Grave 95 (No. 8)
Brown clay, blackened
patches inside and out.
Ware unknown, but
field note says
'not usual cooking ware.'
H. 17.0
Rim di. 12.0
Contained residue 4I09:12
and bones 4I09:52

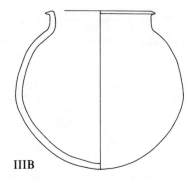

IIIB

341. **6G84:8** (AbS 1934)
Pit in Room 80 (Batch 1701)
A few chips missing.
Orange clay.
Pink core.
Rather patchy cream slip.
Temper of fine black and white grit.
H. 18.2
Rim di. 10.4-10.7
Max. width 20.7

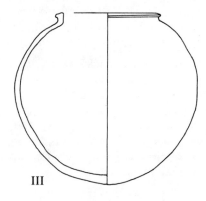

III

342. **No number**
Grave 68 (No. 6)
Condition and ware unknown.
H. 21.0
Rim di. 14.0

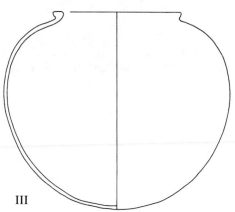

III

343. **6G64:181** (AbS 579)
Grave 1 (No. 1)
A few chips missing.
Ware unknown.
H. 20.2
Rim di. 14.0
Associated with three
tripod legs (AbS 814)

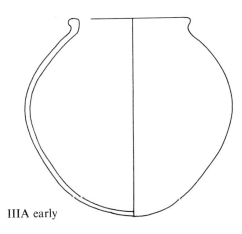

IIIA early

344. **6G54:307** (AbS 1203)
Sounding Level III
fill (Batch 170)
Large sections missing
from rim and body.
Buff clay.
Greenish slip.
Temper unknown.
H. 32.3
Rim di. 12.0-13.3
[Postgate 1977:
fig. 5 no. 10]

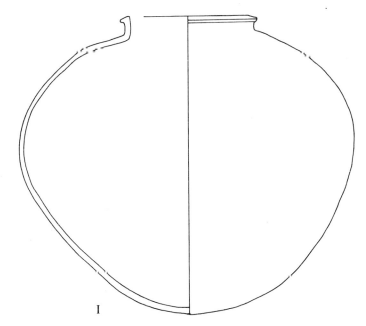

I

345. SIMILAR: **6G54:355**
Sounding Level III floor (Batch 183)
Body sherds only.
Reddish clay, cream surface out, grit temper.   I

346. **5IS:203** (AbS 2035)
Grave 185 (Batch 5372)
Base missing.
Some gaps in shoulder.
Orange clay.
Buff slip.
Grit and white grit temper.
Pres. H. 23.2
Rim di. 15.2
Max. width 32.7

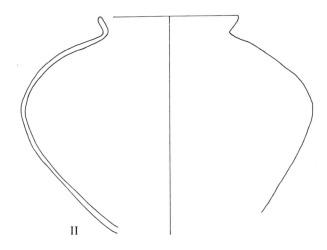

II

347. **6G37:456** (AbS 1423)
    Grave 107 (Batch 571)
    Intact.
    Black clay.
    Surface polished under base.
    Grit temper.
    H. 11.0
    Rim di. 6.9
    Heat-crazed.
    Rim hand-finished.

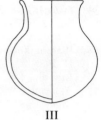

III

348. **6G37:509** (AbS 1462)
    Grave 113 (Batch 577)
    Rim slightly chipped.
    Ware unknown.
    H. 9.6
    Rim di. 6.8

III

349. SIMILAR: **6G63:339** (AbS 1390)
            Grave 73 (No. 4)
            Almost complete.
            Dense red clay, paler slip, very
            sparse temper of sand and mica.
            H. 16.2, rim di. 10.4   IIIA late

350.         **6G37:52** (AbS 622)
            Grave 32 (No. 25)
            Fragmentary: base and half of body only, ware unknown.
            Pres. H. 10.0   IIIB

351. **4I08:28** (AbS 1214)
    Grave 84 (No. 4)
    Small piece missing from body.
    Soft buff clay.
    Cream slip.
    Grit temper.
    (Ware unusual for Abu Salabikh)
    H. 10.2
    Rim di. 6.2
    Smoke-blackened in
    two places under shoulder.

IIIB

352. **6F05:27** (AbS 1931)
    Grave 168 (Batch 6000)
    A few chips, otherwise intact.
    Hard red clay.
    Thick grey surfaces.
    Temper of veg. and some fine grit.
    H. 9.6
    Rim di. 6.6 (reconstruc.)
    Max. width 9.8

IIIA-B

353. **6G47:81** (AbS 1619)
    Room 120 upper layers (Batch 2509)
    Part of rim missing.
    Sandy red clay.
    Cream slip.
    Temper unknown.
    H. 10.7
    Rim di. 8.1
    Very thin-walled.

III

354. **6G37:542** (AbS 1620)
Room 103 fill (Batch 592)
Parts of body missing.
Fine, hard, pink clay.
Pale pink slip.
Fine grit and white grit temper.
H. 9.5
Rim di. 7.1-10.0

II or III

355. **6G64:112** (AbS 400)
Grave 2 (No. 5)
Piece missing from rim.
Red clay.
Buff surface out.
Grit temper.
H. 10.0
Rim di. 7.2
Rim 'frilly' as not really finished off.

IIIA early

356. **5110:33**
Pit in Room 2 (Batch 1006)
Complete but for chips.
Dark red clay, slightly grey core in places.
Temper very sparse grit, perhaps not deliberate.
H. 10.5
Rim di. c. 7.2

III

357. PERHAPS SIMILAR: **6G64:201** (AbS 399)
Surface (Batch 7)
About half extant: base does not join.
Very fine pink clay, no apparent temper.
Pres. H. c. 8.0
Very well-made and fine-walled.    III?

358. **6G36:242**
Grave 116 (Batch 2437)
Fragmentary, salted and badly eroded.
Relationship between non-joining pieces not known.
Pink clay.
Sandy temper.
H. 8.6
Rim di. 6.5
Max. width c. 8.2

IIIB?

359. **6G75:126** (AbS 1970)
Grave 162 (Batch 3616)
Neck chipped, otherwise complete.
Pink clay.
Sparse grit temper.
H. 7.6
Rim di. 6.1
Max. width 7.6

IIIA-B

360. SIMILAR: **6G37:50** (AbS 925)
Room 103 fill (Batch 508)
Intact but for chip from rim.
Pink clay, cream slip, fine sandy temper.
H. 9.2, rim di. 6.3    II or III

361. **6G38:152** (AbS 1378)
Grave 102 (Batch 823)
Complete.
Dark red clay.
Perfunctory buff slip.
Sparse fine grit temper.
H. 10.9
Rim di. 8.5
Red paint applied over grooves in body.

III

362. **6G44:20** (AbS 1744)
Grave 142 (Batch 3101)
Fragments of rim and body missing.
Pinkish clay.
Cream slip.
Fine grit and veg. temper.
H. 16.4
Rim di. 10.5
Neck slightly ridged, shoulder grooved.
No surviving trace of paint.

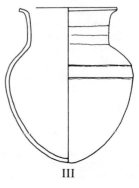

III

363. **6G84:46** (AbS 1929)
Grave 179 (Batch 1712)
Virtually intact: two
small chips from body.
Dense dark orange clay.
Paler slip.
Sparse temper of fine veg.
H. 12.5
Rim di. 8.9-9.0
Ba. di. 3.2
Neck ridged.
Red paint applied over grooves in body.
Shoulder perhaps burnished.

IIIA

364. IDENTICAL: **6G63:367** (AbS 1276)
Grave 100 (Batch 973)
Small pieces missing from rim and body.
Reddish clay, cream slip fired
red in places, temper unknown.
H. 16.8, rim di. 10.6, ba. di. 3.0
Nine deep grooves on neck, two more on shoulder.
Bands of red paint over grooves.
Body lightly burnished. IIIA

365. **6G47:116** (AbS 1596)
Grave 126 (Batch 2551)
Small gaps.
Pink clay.
Cream slip.
Fine grit and veg. temper.
H. 19.5
Rim di. 12.0
Fine-walled and well-made.
No traces of paint or grooves.

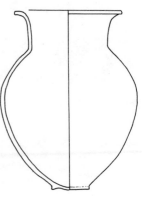

III late

366. **6F05:181** (AbS 2020)
    Grave 183 (Batch 6012)
    A few sherds only.
    Extremely fine, hard, orange
    clay, layered grey in places.
    Very fine, hard grit temper,
    including white grit and much mica.
    Red paint.
    Shoulder has streaky horizontal burnishing.
    Pres. H. 6.5
    Rim di. c. 11.6

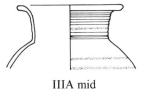

IIIA mid

367. **6G85:25** (AbS 1928)
    Grave 163 (Batch 1804)
    Virtually complete.
    Pink clay.
    Paler surface.
    Sandy temper.
    H. 16.4
    Rim di. 13.4
    Max. width 15.2
    Well-made and finished.

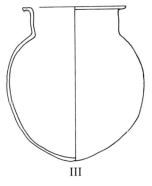

III

368. SIMILAR: **6G85:28**
        Grave 163 (Batch 1804)
        Body sherds only.
        Red clay, white slip, sparse sandy temper.    III

369. FAIRLY SIMILAR: **5I10:166** (AbS 698)
        Grave 41 (No. 2)
        Rim and neck missing.
        Temper unknown.
        Pres. H. 11.0    III

370. PROBABLY SIMILAR: **6G37:101** (AbS 858)
        Grave 38 (No. 27)
        Rim missing, rest fragmentary.
        Ware unknown.
        Pres. H. 22.5
        Incised line around base of neck. IIIB

371. **6G54:141** (AbS 1070)
    Grave 48 (No. 11)
    Chipped.
    Fine pink clay.
    Cream surface.
    Fine white grit temper.
    H. 18.0
    Rim di. 11.4
    Max. width 17.0
    Three horizontal grooves on upper
    body, perhaps markers for paint no
    longer preserved, like no. 361

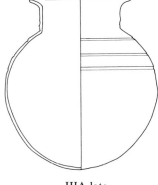

IIIA late

372. **6G54:150** (AbS 1077)
 Grave 48 (No. 12)
 Condition and ware unknown.
 H. 19.5
 Rim di. 10.0
 Ba. di. 3.0

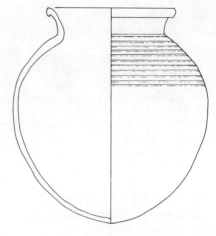

373. **6F05:168** (AbS 2022)
 Grave 183 (Batch 6012 + 6018)
 Much of middle body missing.
 Orange clay.
 Pink slip out.
 Inner surface yellowish.
 Sandy temper with
 occasional white grit.
 H. 19.6
 Rim di. 11.6-11.8
 Horizontal scoring on shoulder.

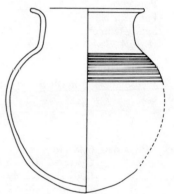

IIIA mid

374. SIMILAR: **6G63:315** (AbS 1413)
 Grave 73 (No. 7)
 Complete but for chips.
 Red clay, fine sandy temper.
 H. 14.8, rim di. 9.9
 Series of shallow horizontal
 grooves on upper body.    IIIA late

375. **6G95:1** (AbS 2023)
 Grave 163 (Batch 3700)
 Nearly half rim and body
 missing; brittle and flaky.
 Red clay.
 Cream slip (mostly rubbed off)
 Rather sparse grit temper.
 H. 15.8
 Rim di. 10.6
 Max. width 14.2

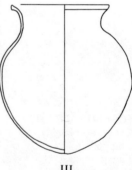

III

376. **6F05:22**
 Grave 168 (Batch 6000)
 Some gaps.
 Pinky orange clay.
 Temper of fine grit and fine veg.
 H. 16.8
 Rim di. 10.4
 Well-made.

377. SIMILAR: **6G63:82** (AbS 1104)
 Grave 73 (no. 33)
 Much of rim missing.
 Buff clay, temper unknown.
 H. 17.5, rim di. c. 10.5   IIIA late

IIIA-B

378. **6G37:115** (AbS 935)
   Grave 32 (No. 13)
   Fragmentary – about half missing.
   Ware unknown (except 'fine')
   H. 18.4
   Rim di. 8.5
   Max. width 15.0

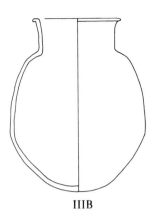

IIIB

379. **6G37:108** (AbS 857)
   Grave 32 (No. 7)
   Intact.
   Ware unknown.
   H. 15.0
   Rim di. 9.7

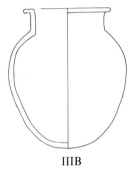

IIIB

380. **6G38:88** (AbS 1029)
   Grave 51 (No. 5)
   Large piece missing from
   body and a little from rim.
   Red clay.
   Fine cream slip out (mostly eroded)
   Fine sandy temper.
   H. 15.0
   Rim di. 9.5
   Underneath of base polished.
   Faint traces of red paint in grooves.

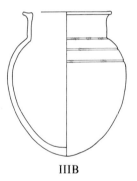

IIIB

381. **6F05:159** (AbS 2031)
   Grave 182 (Batch 6015)
   Intact.
   Ware unknown.
   H. 17.6
   Rim di. 10.0

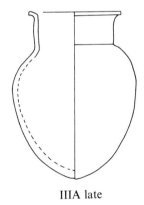

IIIA late

382. IDENTICAL: **5I11:118** (AbS 1111)
   Grave 56 (No. 3)
   Intact.
   Buff clay, greenish slip, temper unknown.
   H. 17.0, rim di. 10.4   III

383. **5I21:88** (AbS 746)
     Pit in Room 6 (Batch 1117)
     Much of lower body missing.
     Ware unknown.
     H. 20.0
     Rim di. 10.6

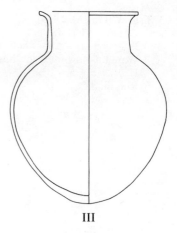

III

384. VERY SIMILAR: **5I21:147** (AbS 784)
                    Grave 31 (No. 2)
                    Condition unknown.
                    Pink clay, buff slip out, fine grit temper.
                    H. 15.8, rim di. 8.9
                    Fine and well-made.    IIIA late

385. **6F05:155** (AbS 2009)
     Grave 182 (Batch 6015)
     Intact but for small
     piece of rim and neck.
     Pink clay.
     Cream slip.
     Temper of grit and black grit.
     H. 23.9
     Rim di. 10.8
     Max. width 15.6
     Lower body scraped down.

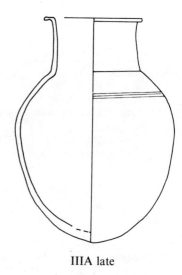

IIIA late

386. **5I21:150 + 151** (AbS 782)
     Grave 28 (No. 14)
     Condition and ware unknown.
     H. 24.1
     Rim di. 13.4
     Max. width 22.3
     Ridges on shoulder.

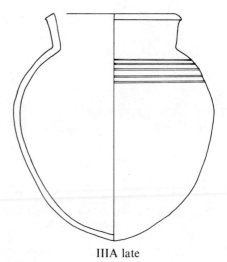

IIIA late

387. **6G47:194** (AbS 1768)
Grave 151 (Batch 2587)
Chips from most parts.
Red clay.
Cream slip.
Fine grit temper.
H. 16.2
Rim di. 11.4
Max. width 15.0
Base scraped down outside.

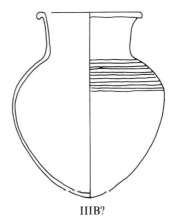

IIIB?

388. **6G75:169** (AbS 2011)
Grave 184 (Batch 3623)
Some small gaps.
Orange clay.
Yellow slip.
Fine grit temper.
H. 15.8
Rim di. 11.4
Max. width 15.0
Base scraped down outside.

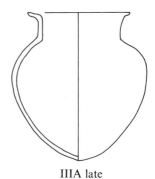

IIIA late

389. **6G84:16**
Pit in Room 80 (Batch 1705)
Red clay.
Paler slip out.
Rather sparse, fine grit temper.
H. 15.6
Rim di. c. 8.4

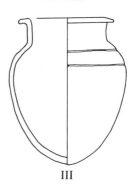

III

390. **4I09:216** (AbS 1401)
Grave 83 (No. 3)
Piece of rim missing.
Yellowish clay.
Traces of cream slip.
Temper unknown.
H. 16.4
Rim di. 10.2
Contained human bone 4I09:233

391. VERY SIMILAR: **6G63:314** (AbS 1386)
Grave 73 (No. 6)
Part of rim missing.
Red clay, temper unknown.
H. 18.6, rim di. 11.9   IIIA late

392. SIMILAR: **6G62:40** (AbS 1110)
Grave 77 (No. 2)
Part of rim and body missing.
Pink clay, fine cream slip, sparse grit temper.
H. 13.8, rim di. 9.6   III

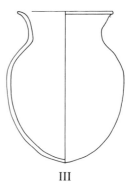

III

393. **6G63:317** (AbS 1479)
     Grave 73 (No. 8)
     Almost complete.
     Fine red clay.
     Well-smoothed surface.
     Grit temper.
     H. 14.8
     Rim di. 9.5

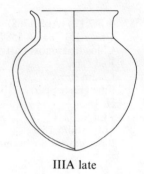

IIIA late

394. SIMILAR: **5I21:164** (AbS 723)
                Grave 26 (No. 27)
                Some gaps in body.
                Dense red clay, paler surface, very
                sparse temper of sand and white grit.
                H. 17.8, rim di. 10.4    IIIA late

395.            **6G63:337** (AbS 1411)
                Grave 73 (No. 3)
                A few pieces missing from body.
                Red clay, temper unknown.
                H. 16.1, rim di. 12.1    IIIA late

396.            **6G63:340** (AbS 1425)
                Grave 73 (No. 5)
                Complete.
                Reddish clay, cream slip, temper unknown.
                H. 19.0, rim di. 11.9    IIIA late

397.            **6G63:110** (AbS 1112)
                Grave 73 (No. 37)
                Complete.
                Buff clay, temper unknown.
                H. 17.6, rim di. 10.5    IIIA late

398.            **6G37:127** (AbS 924)
                Grave 38 (No. 15)
                Fragmentary: only part of body extant.
                Fine cream slip, no other details.
                Pres. H. 15.0
                Fine and well-made.    III

399. **6G37:58** (AbS 542)
     Grave 37 (No. 5)
     Piece of rim missing.
     Ware unknown.
     H. 14.5
     Rim di. 10.4

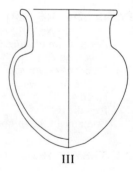

III

400. **6G44:30** (AbS 1743)
     Grave 140 (Batch 3104)
     Intact.
     Pink clay.
     Cream slip.
     Temper of grit
     and probably some veg.
     H. 9.2
     Rim di. 6.5

III

401. **6G39:7**
Pit in or near south wall
of Room 115 (Batch 2303)
Some large gaps.
Fine buff clay.
Temper unknown.
H. 16.7
Rim di. 10.2–10.6

402. SIMILAR: **6G36:272**
Pit in Room 119 (Batch 3500)
Rim and much of upper body missing.
Red clay, cream slip out,
pinkish in, grit and veg. temper.
Pres. H. 17.5, max. width 13.2    IIIA early

403.　　　　**4I09:221**
Grave 93 (No. 3)
Fragmentary and eroded.
Red clay, cream slip out, fine grit temper.
H. 12.0 (v. approx.), rim di. c. 8.5    IIIB

404. **6G37:95** (AbS 644)
Grave 32 (No. 5)
Piece of rim missing.
Ware unknown.
H. 15.5
Rim di. 10.5

405. SIMILAR: **4I09:92** (AbS 1168)
Grave 83 (No. 14)
Two small chips.
Reddish clay, temper unknown.
H. 16.4, rim di. 10.0    III

406.　　　　**4I09:183**
Grave 93, but not definitely
part of deposit (Batch 1432)
Condition unknown.
Red clay, grit temper.
Pres. H. c. 18.0, rim di. c. 9.4
(Not included in Postgate 1985)    IIIB

407. **4I09:85** (AbS 1161)
Grave 83 (no. 7)
A little of rim and body missing.
Red clay.
Temper unknown.
H. 18.4
Rim di. 10.6
Ba. di. 5.4
Base cut.

408. VERY SIMILAR: **6G36:170** (AbS 1617)
Grave 127 fill (Batch 2473)
Most of rim and neck missing.
Dark red clay, pale pink slip,
grit and white grit temper.
H. 19.0, rim di. c. 9.0
Base shaved with a knife.    IIIA-B

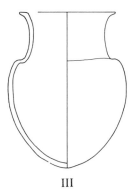

III

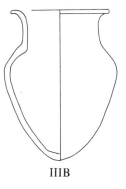

IIIB

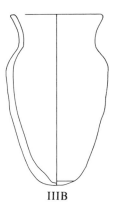

IIIB

409. **6G75:121** (AbS 1932)
Grave 162 (Batch 3615)
Nearly half of rim missing.
Dense red clay.
Somewhat patchy cream slip.
Sparse, sandy temper.
H. 17.0
Rim di. c. 11.5

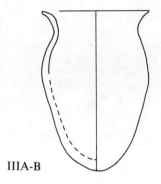

IIIA-B

410. **6F06:34** (AbS 1979)
Grave 181 (Batch 6205)
One or two gaps.
Dense red clay.
Pink slip.
Fine sparse sandy temper.
H. 17.8
Rim di. 9.4–9.8
Max. width 13.1

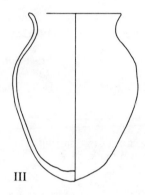

III

411. **6G37:90** (AbS 646)
Grave 38 (No. 28)
Complete.
Ware unknown.
H. 15.8
Rim di. 9.5

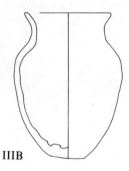

IIIB

412. **6G47:165** (AbS 1618)
Grave 124 (Batch 2550)
Red clay.
Cream slip.
Grit temper.
H. 15.1
Rim di. 10.5

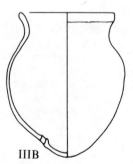

413. VERY SIMILAR:  **5I10:151** (AbS 926)
Grave 19 (No. 2)
Complete.
Red clay, heavy grit temper.
H. 12.0, rim di. 8.8
[Postgate and Moorey 1976:fig. 8 no. 22]    IIIB

IIIB

414. SIMILAR: **4I09:9** (AbS 1096)
Grave 95 (no. 10)
Intact.
Red clay, grit temper.
H. 12.0, rim di. 8.8
Contained tiny open vessel no. 133,
and charcoal and fragments of bone 4I09:54    IIIB

415. **6FS:25** (AbS 1937)
Grave 173 (Batch 5212)
Intact but cracked.
Dark red clay, with red
and brown streaks in section.
Buff to brownish slip.
Sparse sandy temper.
H. 15.8
Rim di. 9.1–9.6
Base scraped down on out-
side, and has single hole.
Fire-blackened in places.

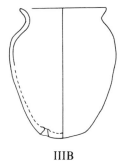

IIIB

416. **6G52:2** (AbS 507)
Grave 17 (No. 2)
Intact.
Ware unknown.
H. 17.5
Rim di. 9.7

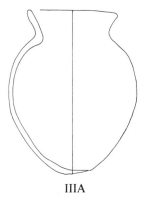

IIIA

417. **6G75:168** (AbS 1968)
Grave 184 (Batch 3623)
Complete.
Fine red clay.
Sparse sandy temper.
H. 16.2
Rim di. 8.8–9.4
Max. width 13.5

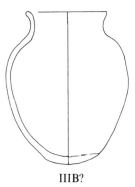

IIIB?

418. **5IS:287**
Grave 193 (Batch 5385)
Some of rim missing.
Pink clay.
Buff patches out.
Hard grit temper with mica.
H. 18.9
Rim di. (reconstruc.) 10.0
Ba. di. 6.6–7.2
Base shaped with knife or similar.

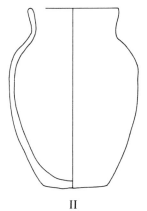

II

419. VERY SIMILAR: **6G37:119** (AbS 932)
Room 102, cut (Batch 521)
Condition and ware unknown.
H. 16.0, rim di. 8.6    II?

420. **6G37:109** (AbS 856)
Grave 32 (No. 10)
Intact.
Ware unknown.
H. 16.7
Rim di. 9.3
Ba. di. 4.2

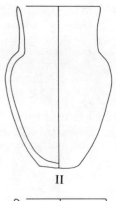

II

421. **6G36:170** (AbS 1617)
Grave 127 fill (Batch 2473)
Much of rim missing.
Dark red clay.
Pale pink slip.
Grit and white grit temper.
H. 18.5
Rim di. 9.0

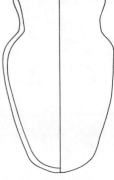

IIIA-B

422. **5IS:282**
Grave 193 (Batch 5385)
Half rim missing.
Pink clay.
Buff patches on surface.
Hard grit temper including mica.
H. 15.5
Rim di. (reconstruc.) 10.0
Ba. di. 6.3
Base 'flat', but pot does not stand well.

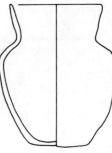

II

423. **6G64:672** (AbS 1072)
Room 39, pit in doorway (Batch 61)
Shoulder chipped.
Pale pink clay.
Thick slurry cream slip.
Fine sand temper.
H. 12.3
Rim di. 8.0
Ba. di. c. 4.5
Crudely made.

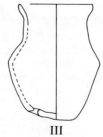

III

424. **4I09:226** (AbS 1437)
Grave 95 (No. 2)
Intact.
Red clay.
Temper unknown.
H. 12.5
Rim di. 9.6
Ba. di. 6.5

IIIB

425. **6F06:33** (AbS 1974)
Grave 181 (Batch 6205)
Quarter of rim missing.
Brittle brown-orange clay.
Yellow to buff slip.
Fine grit temper.
H. 12.5
Rim di. 9.4–10.4
Max. width 11.5

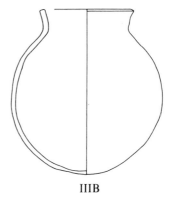

III

426. **6G38:103** (AbS 1034)
Grave 51 (No. 8)
Some large gaps in body.
Buff clay.
Soft temper of veg. and fine grit.
H. 17.6
Rim di. 9.6–9.8
Fine and well-made.

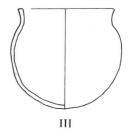

IIIB

427. **6G47:138** (AbS 1589)
Grave 120 (Batch 2534)
Rim chipped.
Pink clay.
Possible white slip.
Temper of veg.
and sparse fine sand.
H. 11.0
Rim di. 10.0
Max. width 11.6

III

428. **6FS:23**
Grave 173 (Batch 5212)
Half of rim and portion of
body missing, surface eroded.
Dark red clay.
Pale pink slip.
Sandy temper.
H. 10.6
Rim di. c. 10.6
Max. width c. 12.0

IIIB

429. **6G84:44** (AbS 1981)
Grave 179 (Batch 1712)
A quarter of rim and body missing.
Red clay.
Cream to pale pink slip.
Fine grit temper.
H. 11.0
Rim di. 9.2–9.6
Ba. di. 6.7–6.8
Base scraped.
Rough reserve-slip effect on shoulder.

IIIB

430. **5I21:157** (AbS 779)
Grave 28 (No. 11)
Complete.
Ware unknown.
H. 13.2
Rim di. 10.4

IIIA late

431. **6G75:241**
Grave 191 (Batch 3637)
Much of body gone and some
of rim, but good profile.
Buff clay.
Temper of sparse fine veg.
and quartz, much black grit.
H. 13.4
Rim di. 10.0
Ba. di. 6.2

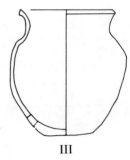

III

432. SIMILAR: **6G36:156** (AbS 1588)
Grave 127 (Batch 2463)
Profile only.
White clay, coarse veg. temper.
H. 12.8, rim di. 9.0, ba. di. 4.7     IIIA-B

433. **6G39:10**
Pit in or near south wall
of Room 115 (Batch 2303)
About half of rim and neck only.
Red clay.
Veg. and sand temper.
Pres. H. 6.0
Rim di. c. 10.0
Cut marks on rim, per-
haps made after firing.

III

434. **4I09:84** (AbS 1160)
Grave 83 (No. 6)
Much of rim missing
and a few chips from body.
Pink clay.
Greenish surface.
Grit temper.
H. 16.0
Rim di. 7.2–10.0
Ba. di. 4.2–4.6
Well-made.
Base shaved down.

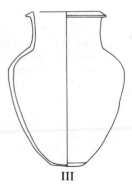

III

435. **4I09:76**
    Grave 78 (No. 5)
    About two thirds extant.
    Brown clay.
    Grit temper.
    H. 17.0
    Rim di. 10.6
    Probably burnt as
    fire-blackened in places.
    Base scraped down outside.

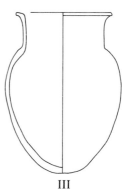

III

436. **6F05:21**
    Grave 168 (Batch 6000)
    Some large gaps in base
    and body, surface eroded.
    Red clay.
    Sandy temper.
    H. c. 19.4
    Rim di. 9.0
    Ba. di. (reconstruc.) 5.2

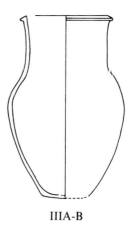

IIIA-B

437. **6FS:22** (AbS 1935)
    Grave 173 (Batch 5212)
    Rim slightly chipped, neck
    cracked, otherwise intact.
    Pink clay.
    Cream slip out
    (inside not visible)
    Sand temper.
    H. 35.8
    Rim di. 15.4–15.7
    Max. width 20.5
    Light horizontal scoring on shoulder.

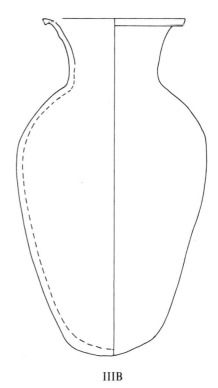

IIIB

438. **5I21:153** (AbS 574)
Grave 28 (No. 8)
Intact.
Ware unknown.
H. 25.0
Rim di. 12.3
Ba. di. 5.8

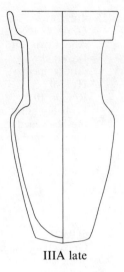

IIIA late

439. **6G64:311** (AbS 536)
Grave 1 (No. 50)
Complete.
Ware unknown.
H. 32.5
Rim di. 11.4
Contained conch 6G64:503
Contents sampled as 6G64:482
[Postgate and Moorey 1976:fig. 8 no. 15]

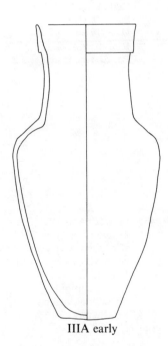

IIIA early

440. **6G54:115** (AbS 1086)
Grave 60 (No. 6)
Most of rim and neck missing.
Fine reddish clay.
Cream slip.
Smoothed to near burnish in places.
Temper unknown.
H. 25.2
Rim di. (reconstruc.) 11.2
Ba. di. 3.7–4.2
Body shaved after application of slip.

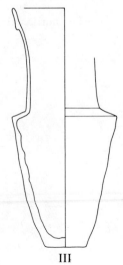

III

441. **6G37:112** (AbS 862)
Grave 32 (No. 16)
Complete.
Ware unknown.
H. 23.5
Rim di. 9.5
Ba. di. 4.0

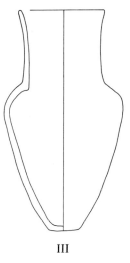

III

442. **6G37:546** (AbS 1615)
Grave 135 fill (Batch 584)
Piece missing from rim.
Pink clay.
Cream slip.
Sandy temper with mica.
H. 20.8
Rim di. 10.4
Oval.
Lower body has traces of polish.

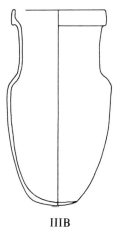

IIIB

# LARGE STORAGE JARS

Large storage jars are usually only found whole by lucky chance. Nos. 443 and 444 had been left against the wall where they originally stood when the building was re-made. No. 444 had been effectively halved in capacity by the addition of a false bottom of bitumen. Something could have been stored in the bottom and sealed with the bitumen, but this is unlikely as the base was filled with sand and sherds. More likely the newly-raised base was to make the jar more accessible. Storage jars at all periods were often set into the floor they stood on, and frequently had pointed bases for just this purpose. Bitumen had also been used on no. 445, this time to block cracks caused during firing. The vessel is quite mis-shaped, but presumably had been used all the same. Perhaps a storage jar was too expensive to discard if at all functional. No. 446 had obviously had firing problems too. Nos. 446 and 447 have ring-bases, but could not possibly have stood on them with any degree of safety, so may well originally have been set into the floor as well.

*All illustrations in this section at 1:8*

443. **4J97:105** (AbS 2242)
Room 50, set into north face of
phase 3 wall (Batch 4469)
Some of rim and body missing.
Pink clay.
Carefully smoothed surface.
Grit and fine grog temper.
H. 100.0
Rim di. 24.0
Max. width 60.0
Two scratched 'pot marks'
high on outside shoulder.
Presumably coil-built.
[Postgate 1984:fig. 7 no. 7]
Contained other vessels –
see Appendix D.

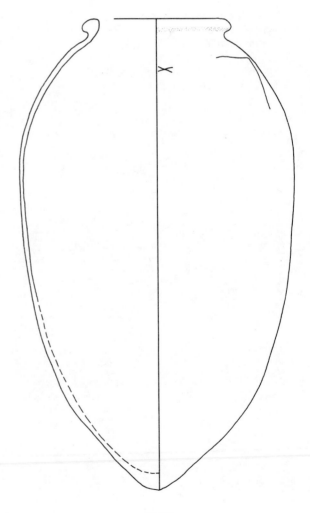

II-III

444. **4J97:153**
     Room 50, set into north
     face of phase 3 wall
     (Batch 4469)
     Almost complete when
     found, but not
     restored (drawn *in situ*)
     Green clay.
     Sandy temper.
     H. 84.0
     Rim di. 30.4
     Max. width 68.0
     False bottom of
     bitumen (4J97:288)
     Presumably coil-built.
     [Postgate 1984:fig. 7 no. 8]

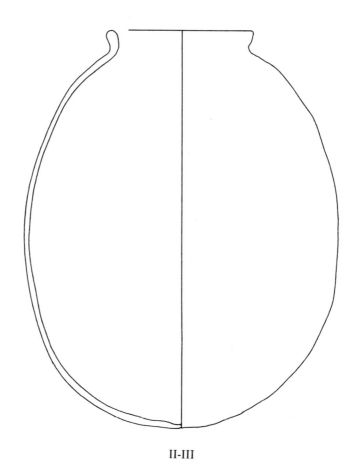

II-III

445. **1T:59**
     Grave 138 (Batch 4050)
     Parts of rim
     and body missing.
     Fine greenish clay.
     Temper unknown.
     Pres. H. 32.0
     Rim di. 10.5
     Very badly warped
     and cracked and
     mended with bitumen.
     Diagonal reserve-slip
     on shoulder.

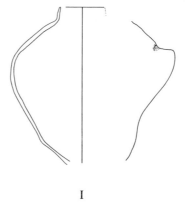

I

446. **6G45:108**
   Room 73 floors (Batch 2939)
   Gaps, but good profile.
   Green clay.
   Veg. temper.
   H. 60.0
   Rim di. c. 9.4
   Ba. di. c. 7.4
   Overfired – shoulder
   deformed in places.
   Lower body scraped in-
   side, and at least one of
   cracks mended with bitumen.

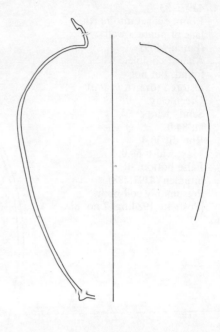

IIIA

447.  SIMILAR: **6G63:423 + 424**
         Grave 86 (No. 3)
         Rim, neck and some of body missing.
         Greenish clay, grit temper.
         Pres. H. 37.6, ba. di. 13.2
         Ring-base pinched.    IIIA early

# FLAT-BASED JARS

The relatively large number of small, squat jars shown below with string-cut base and usually with plain rim can probably be explained partly by the fact that they survive well, being relatively thick-walled and tough. String-cut bases are not in fact common among sherd batches, excepting those of conical bowls, and round and ring-bases seem to have been much more popular for jars at Abu Salabikh.

Both ED II and ED III levels at the Lower Diyala sites seem to have been rich in flat-based jars, though one knows nothing of the sherd evidence of course. The ED II specimens have narrow necks and long bodies (Delougaz 1952 Pl. 72 a-g). The nearest shapes among the Abu Salabikh jars are nos. 497-502, and while these encompass nearly all the ones that are or could be ED II there are others too (like no. 497), and in any case the preference for narrow necks does carry over into ED III at the Diyala sites, suggesting this phenomenon might better be seen as a regional tendency for the moment (Delougaz 1952 Pl. 98 b-j).

Our ED III small flat-based jars are at once uniform and diverse: the careless manufacture means that no two are ever identical, yet no significant variations can be spotted either. The low, squat form has a long life and persists into the second millennium elsewhere (for example, Delougaz 1952 B.174.220a). Masses of these vessels were found in the Royal Cemetery at Ur, to judge from the numbers surviving in the relevant museums.

The slightly larger flat-based form (nos. 448-453) is a late ED III type, especially that with pouring lip. These are common at Kish in graves with ED IIIB types (included in Mackay's type KA) and at Khafajah are first found in Houses 2 (Delougaz 1952 B.175.224, B.176.224 etc.).

The pouring lip on some of the larger jars strongly suggests a use involving liquids, though it is doubtful whether anyone who has actually tried to skim milk would use one of these to do so, as suggested by Mackay (1929 p. 34). What was kept in the smaller ones is open to guesswork: presumably they were for storage, as the high shoulder and slight restriction at the neck would have made them awkward to eat or drink from. They might have been useful for letting small quantities of hot fat cool: it would have been fairly safe from spilling, as the flat bases with low centre of gravity are stable on all but the most unaccommodating surfaces.

All have string-cut base.

448. **6G39:6** (AbS 1392)
Pit in or near south-east
wall of Room 115 (Batch 2303)
Most of rim missing.
Red clay.
Sandy temper.
H. 11.6
Rim di. c. 7.5 (oval)
Ba. di. 6.8
String-cut base.
Perhaps partly hand-shaped.

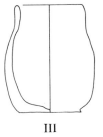

III

449. **6G36:206** (AbS 1763)
Grave 127 (Batch 2473)
Parts of rim and neck missing.
Pink clay.
Cream slip.
Grit and veg. temper.
H. 10.2
Rim di. 7.0
Ba. di. 4.2

IIIA-B

450. SIMILAR: **5I11:62** (AbS 897)
Grave 44 (No. 3)
Condition and ware unknown.
H. 13.0, rim di. 9.0, ba. di. 6.2    III

451. **4J97:84**
Grave 200 (Batch 4406)
Condition and ware unknown.
H. 12.2
Rim di. 12.0
Ba. di. 5.2

IIIB

452. **6G37:551** (AbS 1614)
Grave 135 fill (Batch 584)
Intact.
Cream slip.
Temper probably grit.
H. 15.8
Rim di. 9.0
Ba. di. 5.0

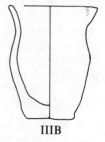

IIIB

453. **6G56:56** (AbS 1273)
Pit in Room 57 (Batch 2019)
Complete but for piece of rim.
Buff clay.
Cream slip.
Temper unknown.
H. 14.7
Rim di. 8.2-8.8
Ba. di. 5.0-5.9

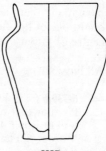

III

454. **6G86:250**
Ash Tip (Batch 1959)
Half upper body missing.
Pink clay.
Paler surface.
Sandy temper.
H. 9.4
Rim di. 6.0
Ba. di. 4.0

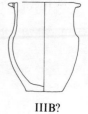

IIIB?

455. **6G62:104** (AbS 1205)
Room 66, inside drain (Batch 2233)
Rim and base chipped.
Red clay.
Buff slip.
Grit temper and
probably some veg. too.
H Rim di. 7.0
Ba. di. 4.3
Pink 'wash' over most of surface
- perhaps a post-depositional effect.

post-ED

456. **5I11:99** (AbS 1075)
Room 1, late cut (Batch 1235)
Part of rim and shoulder missing, base chipped.
Pink clay.
Buff slip out.
Veg. temper.
H. 8.8
Rim di. 6.2
Ba. di. 3.7-4.2

III

457. **6G55:103** (AbS 475)
Surface (Batch 346)
Intact.
Ware unknown.
H. 8.8
Rim di. 6.1
Ba. di. 4.4

III?

458. **6G63:85 + 88** (AbS 1103)
Grave 73 (No. 30)
Rim chipped, and pieces missing from side.
Dense red clay.
Cream slip out.
Sparse sandy temper.
H. 9.0
Rim di. 5.0
Ba. di. 4.0

IIIA late

459. FAIRLY SIMILAR: **6G63:404** (AbS 1385)
Pit in Room 63 (Batch 987)
Intact but for small chip from rim.
Red clay, yellowy surface, grit temper.
H. 8.1, rim di. 6.0, ba. di. 4.3    III

460. **6G37:548** (AbS 1622)
Grave 135 fill (Batch 584)
Virtually complete.
Red clay.
Pale pink surface.
Fine sparse temper
of grit and mica.
H. 8.9
Rim di. 5.2
Ba. di. 5.3

IIIB

461. **6G63:121** (AbS 1095)
Grave 75 (No. 7)
Intact but for chip from rim.
Red clay.
Brownish surface.
Fine sandy temper including mica.
H. 6.9
Rim di. 5.2
Ba. di. 4.6

IIIB

462. SIMILAR: **4I09:29** (AbS 1158)
              Grave 76 (No. 6)
              Intact.
              Pale pink clay, cream surface, grit temper.
              H. 6.8, rim di. 5.5, ba. di. 3.5-4.0
              Base very uneven.    IIIB

463. **6GS:8**
     6G24/25 surface (Batch 6301)
     Half of rim missing, and a large chip from body.
     Red clay.
     Sandy temper, like a conical bowl.
     H. 6.9
     Rim di. (reconstr.) 5.5
     Ba. di. 4.4

III

464. **5I10:35** (AbS 412)
     Pit in Room 2 (Batch 1006)
     Condition and ware unknown.
     H. 7.1
     Rim di. 5.2
     Ba. di. 4.6

III

465. **6G64:509** (AbS 923)
     Grave 27 (No. 2)
     Large piece missing from side.
     Pink clay.
     Buff slip.
     Fine grit and veg.-temper.
     H. 7.1
     Rim di. 7.0
     Ba. di. 4.3

IIIA

466. VERY SIMILAR: **6G64:474** (AbS 725)
                   Grave 1 (No. 54)
                   Complete but for chips.
                   Pale pink clay, cream surface, grit temper.
                   H. 9.2, rim di. 6.1, ba. di. 3.7
                   [Postgate and Moorey 1976:fig. 8 no. 23]    IIIA early

467. SIMILAR: **6G55:87** (AbS 402)
              Grave 12 (No. 7)
              Condition and ware unknown.
              H. 9.2, rim di. 6.6, ba. di. 3.9    III

468.              **6G37:141** (AbS 1093)
                  Grave 109 (Batch 523, inside
                  conical bowl no. 61 above)
                  Intact.
                  Ware unknown (except red surface)
                  H. 6.6, rim di. 4.6, ba. di. 2.8    II or III

469. **5I21:42** (AbS 474)
     Room 4 fill (Batch 1109)
     Rim missing.
     Pale pink clay.
     Cream slip out.
     Grit temper.
     H. 7.2
     Rim di. 5.2
     Ba. di. 3.5
     Heavily smoke-blackened in and out
     (probably post-depositional)

III

470. SIMILAR: **6G65:232** (AbS 761)
     Grave 54 (No. 4)
     Nearly complete.
     Dark red clay, slightly paler
     surface, no apparent temper.
     H. 8.5, rim di. 5.8, ba. di. 3.6 III

471.     **6G37:550** (AbS 1621)
     Probably Grave 135 (Batch 584)
     Rim and neck missing.
     Pink clay, cream slip, temper unknown.
     Pres. H. 7.8, ba. di. 4.1 IIIB

472. **5I21:173** (AbS 690)
  Grave 31 (No. 4)
  Intact.
  Light pink clay.
  Good cream slip.
  Fine grit temper.
  H. 7.7
  Rim di. 5.0
  Ba. di. 4.5

IIIA late

473. SIMILAR: **6G36:98** (1586)
     Grave 122 (Batch 2434)
     Intact.
     Pink to cream surface.
     H. 9.4, rim di. 5.5, ba. di. 4.9-5.4 III

474.     **5I21:108** (AbS 532)
     Grave 26 (No. 32)
     Intact.
     Pink to buff surface, fine grit temper.
     H. 8.0, rim di. 5.7, ba. di. c. 4.8
     Well-made. IIIA late

475.     **5I21:152** (AbS 580)
     Grave 28 (No. 9)
     Condition and clay unknown.
     H. 8.4, rim di. 5.7, ba. di. 4.1 IIIA late

476.     **6G62:5**
     Grave 61 (No. 9)
     About half extant.
     Overfired green clay, grit temper.
     H. 6.8, rim di. 5.8, ba. di. 3.8 III

477. **6F05:16** (AbS 1948)
  Grave 168 (Batch 6000)
  Intact but for scratches.
  Pink clay.
  Thick cream slip.
  Temper of much sand and some veg.
  H. 6.8
  Rim di. 5.6-5.8
  Ba. di. 4.2-4.6

IIIA-B

478. VERY SIMILAR: **5I21:107** (AbS 534)
      Grave 26 (No. 33)
      Intact.
      Smooth red clay, fine sparse grit temper.
      H. 8.5, rim di. 7.1, ba. di. c. 5.0 IIIA late

479. SIMILAR: **6G64:393** (AbS 473)
  Grave 1 (No. 53)
  Condition and clay unknown.
  H. 8.4, rim di. 6.3, ba. di. 3.8   IIIA early

480.          **5I21:230** (AbS 638)
  Grave 42 (No. 3)
  Intact but for chips in surface.
  Dense dark red clay, sparse
  sandy temper including mica.
  H. 8.5, rim di. 6.2, ba. di. c. 3.4   IIIA

481. **6G38:150** (AbS 1379)
  Room 111, late floors
  (Batch 820, inside
  spouted jar no. 634 below)
  Intact.
  Ware unknown (buff surface)
  H. 8.0
  Rim di. 6.0
  Ba. di. 4.3
  Contained fish-bone 6G38:161

II or III

482. **5I21:215** (AbS 756)
  Grave 35 (No. 5)
  Tiny chip from rim.
  Red clay.
  Grit temper.
  H. 8.5
  Rim di. 6.5
  Ba. di. 4.1

IIIA early

483. SIMILAR: **6G65:295** (AbS 1206)
  Grave 87 (No. 2)
  Intact.
  Red clay, grit temper.
  H. 8.5, rim di. 5.3, ba. di. 3.7   IIIA early

484.          **6G65:19** (AbS 411)
  Grave 3 (No. 4)
  Condition and ware unknown.
  H. 6.7, rim di. 6.5   III, prob. IIIB

485. **6G84:94** (AbS 2075)
  Grave 187 (Batch 1723)
  Some of rim missing.
  Orange clay.
  Buff slip out.
  Grit temper.
  H. 8.2
  Rim di. 6.1
  Ba. di. 3.8-4.0

IIIA

486. FAIRLY SIMILAR: **6F05:205** (AbS 2039)
  Grave 182 (Batch 6024)
  Fragments of rim and body missing.
  Pink clay, cream slip, grit temper.
  H. 9.9, rim di. 6.2, ba. di. 4.8   IIIA late

487. **6G47:62** (AbS 1587)
  Grave 119 (Batch 2515)
  Tiny gap in one side.
  Pink clay.
  Buff slip.
  Grit temper.
  H. 10.2
  Rim di. 4.9
  Ba. di. 4.5

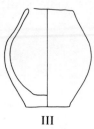

III

488. **6G64:737** (AbS 1275)
Grave 88 (No. 9)
Intact.
Reddish clay, temper unknown.
H. 9.2
Rim di. 5.9
Ba. di. 4.2

II-IIIA

489. **6G47:57** (AbS 1585)
Grave 118 (Batch 2515)
Intact.
Red clay.
Fine grit temper.
H. 9.3
Rim di. 5.1
Ba. di. 3.7

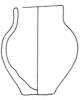

IIIA late

490. VERY SIMILAR: **6G75:362** (AbS 2215)
Grave 162 (S) (Batch 3674)
Intact.
Cream surface, grit temper.
H. 8.5, rim di. 4.9-5.2, ba. di. 4.2    IIIA-B

491. **6G75:428**
Pit into Grave 162 (S) (Batch 3644)
Almost complete.
Pink clay.
Cream slip.
Sandy grit temper.
H. 10.7
Rim di. 6.4
Ba. di. 5.0-5.2

IIIB

492. **5I21:174** (AbS 726)
Grave 28 (No. 13)
Complete but for small chips.
Pink clay.
Sandy temper.
H. 8.6
Rim di. 7.0
Ba. di. 4.8
Blackened inside.

IIIA late

493. SIMILAR: **5I10:178** (AbS 882)
Surface (Batch 1001)
Rim and much of upper body missing.
Red clay, grit temper.
Pres. H. 9.6, ba. di. 4.3
Clumsy and heavy.    III

494. **6G75:144** (AbS 1971)
Grave 162 (Batch 3618)
Broken in excavation: a few chips now missing.
Dense red clay.
Pale pink slip out.
Sandy temper.
H. 9.3
Rim di. 6.9-7.1
Ba. di. 5.4

IIIA-B

495. **6G95:8** (AbS 1940)
Cut into bitumen area
in Room 85 (Batch 3703)
Half rim and neck eroded away.
Red clay.
Traces of buff slip.
Sparse grit temper.
H. 8.2
Rim di. (reconstruc.) 7.4
Ba. di. 4.0-4.2

III

496. **6G77:46** (AbS 2012)
Ash Tip near Grave 186 fill (Batch 3904)
About half extant:
part of shoulder missing.
Browny orange clay.
No apparent inclusions.
H. 7.6
Rim di. c. 5.2
Ba. di. 2.5

II or III?

497. **6G37:114** (AbS 860)
Grave 32 (No. 12)
Intact but for chip from rim.
Pale pink clay.
Buff slip.
Grit temper.
H. 9.0
Rim di. 6.0
Ba. di. 3.5
Light and thin-walled.

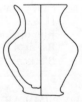

IIIB

498. SIMILAR: **6G64:219** (AbS 401)
Grave 1 fill (No. 8)
Rim missing.
Red clay, sandy grit temper.
Pres. H. 10.0, ba. di. 4.0   IIIA early

499. **6G38:77** (AbS 691)
Fill to east of Room 114 (Batch 808)
Intact.
Buff surface.
Grit temper.
H. 9.4
Rim di. 5.8
Ba. di. 4.5
Well-made.

II or III

500. **6G63:431** (AbS 1398)
Grave 86 (No. 5)
Intact.
Reddish clay.
Temper unknown.
H. 9.7
Rim di. 4.5
Ba. di. 4.3

IIIA early

501. SIMILAR: **6G37:68** (AbS 859)
Grave 38 (No. 31)
Rim missing.
Dense red clay, buff slip out, fine sparse grit temper.
Pres. H. 7.5
Base formed with knife, not string-cut.    II

502. **5IS:277** (AbS 2125)
Grave 193 (Batch 5385)
Intact but for chip from rim.
Red clay.
Buff slip out.
Fine grit temper.
H. 11.4
Rim di. 5.1
Ba. di. 2.9
Lower body scraped with knife or similar; base cut.

II

503 **5I11:80** (AbS 636)
Grave 53 (No. 2)
Intact.
Slurry buff surface.
Grit temper.
H. 13.8
Rim di. 6.7
Ba. di. c. 4.5

III

504. SIMILAR: **6G37:217** (AbS 1198)
Grave 89 (No. 2)
Complete.
Overfired green clay, temper unknown.
H. 9.2, rim di. 5.8, ba. di. 3.4    IIIA-B

505. **6G75:139** (AbS 1969)
Grave 162 (Batch 3618)
Intact.
Orange clay.
Cream slip.
Grit temper.
H. 10.4
Rim di. 5.0
Ba. di. 4.8-5.0
Two crude holes drilled from outside
of neck, only one having gone through.

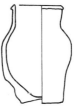

IIIA-B

506. **6F06:16**
Pit in Room 90 (Batch 6203)
Part of rim and body missing.
Orange clay.
Grit and white grit temper.
H. 8.8
Rim di. 6.0
Ba. di. 3.8
Two holes drilled in neck.

IIIA-B

507. **6G75:269** (AbS 2128)
Grave 195 (Batch 3645)
Intact but for chips from rim.
Red clay.
Grit temper.
H. 10.5
Rim di. 5.4-5.6
Ba. di. 4.5-4.7
Irregular and clumsy.

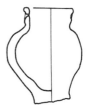

IIIB or later

508. **6G63:118** (AbS 1114)
Room 61 fill (Batch 920)
Intact.
Red clay.
Fine grit temper including mica.
H. 9.6
Rim di. 6.0
Ba. di. 4.7

III

509. **5I11:28** (AbS 505)
Pit in Room 7 (Batch 1208)
Intact but for surface chips.
Buff clay.
Cream surface.
Heavy grit temper.
H. 8.6
Rim di. 5.8
Ba. di. 4.5

III

510. **6G36:43** (AbS 1584)
Grave 115 lower fill (Batch 2411)
Most of rim missing.
Dark red clay.
Cream slip.
Sparse grit temper.
H. 8.6
Rim di. 5.5
Ba. di. 6.0

III

511. **6G74:79** (AbS 637)
Room 54 fill (Batch 605)
About one quarter of neck missing.
Pink clay.
Patchy buff slip.
Grit and probably fine veg. temper.
H. 9.7
Rim di. 7.2
Ba. di. 3.6

III

512. **6G44:37** (AbS 1742)
Grave 150 (Batch 3113)
Rim and surface chipped and abraded.
Reddish clay.
Cream slip out.
Sandy temper.
H. 7.4
Rim di. 4.0
Ba. di. 4.1

IIIB

513. **6G62:16** (AbS 1107)
Grave 61 (No. 14)
Complete but for chip from rim.
Pale pink clay.
Slurry cream slip.
Grit temper.
H. 7.8
Rim di. 6.0
Ba. di. 4.5

III

514. **5I10:172** (AbS 1016)
Surface (Batch 1040)
About half rim missing.
Pink clay.
Good cream slip.
Fine sand and fine veg. temper.
H. 8.7
Rim di. 6.0
Ba. di. 4.8

III?

515. **6G85:103** (AbS 2032)
Grave 171 (Batch 1820)
Small piece missing
from body.
Pink clay.
Cream slip.
White grit temper.
H. 8.8
Rim di. 6.7
Ba. di. 4.6
Base scraped.

IIIA

# RING-BASED JARS

Ring-bases occur already during the ED I period, and fragments of them are not uncommon among sherds from the West Mound. (One ED I vessel with a ring-base is mentioned here, no. 611.) At this period the rings were very low and not always stuck on separately as they always were by ED III. Round bases were still more popular, however, and rings only become the norm during ED IIIA, continuing to increase in number from then on. There are some from our as yet less fully-investigated ED II deposits, but as they do not fit well with the rest most will be found in the next section.

This section contains an unusually large proportion of ED IIIB jars. Whether this is just a matter of changing fashion, or whether it reflects a change in table-manners is impossible to say. Round bases stand much better on uneven surfaces such as mud floors, while ring-bases prefer a level surface such as a table. There is no contemporary evidence for a sudden appearance of tables or platforms in domestic architecture, nor for floors being smoother. Representations of banqueting scenes from Ur do show servants with what appear to be reed-work hostess-trolleys, but they are laden with joints of meat and generally unidentifiable delicacies rather than pots (e.g. Woolley 1934 Pl. 105). Many of the jars shown here do not in fact stand well by themselves (e.g. no. 566), though once full they only wobble as opposed to falling over. As with the round-based jars, there is a great variety of shapes collected together here, but as they form a continuum they have not been divided.

Like most relatively large types, ring-based jars are best preserved in graves, but the large number of ring-bases found among ED III sherds remind us that they were commonly used by the living too. Pieces of the smaller types are not usually distinguishable from similar round-based forms when fragmented.

Graves and other pot-bearing deposits that are known to be early ED IIIA are less well-represented than ones we can date with confidence to the end of the period, so only a few types can be proven to go back that far. Our earliest examples come from Grave 1 (nos. 522, 530, 555,) with just one that could go back as far as ED II, no. 586, most characterised by the full, rounded body, splayed mouth, band-rim and the relatively low ring-base. These features continue into late ED IIIA, the shoulder moving a little higher, as on no. 519. No. 530 has a higher shoulder and slimmer body, again foreshadowing a shape that is well-represented in late ED IIIA graves, like no. 529.

The slurring or scoring of the shoulder surface is seen already on the Grave I jars, and is in fact a decorative technique of some antiquity, common among ED I sherds on the West Mound. It continues in use on various shapes through to the end of ED IIIA (nos. 581 and 566) but is not represented on the ED IIIB jars, except the slightly doubtful no. 583.

The single tiny lug on nos. 518, 521, and 526-528 is almost like a throwback to ED I single-handled jars, though in fact the lug is quite different. The high carinated shoulder and tapering body shown by nos. 527 and 528 is well-represented in late ED IIIA graves: nos. 535-541. A late ED jar with single lug is among the collection from the 'maquette architécturale' from Mari (Parrot 1967 fig. 314 no. 3228).

Most of the general shapes described above continue into ED IIIB, but with conveniently typical characteristics. The round-bodied form first noticed in Grave 88 (no. 586) becomes longer as with nos. 549-552. Jars with sharply angled shoulder (e.g. no. 537) lose their wide mouths and become wider at the shoulder, like no. 544, or nos. 559-560. Very long bodies enjoy a revival during the early Akkadian period, to which no. 548 should probably be dated. Wide splayed band-rims give way to straight ones (as on no. 568) and plain or turned-over rims are used more. The ring-bases themselves get taller and contain a higher proportion of vegetable matter. They also tend to come off: stray rings are more common in sherd batches from later parts of the site.

One unmistakeably different jar shape is introduced at this period, with absurdly wide shoulder and base (nos. 567-572, and 574-575). These are a feature of the 'A' Cemetery assemblage at Kish (Mackay 1929 Pl. LI nos. 12, 14-17) No. 575 is interesting with its red wash, an unusual decorative feature for this period, but paralleled on jars from Ur (Woolley 1934 Pl. 261 no. 158 – not identical, but surely related). No. 573, which is not definitely ED IIIB but looks as though it well might be, has a burnished shoulder, another form of decoration more usually associated with the first part of the Early Dynastic period.

The small ring-based jars, nos. 588-610, form a group on their own, but once again are difficult to separate absolutely from neighbours such as no. 587. All those for which a more exact date can be fixed are ED IIIB, and they are associated with other IIIB forms at Kish (Mackay 1929 Pl. LII type E). Some are exactly like small round-based jars but with ring-bases (nos. 592-597). Others, like nos. 598-607 look more as though they are trying to be a very clumsy and cheap imitation of the ostrich-egg vase, already fairly crude in its original vulgar splendour. Fragments of one such vessel have been found at Abu Salabikh (Postgate 1980:95). While the larger ring-based jars are presumably storage-vessels, it is hard to imagine what use could be contrived for a fake ostrich-egg.

516. **6G63:6** (AbS 1076)
    Pit in Room 61 (Batch 904)
    Intact but for much of
    rim, and chips from base.
    Dark red clay.
    Sparse fine grit temper.
    H. 10.0
    Rim di. 6.7
    Ba. di. 5.0
    Ring-base added in veg.-tempered clay.

post-ED?

517. **6G36:243** (AbS 1767)
    Grave 116 (Batch 2487)
    Intact.
    Red clay.
    Grit temper.
    H. 11.0
    Rim di. 6.0-6.4
    Ba. di. 5.0-5.2
    Ring-base added in coarse, veg.-tempered clay.

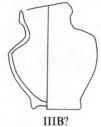

IIIB?

518. **6G85:67** (AbS 1915)
    Grave 171 (Batch 1809)
    Intact but for two thirds of ring-base.
    Red clay.
    Cream slip out on upper
    body, patchy on lower.
    Sandy temper.
    H. 10.8
    Rim di. 8.2
    Ba. di. c. 6.2
    Horizontal reserve-slip on shoulder.
    Single lug.
    Ring-base added in straw-tempered clay.

IIIA

519. **6G63:69+83** (AbS 1202)
    Grave 73 (No. 31)
    Parts of rim and body missing.
    Red clay.
    Temper unknown.
    H. 20.4
    Rim di. 11.4
    Ba. di. 7.4 – 8.0
    Ring-base added in coarser clay.

520. VERY SIMILAR: **6F05:157** (AbS 2013)
        Grave 182 (Batch 6015)
        Intact.
        Buff slip, grit temper.
        H. 16.4, rim di. 10.4, ba. di. 7.7
        Ring-base added in veg.-tempered clay. IIIA late

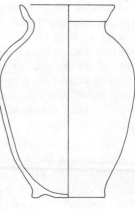

IIIA late

521. **6F05:170**
Grave 183
(Batch 6012)
Profile of
upper body only.
Dark orange clay.
Cream slip out.
Rather sparse
grit temper.
Pres. H. 9.8
Rim di. 11.6
Max. pres. width c. 17.0

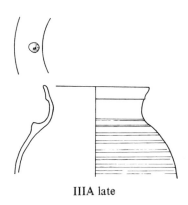

IIIA late

522. **6G64:598** (AbS 724)
Grave 1 (No. 56)
Condition and ware unknown.
H. 21.3
Rim di. 11.8
Ba. di. 8.2
Incised (or perhaps
raised) lines on shoulder.
[Postgate and Moorey 1976:fig. 7 no. 9]

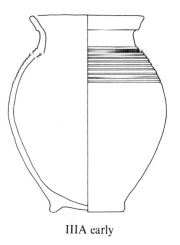

IIIA early

523. **6G44:21** (AbS 1746)
Grave 142 (Batch 3101)
Intact.
Pinkish clay.
Cream slip.
Grit temper.
H. 15.7
Rim di. 10.5
Ba. di. 6.5

III

524. **6F05:165** (AbS 2007)
Grave 182 (Batch 6015)
Intact.
Orange clay.
Rather patchy buff slip.
Grit temper.
H. 21.5
Rim di. 10.3-10.5
Ba. di. 10.2
Ring-base added in veg.-tempered clay.

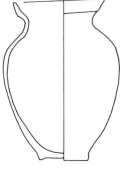

IIIA late

525. IDENTICAL: **6G85:38** (AbS 1854)
                     Grave 165 (Batch 1805)
                     Intact but for small chips.
                     Orange clay, buff slip, sandy temper.
                     H. 17.4, rim di. 10.8, ba. di. 6.9
                     Ring-base added in veg.-tempered clay.  IIIA

526. **6G84:43** (AbS 1966)
        Grave 179 (Batch 1712)
        Virtually complete.
        Pink clay.
        Cream slip.
        Fine grit temper.
        H. 14.1
        Rim di. 7.8
        Ba. di. 4.2
        Shoulder bears horiz-
        ontal lines of raised slip.
        Ring-base added in veg.-tempered clay.

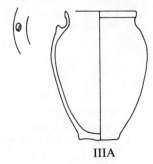

IIIA

527. **6G85:68** (AbS 1916)
        Grave 171 (Batch 1809)
        Intact but for tiny
        chips in body and neck.
        Red clay.
        Cream slip on one side.
        Sparse sandy temper.
        Reserve-slip on shoulder.
        H. 22.2
        Rim di. 10.5
        Ba. di. 6.4-6.6
        Single pointed lug on shoulder.
        Ring-base added in veg.-tempered
        clay and squashed on one side.

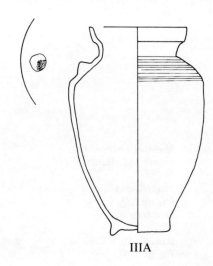

IIIA

528. **6G85:65** (AbS 1914)
        Grave 171 (Batch 1809)
        Complete but for chips.
        Red clay.
        Thin, patchy cream slip.
        Sparse sandy temper.
        Reserve-slip on shoulder.
        H. 22.8
        Rim di. 11.2
        Ba. di. 6.5

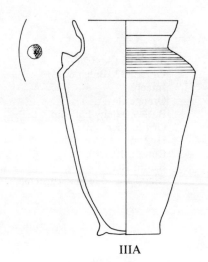

IIIA

529. **6G54:86** (AbS 643)
Grave 48 (No. 9)
Some gaps.
Ware unknown.
H. 18.6
Rim di. 10.5
Ba. di. 5.5
Ring-base added, presumably
in veg.-tempered clay.

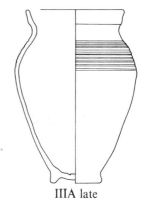

IIIA late

530. VIRTUALLY IDENTICAL: **6G64:604** (AbS 821)
Grave 1 (No. 57)
A quarter of rim missing,
and some body pieces.
Red clay, cream slip, sparse sandy temper.
H. 21.0, rim di. 11.0, ba. di. 6.4-6.6
Reserve slip on shoulder, becoming
heavier lower, producing ridged effect. IIIA early

531. VERY SIMILAR: **6G54:79** (AbS 1069)
Grave 48 (No. 10)
Part of neck, shoulder, and
a little of body missing.
Buff clay, temper unknown.
H. 18.0, rim di. 9.5, ba. di. 6.0
Ring-base added in coarser clay.
Shoulder has ribbed surface. IIIA late

532. **6G54:152** (AbS 1079)
Grave 48 (No. 13)
Some of rim missing, chips from body.
Yellowish surface, with red
patches, temper unknown.
H. 19.5, rim di. 10.3, ba. di. 5.6
Ring-base added in coarser clay.
Spiral groove on shoulder. IIIA late

533. SIMILAR: **6G63:102** (AbS 1105)
Grave 73 (No. 34)
Small pieces missing from body and rim.
H. 20.0, rim di. 11.6, ba. di. 8.0
Ring-base added in coarser clay.
No ribbing or scoring on shoulder. IIIA late

534. **5I21:175** (AbS 753)
Grave 28 (No. 12)
Intact.
Ware unknown.
H. 16.5
Rim di. 9.9
Ba. di. 6.5
Ring-base added in coarser clay.

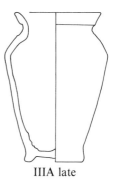

IIIA late

535. **6G63:211** (AbS 1201)
    Grave 79 (No. 13)
    Some of rim and body missing.
    White clay.
    Veg. temper and a little fine sand.
    H. 26.2
    Rim di. 15.0
    Ba. di. 12.1
    Ring-base added in coarser clay.

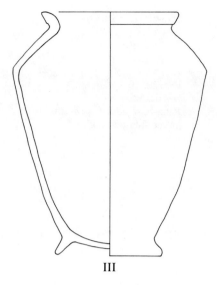

III

336. **5I21.314** (AbS 1285)
    Grave 96 (No. 6)
    Part of rim missing.
    Buff clay.
    Cream slip.
    Temper unknown.
    H. 17.6
    Rim di. 10.2
    Ba. di. 5.6-6.0
    Ring-base added in coarser clay.
    Sieve bowl no. 119 found in mouth.

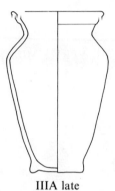

IIIA late

537. **5I21:154** (AbS 571)
    Grave 28 (No. 10)
    Intact.
    Ware unknown.
    H. 21.5
    Rim di. 10.9
    Ba. di. 5.8
    Ring-base added, presumably
    in veg.-tempered clay.

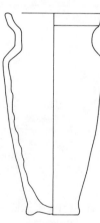

538. IDENTICAL: **5I21:237** (AbS 927)
                Grave 42 (No. 10)
                Rim and neck broken.
                Ware unknown.
                Pres. H. 21.3, ba. di. 5.7
                Ring-base added in coarser clay. IIIA late

IIIA late

539. VERY SIMILAR: **5I21:128** (AbS 654)
                Grave 26 (No. 29)
                Complete.
                Ware unknown.
                H. 21.0, rim di. 10.8, ba. di. 5.2
                Pinched ring-base. IIIA late

540.            **5I21:122** (AbS 655)
                Grave 26 (No. 31)
                Condition and clay unknown.
                H. 22.0, rim di. 10.3, ba. di. 7.3 IIIA late

541. **5I21:129** (AbS 535)
　　Grave 26 (No. 30)
　　Condition and ware unknown.
　　H. 21.5
　　Rim di. 10.4
　　Ba. di. 6.3

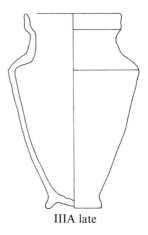

IIIA late

542. **6G38:105** (AbS 920)
　　Grave 51 (No. 9)
　　Condition and ware unknown.
　　H. 21.7
　　Rim di. 10.5
　　Ba. di. 8.0
　　Ring-base added, presumably
　　in veg.-tempered clay.

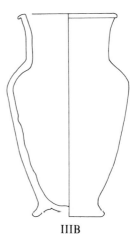

IIIB

543. **6G47:164** (AbS 1611)
　　Grave 124 (Batch 2550)
　　Cracked and chipped.
　　Orange clay.
　　Brown slip.
　　Temper of fine sand including mica.
　　H. 19.5
　　Rim di. 10.0
　　Ba. di. 10.0
　　Ring-base added in veg.-tempered clay.

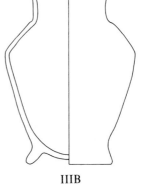

IIIB

544. **6G75:282** (AbS 2130)
Grave 198 (Batch 3658)
Complete but for chips
and some of ring-base.
Pink clay.
Cream slip.
Grit temper.
H. 22.4
Rim di. 10.0
Ba. di. 9.8
Ring-base added
in veg.-tempered clay.

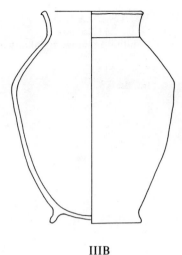

IIIB

545. VERY SIMILAR: **6G36:36** (AbS 1593)
Grave 115 + 117 (Batch 2415)
Fragmentary: two non-joining sections.
Red clay, fine grit temper.
Rim di. 10.0, ba. di. 10.9  III

546.                    **6G66:25** (AbS 413)
Grave 5 (No. 9)
Complete but for chips.
Pink clay, buff slip, sandy grit temper.
H. 22.5, rim di. 11.5, ba. di. 9.4
Ring-base added in coarse veg.-tempered clay.
Neat and well-made. IIIB

547. **6G63:159**
Pit in south wall of Room 61 (Batch 926)
Rim and body fragmentary.
Red clay.
Grit temper.
H. 21.1
Rim di. c. 11.8
Ba. di. 9.5
Ring-base added in chaff-tempered clay.

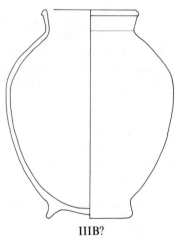

IIIB?

548. **6G75:263** (AbS 2126)
Grave 195 (Batch 3643)
Intact but for small chip.
Greenish clay.
Black grit temper.
H. 23.2
Rim di. 8.6
Ba. di. 7.4
Ring-base added in straw-tempered clay.

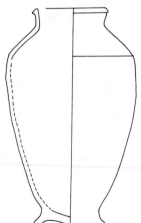

IIIB or later

549. **6G75:490** (AbS 2211)
Room 54, floor (Batch 4500)
Quarter of rim missing.
Pink clay.
Sandy grit temper.
H. 25.8
Rim di. 10.8
Ba. di. 10.0-10.5
Ring-base added in veg.-tempered clay.

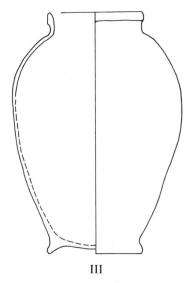

III

550. SIMILAR: **6G37:379** (AbS 1382)
Pit in Room 103 (Batch 564)
Virtually complete.
Buff clay, cream slip, temper unknown.
H. 27.4, rim di. 11.2, ba. di. 11.5
Ring-base added in coarser clay. III

551. **6G75:237** (AbS 2070)
Grave 190 (Batch 3635)
Nearly complete.
Pinky-brown clay.
Poorly applied buff slip.
Fine hard grit and veg. temper.
H. 28.4
Rim di. 11.4-11.6
Ba. di. 11.6
Ring-base added in
fine veg.-tempered clay.

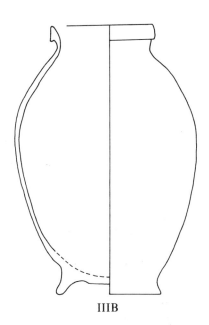

IIIB

552. **6G45:41** (AbS 1613)
Room 74, fill (Batch 2917)
Fragments of rim and base missing.
Pink clay.
Possible cream slip.
Temper unknown.
H. 21.8
Rim di. 10.9
Ba. di. 10.0
Ring-base added in veg.-tempered clay.

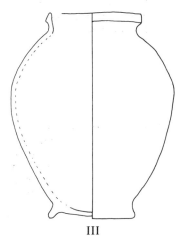

III

553. SIMILAR: **6G63:427** (AbS 1388)
          Grave 100 (Batch 977)
          Most of base missing, also parts of rim and body.
          Reddish clay, cream slip, temper unknown.
          H. c. 23.0, rim di. 12.0, ba. di. c. 9.5
          Ring-base added in veg.-tempered clay. IIIĀ

554.      **6G37:77** (AbS 572)
          Grave 38 (No. 29)
          Some chips from rim.
          Ware unknown.
          H. 25.0, rim di. 11.5, ba. di. 10.5
          Ring-base added, presumably in veg.-tempered clay. IIIB

555. **6G64:478** (AbS 697)
     Grave 1 (No. 51)
     Some small chips.
     Ware unknown.
     H. 22.4
     Rim di. 13.5
     Ba. di. 9.8
     Ring-base of same clay as pot.
     [Base probably drawn too thick]

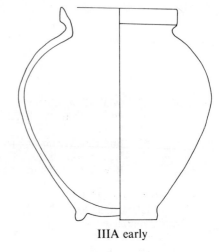

IIIA early

556. SIMILAR: **6G65:38** (AbS 414)
          Grave 3 (No. 2)
          Condition and ware unknown (except cream slip)
          H. 26.3, rim di. 11.5, ba. di. 11.6
          Ring-base added in veg.-tempered clay. III, prob. IIIB

557. **6F05:165** (AbS 2007)
     Grave 182 (Batch 6015)
     Intact.
     Rather patchy buff slip.
     Grit temper.
     H. 21.5
     Rim di. 10.3-10.5
     Ba. di. 10.2
     Ring-base made separately
     in veg.-tempered clay, not
     high enough to support pot.

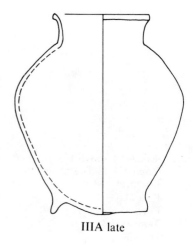

IIIA late

558. VERY SIMILAR: **6G47:79** (AbS 1595)
              Grave 120 (Batch 2534)
              Profile extant, excluding ring-base.
              Red clay, fine cream slip, temper
              of sparse grit and fine veg.
              H. 21.7, rim di. 12.0, ba. di. prob. 7.8
              Ring-base of veg.-tempered clay: traces adhere to underneath of pot.
              Traces of veg.-tempered clay inside too, presumably introduced while
              fixing ring-base. III

559. **6G37:113** (AbS 893)
Grave 32 (No. 9)
Intact, but ring-base broken underneath.
Ware unknown.
H. 19.7
Rim di. 9.6
Ba. di. prob. around 9.0
Ring-base added, presumably
in veg.-tempered clay.

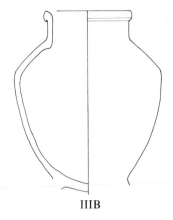

IIIB

560. **6G36:210** (AbS 1765)
Grave 152 (Batch 2488)
Part of rim and body missing.
Pinkish clay.
Cream slip.
Temper unknown.
H. 21.2
Rim di. 11.0
Ba. di. 11.0

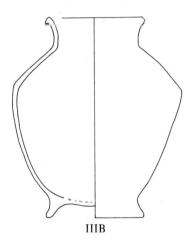

IIIB

561. SIMILAR: **6G76:601** (AbS 1745)
Grave 146 (Batch 2633)
Rim chipped.
Yellowish clay, possible cream slip, temper unknown.
H. 15.4, rim di. 9.5, ba. di. 11.5   IIIB

562.          **6G63:150** (AbS 1106)
Grave 73 (No. 35)
Fragmentary: profile only.
Red clay, sandy temper including mica.
H. 20.5, rim di. 11.0, ba. di. 10.5
Ring-base added in coarser clay.   IIIA late

563. **6F06:19** (AbS 1965)
Grave 181 (AbS 6205)
Intact.
Overfired green clay.
Grit temper.
H. 19.6
Rim di. c. 9.4 (warped)
Ba. di. 9.5
Ring-base added in veg.-tempered clay.
Crack in bottom smeared with bitumen.

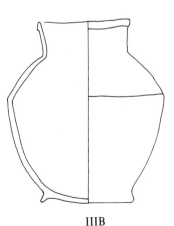

IIIB

564. **6G45:48** (AbS 1747)
    Grave 143 (Batch 2919)
    Some small gaps.
    Pinkish clay.
    Cream slip.
    Fine light grit temper.
    H. 23.3
    Rim di. 11.5
    Ba. di. 12.0
    Ring-base added.

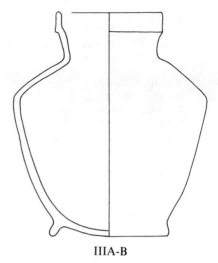

IIIA-B

565. SIMILAR: **6G38:102** (AbS 919)
    Grave 51 (No. 7)
    Intact.
    Ware unknown.
    H. 21.0, rim di. 11.0, ba. di. 12.0
    Ring-base added in coarser clay.    IIIB

566. **6F05:6** (AbS 1936)
    Grave 168 (Batch 6000)
    Complete.
    Pinky yellow clay.
    Yellow slip.
    Grit, veg., and sand temper.
    H. 23.0
    Rim di. 10.6-10.9
    Ba. di. 10.6
    Ring-base added in veg.-tempered clay.

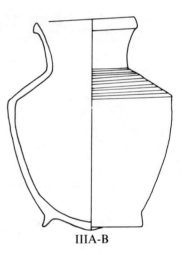

IIIA-B

567. **6G47:139** (AbS 1590)
    Grave 120 (Batch 2534)
    Part of body missing.
    Pinkish clay.
    Cream slip.
    Fine grit temper.
    H. 17.3
    Rim di. 10.6
    Ba. di. 11.7
    Ring-base added
    in veg.-tempered clay.
    Shoulder bears horiz-
    ontal lines of raised slip.

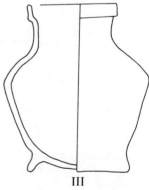

III

568. **6G76:601** (AbS 1745)
    Grave 146 (Batch 2633)
    Small piece of rim missing.
    Yellowish fabric.
    Perhaps white slip.
    Temper unknown.
    H. 15.4
    Rim di. 9.5
    Ba. di. 11.5

IIIB

569. SIMILAR: **6G63:308** (AbS 1387)
    Grave 73 (No. 2)
    Small gaps near base.
    Buff clay, cream slip, temper unknown.
    H. 24.0, rim di. 12.4, ba. di. 13.0
    Ring-base added in coarser clay.
    Incised nicks at base of neck.    IIIA late

570. **6G75:356**
    Grave 162 (S) (Batch 3670)
    Base missing, and half of rim.
    Pink clay.
    Cream slip.
    Sandy temper.
    H. 17.8
    Rim di. (reconstruc.) 9.6
    Ba. di. probably around 11.0
    Ring-base originally
    added in veg.-tempered clay.

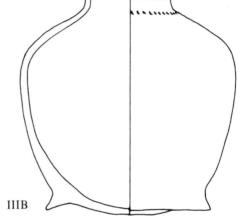

IIIA-B

571. SIMILAR: **6G56:87** (AbS 1476)
    Grave 68 (No. 5)
    Rim missing.
    Red clay, grit temper.
    Pres. H. 19.2, ba. di. 10.0
    Ring-base added in veg.-tempered clay. III

572. **6G37:526** (AbS 1626)
    Grave 135 fill (Batch 584)
    Complete but for chips.
    Pinky yellow clay.
    Cream slip.
    H. 26.5
    Rim di. 12.4
    Ba. di. 19.0
    [Drawing of base
    probably needs correction]

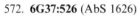

IIIB

573. **6F05:232** (AbS 2071)
    Grave 188 disturbed
    fill (Batch 6027)
    Some gaps in lower body.
    Hard pink clay.
    Buff slip out.
    Fine mixed temper.
    H. 31.5
    Rim di. 11.3-11.5
    Ba. di. 16.2
    Ring-base added
    in straw-tempered clay.
    Shoulder and some
    of body burnished.

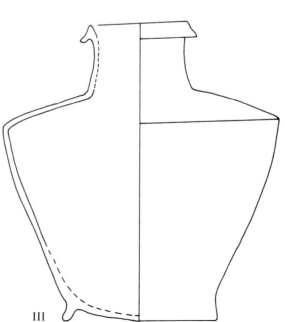

III

574. **6G47:106** (AbS 1592)
     Grave 124 (Batch 2550)
     Parts of rim missing.
     Yellow clay.
     Possible cream slip.
     Grit temper.
     H. 17.6
     Rim di. 11.7
     Ba. di. 16.5

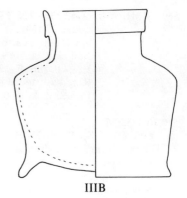

IIIB

575. **6G45:78** (AbS 1766)
     Grave 148 (Batch 2926)
     Fragmentary, but shape clear.
     Red clay, green core.
     Buff slip out and inside neck.
     Heavy grit temper including mica.
     H. 24.6
     Rim di. 11.5
     Ba. di. 16.2
     Very clumsy ring-base added
     in coarse, veg.-tempered clay.
     Traces of red wash.

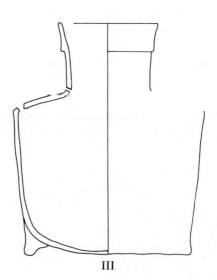

III

576. **6G75:254** (AbS 2124)
     Grave 194 (Batch 3640)
     Some of rim and base missing.
     Pink clay.
     Buff surface out.
     Fine and fairly sparse grit temper.
     H. 16.5
     Rim di. (reconstruc.) 9.0
     Ba. di. c. 11.0
     Ring-base added in veg. tempered clay.

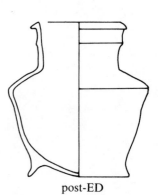

post-ED

577. **6G37:525** (AbS 1612)
     Grave 135 fill (Batch 584)
     Part of rim missing.
     Pinky yellow clay.
     White surface.
     H. 15.7
     Rim di. 9.5
     Ba. di. 9.5
     Ring-base added in veg.-tempered clay.
     Two grooves around shoulder.

IIIB

578. **6F05:171** (AbS 2021)
Grave 183 (Batch 6012)
More than half of rim and neck
missing, and much of upper body.
Dull orange clay.
Cream slip.
Grit temper.
H. 23.0
Rim di. (reconstruc.) 9.0
Ba. di. 11.4

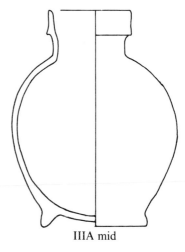

IIIA mid

579. **6F05:51**
Grave 168 (Batch 6004)
Nearly half of upper part
missing, and some of ring-base.
Red clay.
Rather sporadic cream/pale pink slip.
Sparse sandy temper.
Burnt in places.
H. c. 25.0
Rim di. c. 10.5
Ba. di. 12.4
Ring-base added in veg.-tempered clay,
not quite high enough to support body.

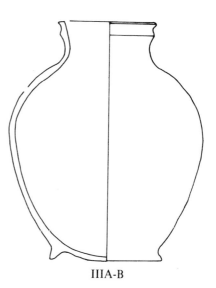

IIIA-B

580. **6G37:179** (AbS 1172)
Grave 89 (No. 12)
Intact.
Buff clay.
Temper unknown.
H. 27.0
Rim di. 15.0
Ba. di. 11.5
Ring-base of same clay as pot.

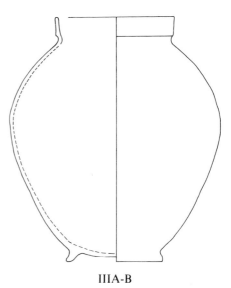

IIIA-B

581. **6F05:173**
Grave 183 (Batch 6012 + 6018)
Two separate parts, not
joining: no proven connection.
Dark orange clay.
Grit and white grit temper.
Pres. H. top 8.0, bottom 11.2
Rim di. 15.6
Ba. di. c. 12.0

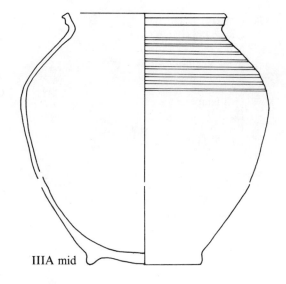

IIIA mid

582. VERY SIMILAR: **5I21:266** (AbS 900)
Grave 26 (No. 43)
Fragmentary: good profile to near base, of which
a third is preserved and which does not join.
Pink clay, buff slip, fine grit temper.
H. prob. c. 23.0, rim di. 14.0, ba. di. c. 12.0
Slip slurred into ridges on shoulder (outside,
not in, as Postgate 1985:fig. 127)   III

583.                    **6G47:119** (AbS 1755)
Grave 126 (Batch 2551)
Much of rim and body lost.
Pink clay, cream slip, fine grit and veg. temper.
H. c. 24.0, rim di. 15.0, ba. di. 13.0
Slip slurred into ridges on shoulder.
Base much thinner than on no. 581   IIIB?

584. **6G37:345** (AbS 1381)
Grave 106, disturbed (Batch 563)
Complete but for chips.
Buff clay.
Cream slip.
Temper unknown.
H. 25.2
Rim di. 10.5
Ba. di. 10.5
Ring-base added in coarser clay.

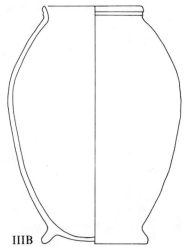

IIIB

585. **6G85:42 + 49** (AbS 1858)
Grave 165 (Batch 1805)
Gaps in body and neck.
Pinky-buff clay.
Greenish slip.
Temper of fine veg. and fine grit.
H. 20.4
Rim di. 10.6
Ba. di. 9.4
Ring-base of same clay as pot.

IIIA

586. **6G64:717** (AbS 1396)
    Grave 88 (No. 14)
    A few small gaps.
    Light pink clay.
    Cream slip.
    Fine grit temper.
    H. 22.1
    Rim di. 13.1
    Ba. di. 10.5

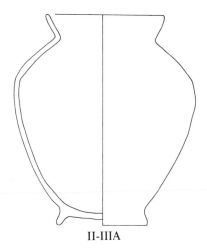

II-IIIA

587. **6G47:118** (AbS 1594)
    Grave 126 (Batch 2551)
    Pieces missing overall.
    Pinkish clay.
    Cream slip.
    Temper unknown.
    H. 19.7
    Rim di. 14.0
    Ba. di. 9.6
    Ring-base added, pre-
    sumably in veg.-tempered clay.

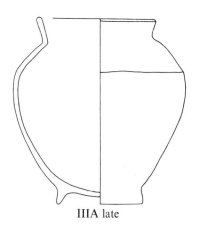

IIIA late

588  **4I09·90** (AbS 1166)
    Grave 83 (No. 12)
    Large gap in body, join to base uncertain.
    Red clay.
    Fine grit and fine veg. temper.
    H. 15.2
    Rim di. 9.6
    Ba. di. 8.0
    Ring-base added in veg.-tempered clay.

589. SIMILAR: **4I09:91** (AbS 1167)
        Grave 83 (No. 13)
        Most of rim and shoulder missing and some of base.
        Pink clay, cream slip out and
        inside rim, grit and veg. temper.
        H. 16.8, rim di. c. 11.0, ba. di. 7.7
        Ring-base added in veg.-tempered clay.  III

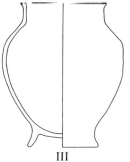

III

590. **6G36:287**
    Pit in west wall of Room 119 (Batch 3504)
    Complete but for chips.
    Fine reddish clay.
    Pinky white slip.
    Fine sparse grit and veg. temper.
    H. 17.2
    Rim di. 10.0
    Ba. di. 8.0
    Ring-base added in veg.-tempered clay.
    Lower body scraped down.

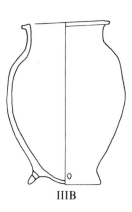

IIIB

591. **6G63:141** (AbS 1099)
     Grave 75 (No. 3)
     About two thirds extant.
     Red clay.
     Greenish slip out.
     Sandy temper.
     H. 16.5
     Rim di. 10.5
     Ba. di. 8.5
     Ring-base added in veg.-tempered clay.

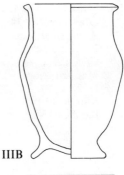

IIIB

592. **6G38:110** (AbS 918)
     Grave 51 (No. 11)
     Rim chipped.
     Ware unknown.
     H. 16.3
     Rim di. 9.6
     Ba. di. 9.1
     Ring-base added.

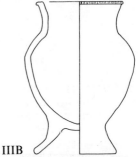

IIIB

593. **4I09:101** (AbS 1169)
     Grave 83 (No. 15)
     Pink clay.
     Cream slip.
     Grit temper.
     H. 17.0
     Rim di. 11.2
     Ba. di. c. 7.6
     Purple stain around inside of rim.
     Ring-base added in veg.-tempered clay.

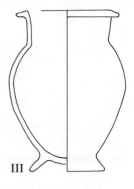

III

594. **4I09:88** (AbS 1164)
     Grave 83 (No. 10)
     One or two gaps.
     Buff clay.
     Firing blushes of green and red.
     Temper unknown.
     H. 17.2
     Rim di. 10.7
     Ba. di. 7.6
     Ring-base added in veg.-tempered clay.

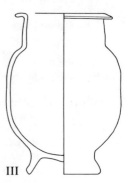

III

595. SIMILAR: **6G56:74** (AbS 1399)
          Grave 99 (No. 2)
          Complete but for chip and part of base.
          Reddish clay, cream slip, temper unknown.
          H. 17.2, rim di. 11.5, ba. di. c. 6.5
          Ring-base added in veg.-tempered clay.
          Contained fish-bone 6G56:28    III

596. PROBABLY SIMILAR: **4I09:89** (AbS 1165)
          Grave 83 (No. 11)
          Fragmentary.
          Pink clay, yellowy slip, soft, sandy temper.
          H. 15.8, rim di. 11.3
          Ring-base added.    III

597. **4I09:87** (AbS 1163)
Grave 83 (No. 9)
Part of base missing,
chips elsewhere.
Buff clay.
Temper unknown.
H. 17.5
Rim di. 10.6
Ba. di. 7.6
Ring-base added in veg.-tempered clay.

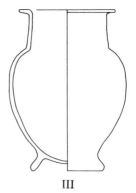

III

598. **6G86:271** (AbS 1967)
Grave 177 (Batch 1955 + 1974)
Intact but for pick-holes.
Hard orange clay.
Cream slip.
Temper of sand and mica.
H. 19.2
Rim di. 9.5
Ba. di. 10.6
High, splayed foot attached
separately by being pushed right
through base and fastened inside.
Black salty deposit over and
under foot and over lower body.

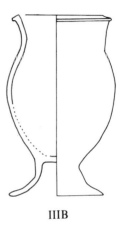

IIIB

599. VERY SIMILAR: **4I09:86** (AbS 1162)
Grave 83 shaft (No. 8)
Parts of base and body missing.
Red clay, cream slip out and inside
neck, fine grit and veg. temper.
Pres. H. 17.0, rim di. 9.9
Ring-base added in veg.-tempered clay.
Four holes in base, traces
of blackening on outside.    III

600. **4I09:18** (AbS 1156)
Grave 76 (No. 4)
Complete.
Buff clay.
Cream slip.
Temper unknown.
H. 20.0
Rim di. 11.5
Ba. di. 10.0
Lopsided.
Ring-base added.

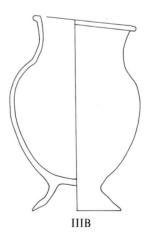

IIIB

601. **4I09:30** (AbS 1159)
     Grave 76 (No. 5)
     Intact.
     Reddish clay.
     Temper unknown.
     H. 24.4
     Rim di. 12.0
     Ba. di. 13.4
     Outer surface black all over
     (recorded as 'burnt' but probably bitumen
     wash as suggested by Postgate, 1985:134)
     Ring-base added.

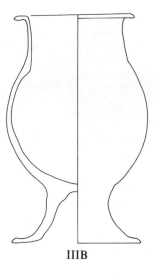

IIIB

602. VERY SIMILAR: **4I09:20** (AbS 1157)
                    Grave 76 (No. 3)
                    Rim slightly chipped.
                    Green clay, grit temper.
                    H. 24.0, rim di. 11.5, ba. di. 12.5
                    Ring-base added. IIIB

603. **6G66:77** (AbS 533)
     Grave 15 (No. 6)
     Foot broken.
     Ware unknown.
     H. 21.8
     Rim di. 10.9
     Ba. di. 11.5
     Ring-base added
     Contained fish bone 6G66:86
     and grain 6G66:87
     [Postgate and Moorey
     1976:fig. 7 no. 10]

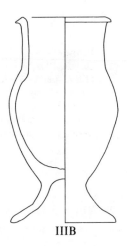

IIIB

604. SIMILAR: **6G66:141** (AbS 645)
              Grave 5 (No. 3)
              Base broken off.
              Ware unknown.
              Pres. H. 16.8, rim di. 11.0
              Ring-base added. IIIB

605. **6G75:281**
     Grave 198 (Batch 3658)
     Half rim and most of base missing.
     Red clay.
     Perfunctory cream slip out.
     Sandy temper.
     Pres. H. 17.4
     Rim di. c. 8.5
     Ring-base added.

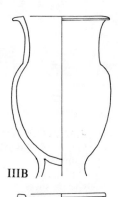

IIIB

606. **6G66:29** (AbS 416)
     Grave 5 (No. 4)
     Intact.
     Ware unknown (except cream surface)
     H. 21.1
     Rim di. 9.9
     Ba. di. 11.6
     Ring-base added.

IIIB

607. SIMILAR: **6G66:32** (AbS 417)
              Grave 5 (No. 7)
              About a third of rim lost.
              Ware unknown.
              H. 19.5, rim di. 11.1, ba. di. 11.8
              Ring-base added.    IIIB

608. **6G55:151** (AbS 752)
Grave 49 (No. 2)
Intact.
Ware unknown.
H. 26.4
Rim di. 10.3
Ba. di. 9.4
Ring-base added.

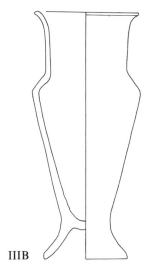

IIIB

609. **6G47:60** (AbS 1598)
Grave 118 (Batch 2515)
Part of rim and stem missing.
Pink clay.
Cream slip.
Fine grit temper.
H. 20.1
Rim di. 11.2
Ba. di. 10.7
Possible bitumen wash,
but may be accidental.
Ring-base added.

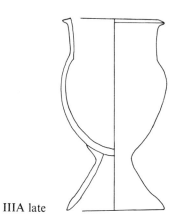

IIIA late

610. **6G47:105** (AbS 1599)
Grave 124 (Batch 2550)
Part of base missing, and rim chipped.
Pink clay.
Bitumen coated.
Grit temper.
H. 21.7
Rim di. 11.6
Ba. di. 12.0
Ring-base of veg.-tempered clay.
Ancient mend to rim.
Ring-base added.

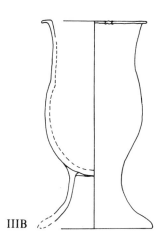

IIIB

611. NOT ILLUSTRATED: **2GS:93** (AbS 1463)
West Mound Room 8 (Batch 5055)
Rim and much of upper body missing.
Reddish brown clay, temper unknown.
Pres. H. 26.4, ba. di. 13.0
Ring-base of same clay as pot.
Finger-nail impressions at base of neck.
[Postgate 1983:fig. 284]   I

# MISCELLANEOUS RING-BASED FORMS

This section contains just those few ring-based jars that seem to have no near neighbours among the rest of the assemblage. Combing on jar shoulders of the later Early Dynastic period, as on no. 612 is not usual at Abu Salabikh, but is known elsewhere (for instance at Khafajah, Delougaz 1952 C.506.470c). No. 613 looks almost as though it belongs to the second rather than the third millennium, but can probably be accommodated in the ceramic assemblage of the Akkadian period for this region.

The sharp shoulder angle and pinched base of no. 614 point to an ED II date, but it is open to debate. Nos. 615 and 616, on the other hand, were found with the rich collection of ED II pottery from Grave 185. No. 615 has a distinctive rim, folded back to lie on the shoulder, and so far only found in ED II deposits at Abu Salabikh (see also no. 790 below). No. 616 could conceivably have had a single handle, but there is not enough of the shoulder left to say if the decoration was concentrated on one part of it, as with no. 712, or not.

No. 617 is one of the few large jars to be found in a grave at the site. Fragments of neck ridge with thumb-marks turn up occasionally among sherds of various ED dates. The style certainly has a long history in the Lower Diyala, where very similar shapes go back to ED I Scarlet Ware (e.g. Delougaz 1952 Pl. 52b). The band-rim marks our specimen as later, apart from the unequivocal context, and in fact one smaller jar of the same type but with band-rim was also found at Khafajah (ibid. C.515.370b).

612. **6G36:34**
    Grave 116 upper fill (Batch 2412)
    Rim missing, a few other gaps.
    Red clay.
    White slip.
    Firing blushes in places.
    H. 22.0
    Ba. di. 11.0
    Max. width 20.0
    Incised band made with three-toothed comb.

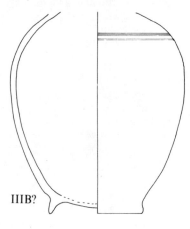

IIIB?

613. **6G75:255** (AbS 2123)
    Grave 194 (Batch 3640)
    Piece missing from near body.
    Pink clay.
    Cream slip out.
    Grit and fine veg. temper.
    H. 22.8
    Rim di. 9.0
    Ba. di. 8.0
    Ring-base broken and mended
    with bitumen in antiquity.

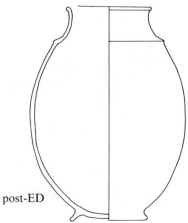

post-ED

614. **6HS:228**
    6H24 surface
    Most of lower body and
    fragment of shoulder extant.
    Red clay.
    Buff surface out.
    Sandy grit temper.
    Pres. H. 8.7
    Ba. di. 3.5
    Base pinched into small
    ring which does not support body.
    Thumb-nail decoration on shoulder.

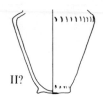

II?

615. **5IS:75** (AbS 1963)
Grave 185 (Batch 5372)
Pinky brown clay.
Greenish slip out.
Fine grit and veg. temper
H. 12.6
Rim di. 12.8
Ba. di. 8.6
Incised decoration not combed.

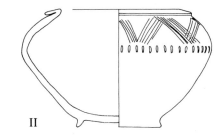

II

616. **5IS:192**
Grave 185 (Batch 5372)
Fragmentary rim and shoulder,
complete but non-joining base.
Pinky-orange clay.
Yellowish to green slip.
Grit and veg. temper.
Pres. H. top 9.0
Pres. H. bottom 5.4
Rim di. c. 16.0
Ba. di. 13.4
Ring-base apparently
made in one with pot.

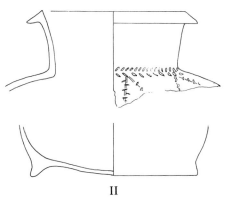

II

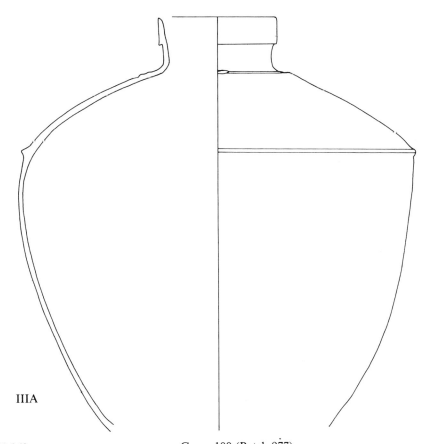

IIIA

617. **6G63:363**
Base and parts of body missing.
Pink clay.
Cream slip.
Sandy temper.

Grave 100 (Batch 977)
Pres. H. 42.0
Rim di. 13.4
Max. width 43.6
Fragment of ring-base probably belongs.

Rib at base of neck probably bore four opposed pairs of
finger-impressions, now badly eroded.

# SPOUTED JARS

The spouted jar first appears in quantity in the Uruk period and becomes one of the hallmarks of the ED ceramic repertoire. Its abrupt removal in ED IIIB is curious in view of its obvious practical advantages. The thousands of spouts found in sherd batches testify to its domestic ubiquity, in spite of the fact that nearly all the whole examples are from graves. Even the smaller types of spouted jar are fragile, being relatively thin-walled and top-heavy, and very few have survived from everyday contexts.

There were plenty of spouted fragments from ED I deposits at Abu Salabikh, but our best collection of whole ED I spouted jars comes from the isolated Grave 160: nos. 694-698. The flat bases, the fine walls and rims, and the comparatively careful manufacture as well as the distinctive shapes distinguish them sharply from later forms. They are also remarkably diverse, in contrast to the marked tendency towards standardization so clear from spouted jars of ED II and ED III graves. Similarities with ED I spouted jars from Khafajah and Tell Agrab can be seen from Delougaz 1952 Pl. 37, and there are echoes of the 'Jamdat Nasr' cemetery at Ur (Woolley 1956 Pl. 61 JN 115, Pl. 64 JN 164). Grave 160 is dated by us to ED I on account of its containing conical bowls (e.g. no. 85), but an early point in this period is probably indicated. No. 704, also from an isolated context, is of a form which continues with little change into ED IIIA, as witnessed by nos. 702 and 703, and no. 705.

ED II types (nos. 675-679, 682-692) tend to be smaller, with plain, upright rim, and base either convex (e.g. nos. 676 and 677), or formed of a low ring pinched out of the bottom of the vessel. On the slim available evidence the latter style is a little later: Grave 81 (no. 677) is certainly earlier than our other ED II contexts. There are a few possibly anomalous forms, such as no. 618, which is not definitely ED II, and nos. 700 and 701, which are not definitely spouted.

If our dating is right – and it does rest rather exclusively on burials at the moment – a fairly neat development can be traced from the usual ED II forms to the late ED IIIA types at the end of the sequence. The generous number of spouted jars from Grave 1 forms a homogeneous group with certain minor variations. No. 673 is very like the slightly earlier nos. 674 and 680, except the spout sticks out more and the base is narrower. Nos. 646-654 on the other hand begin to look more like later forms. Others from the same grave are somewhat individual: nos. 663-665. No. 666 is interesting with its particularly bulbous body; this approximate shape is common in the Royal Cemetery (Woolley 1934 Pl. 264 no. 208). The later ED IIIA Grave 26 contains both spouted jars that are identical to some from Grave 1 (like no. 645) but also others with more angular shoulder, more dominant spout and still narrower base, as nos. 637-638, and, more extreme, no. 625. (Grave 1 also had just one example of this small, narrow-based shape – no. 626.) Other late ED IIIA graves have provided us with just the smallest, most angular and most narrow-based spouted jars of the typology: nos. 621-623, 627, 633, 635.

One must take issue with Delougaz' contention that 'on the whole the ED III forms do not differ greatly from those of ED II' (1952 p. 91). Comparing Pls. 67 and 90 as recommended certainly conveys that impression, but of the six jars illustrated on Pl. 90, three are from Grave 137, one from Grave 131, and one from Grave 133. These three tombs contain a bewildering mixture of ED II and ED III pottery anyway, and whatever the reason for this, cannot be taken as typical ED III.

Spouted jars were occasionally used as ovens at Abu Salabikh, having first been turned upside-down and deprived of their bases (nos. 700-701; there are more convincing examples from subsequent excavation). The unusual ribbed jar (no. 706) has a close parallel from the Temple Oval at Khafajah (Delougaz 1952 D.514.362).

The official function of the spouted jar is not in doubt: it was used as a measure for beer (Postgate 1977 p. 293). No doubt it came in useful for pouring all sorts of other things too. Experiments in measuring the capacities of Abu Salabikh spouted jars have not produced much evidence of standardization, but then measures were not necessarily standardized. This rather Oriental concept was brought home to us in the middle of the measuring operation when we were interrupted by a workman offering to sell straw, which we needed to repair the roof. Straw that season was fetching half a dinar an abba-ful, the amount you can carry in an abba, the traditional woollen cloak. A second workman, not related to the first, offered to lend us his for the transaction, as it was unusually large.

Spouts with pellets underneath as on no. 707 occur occasionally elsewhere at various stages of the Early Dynastic period (for instance at Uch Tepe, Gibson 1981 Pl. 66:15).

Double spouts are sometimes found among sherds at Abu Salabikh, also very occasional fragments of flasks with neck pinched to form a double pourer, like Kish type JB (Mackay 1929 Pl. LII nos. 32-34).

618. **6G37:67**
  Grave 38 (No. 24)
  Some gaps.
  Pink clay.
  White surface
  varying to buff inside.
  Temper unknown.
  H. 18.7
  Rim di. c. 10.0
  (reconstruc.- in fact oval)
  Ba. di. (reconstruc. ) 5.0

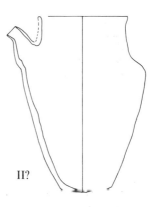

II?

619. **6G54:11** (AbS 397)
  Surface (Batch 102)
  Condition and ware unknown.
  H. 17.8
  Rim di. 10.2
  Ba. di. 4.6
  Ring-base pinched.
  Bitumen inside, and
  on outside of base.

620. IDENTICAL: **6G64:455** (AbS 921)
    Surface (Batch 47)
    Complete.
    Greenish surface, grit temper.
    H. 20.2, rim di. 10.6, ba. di. 4.9
    Ring-base pinched out of pot.
    Spout irregular. IIIA late?

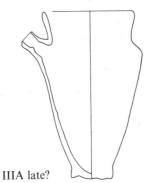

IIIA late?

621. **6G74:353** (AbS 1980)
  Grave 170 (Batch 687)
  Ring-base missing, also
  a little of rim and body.
  Dark red clay.
  Cream slip.
  Sparse temper of fine sand.
  Pres. H. 16.8
  Rim di. 9.2-9.6
  Ba. di. probably around 3.5-4.0
  Ring-base added in veg.-tempered
  clay (frags. clinging to pot).

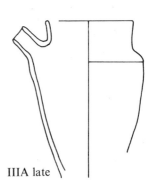

IIIA late

622. **6G47:114** (AbS 1597)
  Grave 126 (Batch 2551)
  Fragments of rim missing.
  Pink core.
  White slip.
  Fine grit temper.
  H. 20.3
  Rim di. 8.6
  Ba. di. 3.1

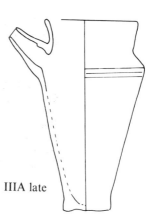

IIIA late

623. **6F05:156** (AbS 2010)
Grave 182 (Batch 6015)
Complete.
Pink clay.
Greenish slip.
Grit temper, in-
cluding black grit.
H. 19.1
Rim di. 10.8
Ba. di. 5.4
Ring-base added in
veg.-tempered clay.

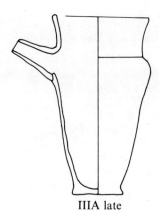

IIIA late

624. **6HS:60**
6H10 sub-surface (Batch 7016)
Rim, spout, and much of
shoulder missing. Very eroded.
Pink clay.
Cream slip.
Sandy temper.
Pres. H. 18.1
Ba. di. 5.5
Max. width (reconstruc.) 11.6

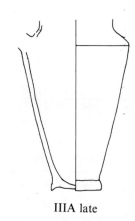

IIIA late

625. **5I21:142** (AbS 669)
Grave 26 (No. 23)
Complete but for chips.
Red clay.
Buff slip.
Grit temper.
H. 21.4
Rim di. 10.8
Ba. di. 5.3

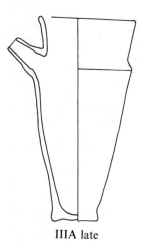

IIIA late

626. SIMILAR:  **6G64:564** (AbS 598)
Grave 1 (No. 68)
Small piece missing near base.
Pale pink clay, greenish slip, grit temper.
H. 24.5, rim di. 11.2, ba. di. 8.2
Ring-base added in veg.-tempered clay. IIIA early

627.            **6G54:63** (AbS 1071)
Grave 48 (No. 14)
Part of rim and body missing.
Buff clay, grit and veg. temper.
H. 21.0, rim di. 10.0, ba. di. 6.0
Ring-base of same clay as pot.
Purple mis-fired patch on body. IIIA late

628. **6F05:189** (AbS 2018)
Grave 183 (Batch 6012)
More than half of
rim and body missing.
Base vitrified and
deformed, as is part of body.
Pink clay.
Buff slip out.
Grit temper.
H. 21.4
Rim di. c. 10.8
Ba. di. c. 5.4
Ring-base added in veg.-tempered clay.

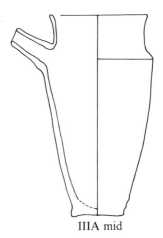

IIIA mid

629. VERY SIMILAR: **6F05:137** (AbS 2019)
Grave 183 (Batch 6012)
Rim chipped, base missing.
Dull orange clay, yellowish slip, grit temper.
Pres. H. 20.0, rim di. 10.8-11.0   IIIA mid

630.                **6G64:607** (AbS 808)
Grave 1 (No. 88)
One or two gaps.
Buff clay, grit and veg. temper.
H. 25.0, rim di. 12.5, ba. di. 6.2
Ring-base added in
coarser veg.-tempered clay.   IIIA early

631. SIMILAR: **6G64:610** (AbS 701)
Grave 1 (No. 90)
Complete but for chips.
Buff clay, grit and veg. temper.
H. 26.2, rim di. 12.7, ba. di. 7.5
Ring-base of same clay as pot.   IIIA early

632.                **6G55:117** (AbS 898)
Pit to east of Room 47 (Batch 351)
Much of rim and shoulder missing.
Pink clay, buff slip, grit and veg. temper.
H. 22.8, rim di. 9.2 (reconstruc.), ba. di. 5.0
Ring-base hand-made and pinched,
perhaps pulled directly out of pot.   III

633. **6G37:199** (AbS 1200)
Grave 89 (No. 14)
Complete but for chips.
Yellow clay.
Temper unknown.
H. 24.4
Rim di. 11.6
Ba. di. 5.9
Ring-base made in one with pot.
[Postgate and Moorey 1977:fig. 5 no. 8]

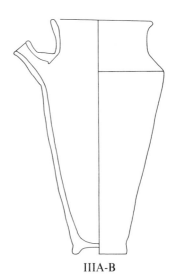

IIIA-B

634. **6G38:149**
Room 111 late floors
(Batch 820) inside
large jar (not restored,
but perhaps upright-
handled) 6G38:151
Spout and parts
of rim and base missing.
Pink clay.
Yellowish slip.
Hard temper of grit and some veg.
H. 25.4
Rim di. (reconstruc.) 10.6
Ba. di. c. 6.2
Ring-base added in
veg.-tempered clay.
Contained small jar,
no. 481

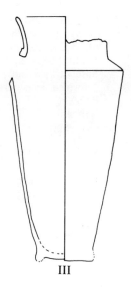

III

635. **6G47:189** (AbS 1748)
Grave 151 (Batch 2587)
Frags. of rim and spout missing.
Reddish clay.
Cream slip.
Fine grit temper.
H. 22.7
Rim di. 10.5
Ba. di. 7.0
Ring-base of same ware as pot.

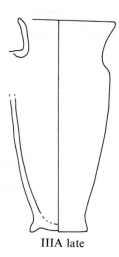

IIIA late

636. **5I21:127** (AbS 674)
Grave 26 (No. 24)
Spout chipped, some
of lower body missing.
Pale pink clay.
Buff slip.
Temper of grit and a little veg.
H. 24.0
Rim di. 10.5
Ba. di. 6.2
Ring-base of same ware as pot.
Carelessly made.

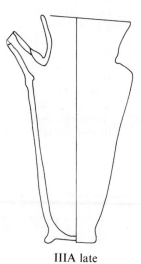

IIIA late

637. **5I21:119** (AbS 722)
Grave 26 (No. 21)
Much of rim and neck missing,
base and lower body damaged.
Buff clay.
Grit and veg. temper.
H. 23.8
Rim di. 11.2
Ba. di. 5.8
Ring-base added separately in
coarse, veg.-tempered clay.

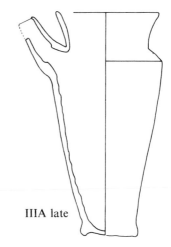

IIIA late

638. VIRTUALLY IDENTICAL: **5I21:123** (AbS 695)
Grave 26 (No. 18)
Base damaged, small gaps elsewhere.
Pink clay, greenish slip, grit and veg. temper.
H. 23.2, rim di. 11.4, ba. di. 6.0
Ring-base added in veg.-tempered clay. IIIA late

639. **6F05:188** (AbS 2018)
Grave 183 (Batch 6018)
Gaps in body and rim.
Rather dense red clay.
Buff slip.
Grit temper.
H. 25.2
Rim di. 11.0
Ba. di. 6.8
Ring-base added in veg.-tempered clay.

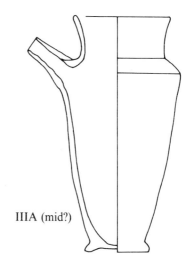

640. SIMILAR: **6G37:500** (AbS 1471)
Grave 112 (Batch 575)
Intact but cracked.
Fabric unknown.
H. 23.1, rim di. 11.6, ba. di. 6.8
Ring-base of same ware as pot. III

IIIA (mid?)

641. **5I21:126** (AbS 688)
Grave 26 (No. 20)
Small gaps overall.
Pink clay, buff slip, fine grit temper.
H. 22.2, rim di. 9.7, ba. di. 6.3
Ring-base of same ware as pot. IIIA late

642. **5I21:117** (AbS 675)
Grave 26 (No. 25)
Gaps in rim, rest chipped.
Pale pink clay.
Greenish slip.
Grit temper.
H. 23.3
Rim di. 11.5
Ba. di. 6.0
Ring-base added in veg.-tempered clay.
[Drawing of profile at base and
spout probably needs correction
but cannot be checked at present]

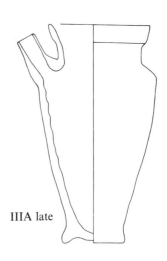

IIIA late

643. VERY SIMILAR: **5I21:249** (AbS 694)
          Grave 26 (No. 26)
          Large gap in body under spout.
          Pink clay, buff slip, grit temper.
          H. 23.0, rim di. 10.8, ba. di. 7.7
          Ring-base of same ware as pot. IIIA late

644. **6F05:146** (AbS 1964)
    Grave 183 (Batch 6012)
    Complete.
    Pinky-buff clay.
    Greenish slip.
    Grit and black grit temper.
    H. 24.2
    Rim di. 10.4
    Ba. di. 6.5
    [Some guess-work in drawing of spout profile]

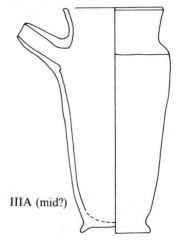

IIIA (mid?)

645. VERY SIMILAR: **5I21:113** (AbS 696)
          Grave 26 (No. 22)
          Much of rim and upper body missing.
          Dense red clay, buff slip
          out, sparse sand and mica temper.
          H. 22.5, rim di. 11.8, ba. di. 5.7
          Ring-base pinched out of bottom of pot. IIIA late

646. **6G64:582** (AbS 895)
    Grave 1 (No. 66)
    Some small gaps.
    Buff clay, fine grit and veg. temper.
    H. 27.5, rim di. c. 10.2, ba. di. 6.8
    Ring-base of same ware as pot IIIA early

647. **6G64:590** (AbS 699)
    Grave 1 (No. 75)
    Tiny chip from rim.
    Pink clay, cream slip, fine grit and veg. temper.
    H. 24.0, rim di. 10.9, ba. di. 7.8
    Ring-base added in veg.-tempered clay. IIIA early

648. **6G64:587** (AbS 665)
    Grave 1 (No. 84)
    Piece missing from rim, surface chipped.
    Red clay, fine grit temper.
    H. 26.6, rim di. 10.2, ba. di. 8.3
    Ring-base added in veg.-tempered clay. IIIA early

649. **6G64:563** (AbS 587)
    Grave 1 (No. 71)
    Slight chips from rim.
    Red clay, buff slip, hard grit temper.
    H. 23.5, rim di. 11.5, ba. di. 7.4
    Ring-base added in veg.-tempered clay. IIIA early

650. SIMILAR: **6G64:602** (AbS 666)
        Grave 1 (No. 79)
        Condition and ware unknown.
        H. 26.0, rim di. 11.2, ba. di. 7.7
        Ring-base added, presumably
        in veg.-tempered clay.    IIIA early

651.          **6G64:587** (AbS 665)
        Grave 1 (No. 84)
        Piece missing from rim, surface chipped.
        Red clay, fine grit temper.
        H. 26.6, rim di. 10.2, ba. di. 8.3
        Ring-base added in veg.-tempered clay.    IIIA early

652.          **6G64:588** (AbS 612)
        Grave 1 (No. 73)
        Complete but for chips.
        Red clay, paler slip, grit temper.
        H. 25.0, rim di. 10.4, ba. di. 8.0
        Veg.-tempered base built on
        over whole of bottom of pot.    IIIA early

653.          **6G64:526** (AbS 590)
        Grave 1 (No. 69)
        Condition and ware unknown.
        H. 25.0, rim di. 11.1, ba. di. c. 8.5
        Ring-base added, presumably
        in veg.-tempered clay.    IIIA early

654.          **6G64:490** (AbS 616)
        Grave 1 (No. 70)
        Condition and ware unknown.
        H. 24.7, rim di. 11.5, ba. di. 8.0
        Ring-base of same clay as pot.    IIIA early

655.          **5I21:247** (AbS 933)
        Pit into Grave 26 (Batch 1142)
        Most of rim missing.
        Pink clay, cream slip, grit temper.
        H. 24.5, rim di. c. 10.0, ba. di. c. 8.0
        Smoothed vertically out,
        producing pseudo-burnished effect.
        Ring-base of same ware as pot.    IIIA late?

656. **6G64:392** (AbS 476)
        Grave 1 (No. 65)
        Intact but for chips from base.
        Pink clay.
        Buff slip.
        Grit temper including mica.
        H. 25.0
        Rim di. 11.0
        Ba. di. 8.4
        Ring-base added
        in veg.-tempered clay.
        [Postgate and Moorey
        1976:fig. 7 no. 8]

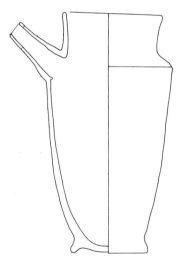

IIIA early

657. VERY SIMILAR: **6G64:554** (AbS 589)
        Grave 1 (No. 72)
        Complete but for chips.
        Red clay, buff slip, grit temper.
        H. 24.5, rim di. 10.8, ba. di. 8.0
        Ring-base added in veg.-tempered clay. IIIA early

658. SIMILAR: **5I21:177** (AbS 588)
        Grave 28 (No. 22)
        Small gap in rim.
        Pink clay, green slip, hard fine grit temper.
        H. 23.5, rim di. 10.7, ba. di. 6.5
        Ring-base added in veg.-tempered clay. IIIA late

659. **6G64:589** (AbS 599)
     Grave 1 (No. 82)
     Virtually complete.
     Pink clay.
     Cream slip.
     Grit temper.
     H. 24.7
     Rim di. 12.8
     Ba. di. 6.2
     Ring-base added in veg.-tempered clay.

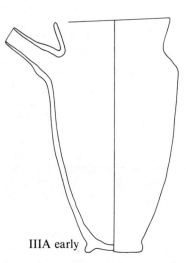

IIIA early

660. **6G64:603** (AbS 623)
     Grave 1 (No. 80)
     Complete but for chips.
     Pink clay.
     Buff surface.
     Grit and veg. temper.
     H. 23.5
     Rim di. 10.3
     Ba. di. 7.0
     Ring-base added in veg.-tempered clay.

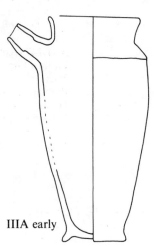

IIIA early

661. **6G64:595** (AbS 818)
     Grave 1 (No. 81)
     Much of body and rim missing.
     Overfired green clay.
     Grit temper.
     H. c. 24.5
     Rim di. c. 9.0
     Ba. di. 6.6
     Ring-base added in veg.-tempered clay.

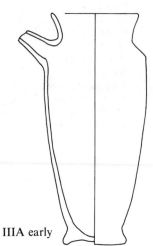

IIIA early

662. **4J97:136**
Animal hole from
surface (Batch 4430)
Rim and spout missing,
upper part fragmentary.
Red clay.
Paler surface.
Sparse grit temper.
Pres. H. 24.4
Max. width (reconstruc.) 11.6
Ba. di. 6.2
Ring-base added in
veg.-tempered clay.

663. **6G64:605** (AbS 816)
Grave 1 (No. 83)
Some gaps and chips.
Buff clay.
Grit and veg. temper.
H. 22.8
Rim di. 9.5-10.2
Ba. di. 7.0
Ring-base added
in veg.-tempered clay.

664. **6G64:609** (AbS 809)
Grave 1 (No. 89)
A little of rim and
upper body missing.
Pink clay.
Cream slip.
Grit temper.
H. 21.8
Rim di. 11.2-11.7
Ba. di. 6.1
Ring-base added in
veg.-tempered clay,
and worn underneath.

665. **6G64:596** (AbS 702)
Grave 1 (No. 77)
Some of rim, much
of base, and
other frags. missing.
Pink clay.
Cream slip.
Grit and veg. temper.
H. 22.7
Rim di. 11.2
Ba. di. 6.0
Ring-base added
in veg.-tempered clay.

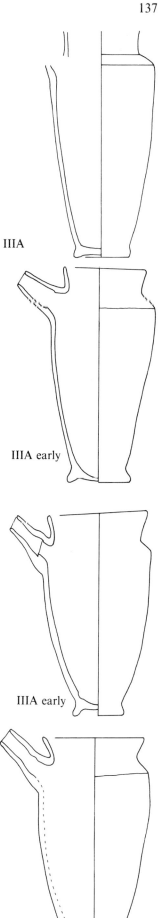

IIIA

IIIA early

IIIA early

IIIA early

666. **6G64:591** (AbS 615)
     Grave 1 (No. 76)
     One or two gaps.
     Dark red clay.
     Cream slip.
     Fine sandy temper.
     H. 24.0
     Rim di. 10.5
     Ba. di. 7.3
     Ring-base added, pre-
     sumably in veg.-tempered clay.

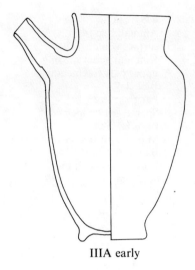

IIIA early

667. **6F05:240**
     Grave 188 (Batch 6027)
     Rim missing and gaps in body.
     Crisp green clay.
     Fine grit temper.
     Pres. H. 23.4
     Max. width 13.9
     Ba. di. 7.4

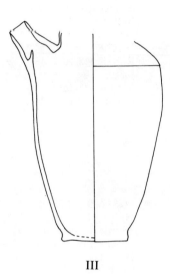

III

668. **6G64:608** (AbS 600)
     Grave 1 (No. 86)
     Condition and ware unknown.
     H. 26.8
     Rim di. 10.7
     Ba. di. 7.4
     Ring-base of same ware as pot.

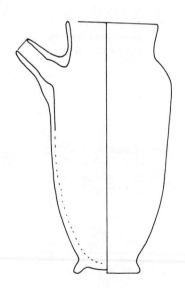

IIIA early

669. **6G62:12** (AbS 1081)
Grave 61 (No. 12)
Complete.
Green clay.
Temper unknown.
H. 24.4
Rim di. 11.1
Ba. di. 6.0
Ring-base added in
coarser, veg.-tempered clay.
Fragments of bone 6G62:22 found inside.

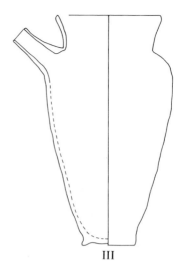

III

670. SIMILAR: **6G64:363** (AbS 754)
Grave 1 (No. 64)
Condition and ware unknown.
H. 24.8, rim di. 11.0, ba. di. 8.0
Ring-base added, presumably in veg.-tempered clay. IIIA early

671.        **5I21:218** (AbS 780)
Grave 35 (No. 7)
Much of upper part missing.
Pink clay, cream slip, grit temper.
H. 22.0, rim di. c. 10.4, ba. di. 6.8
End of spout pinched into triangular form.
Ring-base added, presumably in veg.-tempered clay. IIIA early

672.        **5I21:220** (AbS 781)
Grave 35 (No. 6)
Large chunk missing, including much of rim.
Pink clay, cream slip, fine grit temper.
H. 23.0, ba. di. 6.0
Extra ring of clay used to seal spout from inside.
Bottom of pot shaved and squared off
before ring added in veg.-tempered clay. IIIA early

673. **6G64:309 + 310** (AbS 817 + 822)
Grave 1 (No. 62 + 63)
One or two small gaps, surface eroded.
Pale pink clay.
Buff slip out.
Fine grit and veg. temper.
H. 25.5
Rim di. 11.0
Ba. di. 7.6-8.0
Ring-base added in veg.-tempered clay.

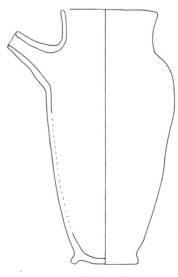

IIIA early

674. **6G64:736** (AbS 1395)
     Grave 88 (No. 12)
     Nearly complete.
     Overfired green clay, temper unknown.
     H. 25.5
     Rim di. 9.8-10.2
     Ba. di. 8.0-8.2
     Pinched ring-base.
     [Postgate and Moorey 1977:fig. 5 no. 4]

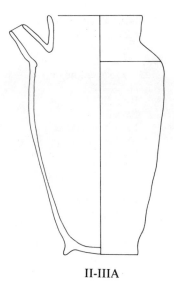

II-IIIA

675. **6G37:280** (AbS 1271)
     Grave 80 (No. 19)
     Rim slightly chipped.
     Buff clay.
     Cream slip.
     Fine sandy temper.
     H. 21.8
     Rim di. 9.8
     Ba. di. 8.5
     Ring-base of same clay as pot.
     Scored line on
     shoulder identical
     to that on no. 682
     Contained bone 6G37:331

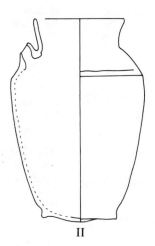

II

676. **5IS:164** (AbS 2037)
     Grave 185 (Batch 5372)
     A third of rim missing,
     and part of body and base.
     Brownish clay.
     Light grey-green slip.
     Temper of veg. and a little grit.
     H. 24.4
     Rim di. c. 10.4
     Ba. di. 10.4
     Interior bitumen coated, running
     into ancient cracks. More bitumen,
     or perhaps smoke-blackening, on rim.

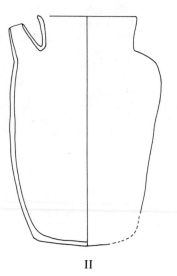

II

677. **5I31:49** (AbS 1209)
  Grave 81 (No. 8)
  Intact but for chips.
  Pink clay.
  Cream slip.
  Fine grit and veg. temper.
  H. 25.5
  Rim di. 11.3
  Ba. di. 9.9
  Contained bone fragments 5I31:84
  [Postgate 1977:fig. 5 no. 3]

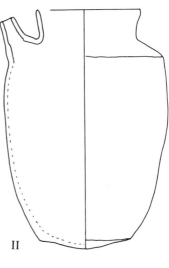

II

678. **5I98:66** (AbS 2232)
  Grave 205 (Batch 7420)
  Some of rim missing,
  and a few chips elsewhere.
  Pink clay.
  Cream slip.
  Grit temper.
  H. 25.6
  Rim di. 9.4 – 10.2
  Ba. di. 9.2
  [Postgate 1984:fig. 7 no. 3]

679. SIMILAR: **4J97:314**
    Inside storage jar
    no. 443 (Batch 4475)
    Base and some of body only.
    Greeny buff clay, grit and veg. temper.
    Pres. H. 16.0, ba. di. 8.8
    Ring-base pinched. II-IIIA

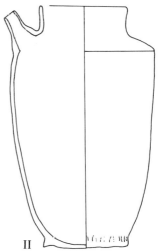

II

680. **6G64:735**
  Grave 88 (No. 11)
  A few pieces missing.
  Brown clay.
  Cream slip out.
  Heavy grit temper.
  H. 26.2
  Rim di. 10.5
  Ba. di. 8.4

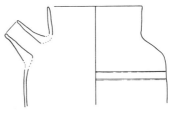

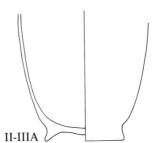

II-IIIA

681. PROBABLY SIMILAR: **6G64:689 + 692**
    Grave 88 (No. 10)
    Fragmentary.
    Pinkish buff clay, cream slip, grit temper.
    Rim di. c. 11.2, ba. di. 7.3-7.5
    [Postgate 1985 fig. 138 – non-joining
    parts shown at different scales] II-IIIA

682. **6G37:225** (AbS 1266)
     Grave 80 (No. 24)
     Almost complete.
     Pink clay.
     Cream slip.
     Sandy grit temper.
     H. 26.9
     Rim di. 10.3
     Ba. di. 8.9
     Pinched ring-base.
     Scored line on shoulder identical
     to that on no. 675

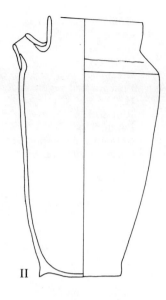

683. **8GS:32** (AbS 1473)
     Grave 110 (no Batch number)
     Incomplete.
     Buff clay.
     Cream slip.
     Grit temper.
     H. 39.6
     Rim di. 9.7
     Ba. di. 10.8
     Ring-base of same clay as pot.
     Inside surface scraped.

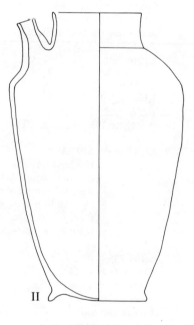

684. **6G37:271** (AbS 1270)
     Grave 80 (No. 21)
     Complete but for chips.
     Buff clay.
     Cream slip.
     Grit and veg. temper.
     H. 29.2
     Rim di. 10.8
     Ba. di. 10.4
     Ring-base of same clay as pot.
     Upper part green and vitrified.

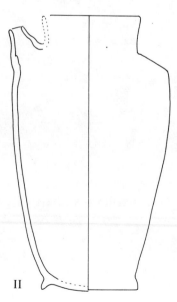

685. **6G38:96** (AbS 870)
Grave 52 (No. 3)
Much of base missing.
Hard pink clay.
Cream slip.
Fine grit temper.
H. 28.0
Rim di. 11.0
Ba. di. (reconstruc.) 10.6
Ring-base pinched directly out of pot.

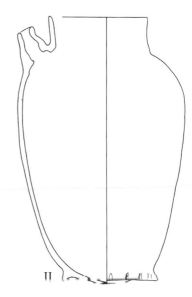

686. SIMILAR: **6G37:247** (AbS 1267)
Grave 80 (No. 23)
Complete but for chip from rim.
Buff clay, cream slip, temper unknown.
H. 31.2, rim di. 11.6, ba. di. 9.8
Pinched ring-base.     II

687.               **6G37:236** (AbS 1268)
Grave 80 (No. 22)
Complete but for chips.
Buff clay, cream slip, temper unknown.
H. 27.7, rim di. 10.6, ba. di. 10.0
Ring-base added in veg.-tempered clay and pinched.     II

688.               **6G37:282** (AbS 1269)
Grave 80 (No. 20)
Complete but for part of rim and spout.
Greenish overfired clay, temper unknown.
H. 27.9, rim di. 10.7, ba. di. 10.0
Pinched ring-base.
Contained bone fragments 6G37:332
[Postgate 1977:fig. 5 no. 7]     II

689.               **6G37:390** (AbS 1383)
Grave 80 (No. 18)
Complete.
Greenish clay, temper unknown.
H. 26.5, rim di. 10.0, ba. di. 9.0
Pinched ring-base.     II

690. **5IS:190** (AbS 2038)
Grave 185 (Batch 5372)
Rim and upper body nearly complete,
also base, but part of lower
body missing so does not join.
Orange clay.
White slip out.
Grit and white grit temper.
Pres. H. top 19.2
Pres. H. base 7.4
Rim di. 11.0
Ba. di. 11.4
Ring-base of same clay as pot
and not tall enough to support it.     II

691. **5I31:32** (AbS 1210)
     Grave 81 (No. 15)
     Parts of rim and body missing.
     Fine red clay.
     Cream slip.
     Temper unknown.
     H. 36.2
     Rim di. 11.5
     Ba. di. 11.9
     Horizontal reserve-
     slip on shoulder.
     Ring-base of same clay as pot.

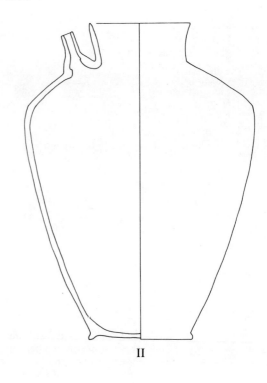

II

692. **6G85:9**
     Grave 161 (Batch 1803)
     Part of rim and shoulder only.
     Pink clay.
     Greeny buff surface.
     Grit temper.
     Pres. H. 7.5
     Rim di. 12.0

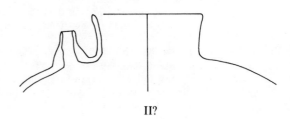

II?

693. **4J88:19**
     Grave 197 (Batch 4205)
     Part of rim and neck only.
     Pink clay.
     Yellowy slip out.
     Grit temper.
     Pres. H. 17.5
     Rim di. (reconstruc.) 12.0
     Max. width c. 23.0
     Found upside-down.

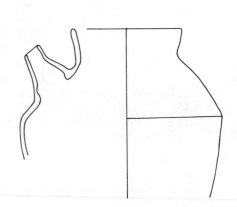

III

694. **0US:20** (AbS 1847)
　　　Grave 160 (Batch 4056)
　　　Half body and much of base missing.
　　　Friable red clay.
　　　Buff slip.
　　　Sparse grit temper.
　　　H. 29.4
　　　Rim di. c. 10.6
　　　Ba. di. (reconstruc.) 10.4
　　　Scraped down inside.
　　　Pinched ring-base.

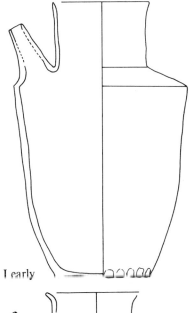

I early

695. **0US:11** (AbS 1843)
　　　Grave 160 (Batch 4056)
　　　Rim and spout chipped.
　　　Buff clay.
　　　Cream slip.
　　　Sand temper.
　　　H. 23.8
　　　Rim di. 10.3
　　　Ba. di. 8.4
　　　Scraped down inside.
　　　Conical bowl no. 85 found inverted over mouth.

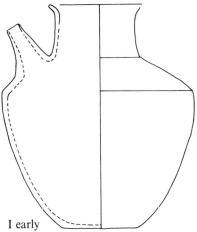

I early

696. **0US:5** (AbS 1840)
　　　Grave 160 (Batch 4056)
　　　Virtually complete.
　　　Fine pink clay.
　　　Buff surface.
　　　Cream slip.
　　　Sand temper.
　　　H. 39.2
　　　Rim di. 11.0
　　　Ba. di. 10.9
　　　Surface scraped inside and out.

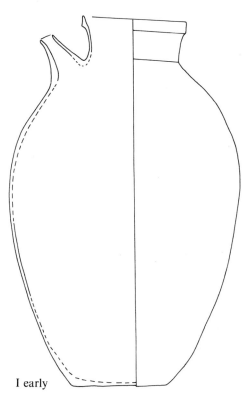

I early

697. **0US:7** (AbS 1841)
Grave 160 (Batch 4056)
Part of rim missing,
end of spout broken.
Pink clay.
Cream slip out.
Sandy temper.
H. 35.0
Rim di. 12.0
Ba. di. 14.8

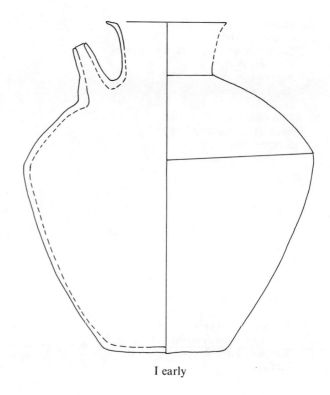

I early

698. **0US:6** (AbS 1848)
Grave 160 (Batch 4056)
Rim missing. Most of
rest extant, but upper
and lower parts do not join.
Pink clay.
Cream slip out.
White grit temper.
Pres. H. top 21.8
Pres H. bottom 15.6
Max. width 33.6
Ba. di. 15.6
Fine and delicate.
Inside scraped down.
Reserve slip on shoulder.

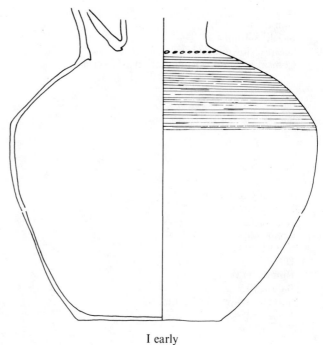

I early

699. **6G84:36**
Room 80 floors (Batch 1709)
Rim and part of shoulder only.
Pink clay.
Buff slip.
Grit and veg. temper.
Pres. H. 6.8
Rim di. 15.6

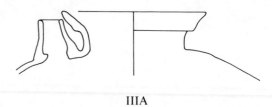

IIIA

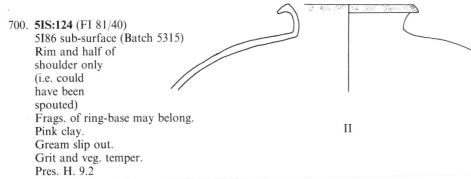

700. **5IS:124** (FI 81/40)
5I86 sub-surface (Batch 5315)
Rim and half of
shoulder only
(i.e. could
have been
spouted)
Frags. of ring-base may belong.
Pink clay.
Gream slip out.
Grit and veg. temper.
Pres. H. 9.2
Rim di. 13.4
A little red paint preserved on rim and inside neck.
Found upside-down: inside burnt.

II

701. SIMILAR: **5IS:125 + 126** (FI 81/16)
5I87 sub-surface (Batch 5313)
Rim and part of shoulder only (could have been spouted).
Buff clay, cream slip out,
temper of grit including much quartz.
Pres. H. 8.0, rim di. 14.0
Traces of red paint on rim.
Found upside-down: inside burnt.    II

702. **5IS:202**
Part of drain in
5I97 (Batch 5333)
Ring-base, some of
lower body, and
tip of spout missing.
Buff clay.
Yellowish slip.
Grit and black
grit temper.
Pres. H. 36.6
Rim di. 12.2
Max. width 33.0

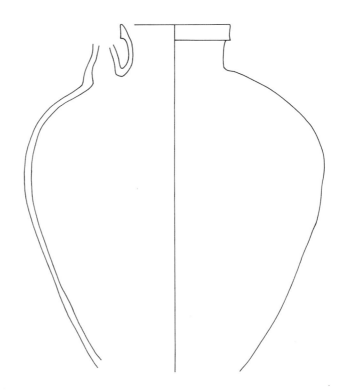

II or III

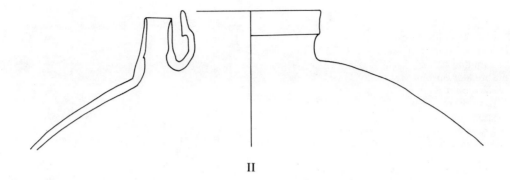

II

703. **5I98:232**
Found complete but for
base, but only rim and
shoulder restored.
Pink clay.
Grit temper.

FI 83/27 (Batch 7417)
Pres. H. 14.8
Rim di. 15.1
[Postgate 1984:fig. 7 no. 6]

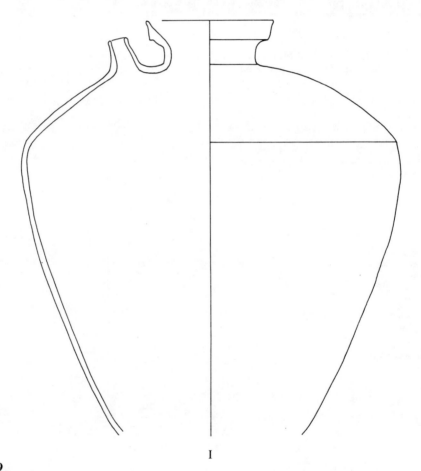

I

704. **1T:9**
Ring-base missing
and some gaps too.
Green clay.
Black surface inside.
Temper unknown.

North-East Mound (Batch 4006)
Pres. H. 44.0
Rim di. 14.0
Max. width 40.0

705. **5I21:370**
   Room 4 floor (Batch 1110)
   Rim complete, one side of
   body extant down to near base.
   Pink clay.
   Cream slip out.
   Grit temper.
   Pres. H. 39.6
   Rim di. 15.4-16.0
   Max. width (reconstruc.) 31.4

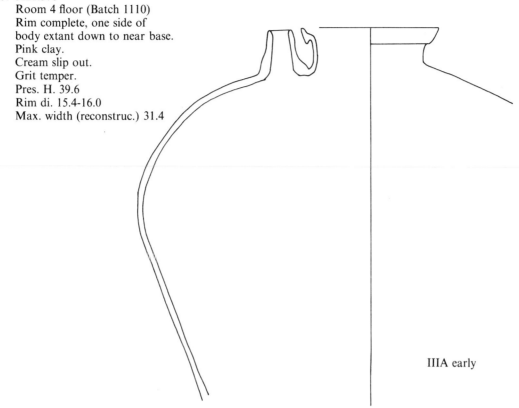

IIIA early

706. **4J98:28**
   (AbS 2033)
   Set into
   floor of
   Room 26
   (Batch 1610)
   Nearly complete
   but for spout.
   Surface
   badly
   flaked
   in places.
   Pink clay.
   Buff slip.
   Grit temper.
   H. 39.0
   Rim di. 19.5-20.0
   Ba. di. 18.7
   Incised nicks at
   base of neck
   (not visible in drawing)
   Contained bottle no. 288

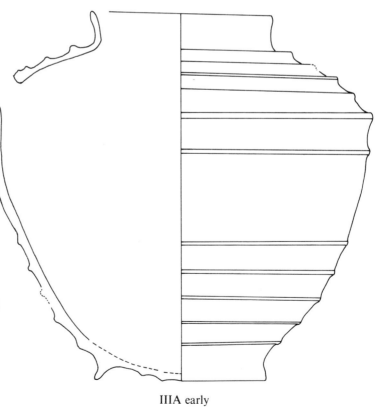

IIIA early

707. **6HS:133**
     FI 83/22 (Batch 7022)
     Most of rim and neck extant,
     and part of shoulder.
     Pink clay.
     Cream slip out.
     Sandy temper.
     Pres. H. 8.3
     Rim di. 11.4
     6 applied pellets around base of spout.
     Surface blackened inside.

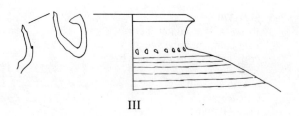

III

708. NOT ILLUSTRATED: **2G36:40**
     Large pit in West Mound Level II (Batch 5403)
     Most of rim and part of shoulder only.
     Orange clay, cream slip out, sandy temper.
     Pres. H. 3.2, rim di. 11.0-11.4
     [Postgate and Moon 1982:fig. 6 no.7] I early

709.               **2G36:42**
     Large pit in West Mound Level II (Batch 5403)
     Fragmentary.
     Pink clay, buff slip out, fine mixed temper.
     Pres. H. 8.2, rim di. 12.2-12.5
     [Postgate and Moon 1982:fig. 5. no. 8] I early

710.               **2G26:86**
     Large pit in West Mound Level II (Batch 5403)
     Fragmentary.
     Pink clay, cream slip out,
     mixed grit and veg. temper.
     Pres. H. 6.6, rim di. c. 8.0
     [Postgate and Moon 1982:fig. 6. no. 9] I early

# SINGLE-HANDLED JARS

As with the stemmed dishes (p. 59 above), the Abu Salabikh corpus of single-handled jars has grown since it was last reported on (Moon 1981), but for ED III at least has not acquired any significantly different types. Again, where possible, recent additions have been used here to illustrate their particular style, but some previously-published items have been included too in order to demonstrate the complete range.

No. 711 may be of ED I date, but more typical of the usual Abu Salabikh style for this period are nos. 713-715, large jars with wing-lugs and elaborate decoration. So far there have not been any large ED I upright-handled jars with broad solid handles from the site, though some of the loose handles found in later context strongly suggest their existence (for instance no. 777). These are limited so far to the Main Mound, and there is virtually no evidence yet of upright handles from the West Mound, not even from the surface.

One or two ED II types have been added to the repertoire. No. 716 has a wing-lug, nos. 712 and 717 are of the upright-handled variety. No. 712 has no extant handle, but the decoration is concentrated round the break where one would expect it, in typical early ED style (compare Delougaz 1952 Pl.78). These jars from Grave 185 look earlier than no. 723, which already displays the proportions of ED III jars, with comparatively wide shoulder, and is without the bevelled-ledge rim characteristic of ED I and II. It has more in common with the early IIIA examples nos. 720-722.

ED III upright-handled jars generally show much diversity of style and decoration. Only one from our collection can be pinned to late IIIA, no. 729, and this has the typically IIIA band-rim and hollow handle, but the lower body is beginning to sag into the 'baggy' shape popular later. Anthropomorphic features are of course a IIIB indicator, and can be seen first on nos. 733-737, which may go back to late IIIA. The solid handles combined with lengthening body, common from the 'A' cemetery at Kish, are well demonstrated by nos. 743-751. No. 742 is perhaps Akkadian.

Disembodied handles of all dates are very common, especially in rubbish contexts, the solid ones in particular being almost indestructible (nos. 753-789). As they do not help much with chronological problems only a few are illustrated.

711. **6G64:61**
  Grave 2 (No. 21)
  Rim and neck only,
  and piece of shoulder.
  Red clay.
  Smooth finish.
  Temper unknown.
  Pres. H. 9.1
  Rim di. 11.8
  Well made and finished.

I?

712. **5IS:76** (AbS 1962)
  Grave 185 (Batch 5372)
  Half of rim and body missing.
  Pinky brown clay.
  Greenish slip.
  Grit and veg. temper.
  H. 28.8
  Rim di. c. 11.8
  Ba. di. 9.8
  Faint diagonal reserve-
  slip over lower body.
  Bitumen painted onto
  shoulder has dripped onto neck.
  No extant lug, but
  vessel is of this type.

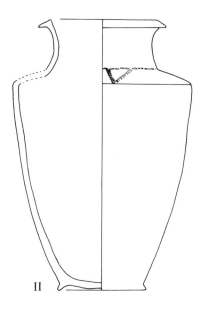

II

713. **2G36:178**
West Mound Level II,
stratified deposit (Batch 5437)
Part of neck and
shoulder only.
Pink clay.
Yellowy slip out.
Pres. H. 9.0
Neck di. 11.8

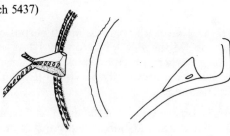

I early

714. NOT ILLUSTRATED: **2GS:91 + 104** (AbS 1474)
West Mound Room 8 (Batch 5055)
Nearly complete.
Reddish clay, greenish slip out, grit temper.
H. 56.6, rim di. 19.6, ba. di. 20.0
Excised triangles.
[Postgate 1978:fig. 3 no. 1;
1983:fig. 286 and Pl. VIIIb]    I

715.                                **2GS:103 +2G03:1** (AbS 1475)
West Mound Room 8 (Batch 5055
+ 5800 + 5801 + 5803)
Quarter of body missing.
Red clay, cream slip out, grit temper.
Burnished out except on rim and neck.
H. 56.8, rim di. 24.6, ba. di. 20.8
[Postgate 1978:fig. 3 no. 2;
1983:fig. 285 and Pl. VIIIa]    I

716. **5IS:219**
Grave 193 (Batch 5380)
Badly salted, and
a few bits missing.
Pink clay.
Yellowy slip.
Sandy temper.
H. 15.4
Rim di. 11.4-11.8
Ba. di. 8.5-9.2

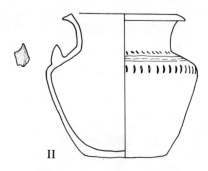

II

717. **6G37:85** (AbS 647)
Grave 38 (No. 25)
Fragmentary.
Pink clay.
Buff slip out.
Fine grit temper.
Pres. H. 16.3
Handle undecorated.

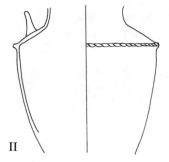

II

718. SIMILAR: **6G38:95** (AbS 755)
Grave 52 (No. 2)
Intact.
Ware unknown.
H. 17.3, rim di. 8.8, ba. di. 6.4
[Postgate and Moorey 1976:fig. 7 no. 3]
[Moon 1981:no. 38]    II

719. **5IS:193**
    Profile of neck to
    just below shoulder.
    Orange clay.
    Yellow slip.
    Grit temper.

Grave 185 (Batch 5372)
Pres. H. 12.4
Max. width (reconstruc.)
c. 31.0
Thin, flat handle attached
by pushing through hole in
shoulder.

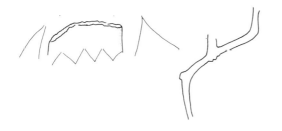
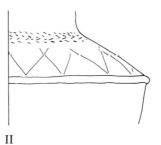

II

720. **5I10:59** (AbS 540)
    Room 2 Level II floor (Batch 1006)
    Upper part only.
    Ware unknown.
    Pres. H. 24.0
    Rim di. 15.2
    [Postgate and Moorey
    1976 Pl. XXVb]
    [Moon 1981:no. 3]

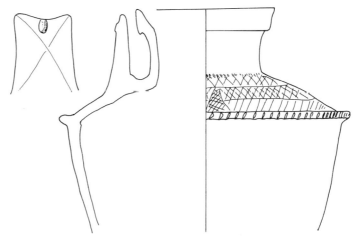

IIIA early

721. SIMILAR: **5I11:95**
        Room 7 fill (Batch 1206)
        Upper part only.
        Pink clay, cream surface, temper unknown
        Pres. H. 14.6, rim di. 16.4
        [Moon 1981:no. 2]   IIIA early

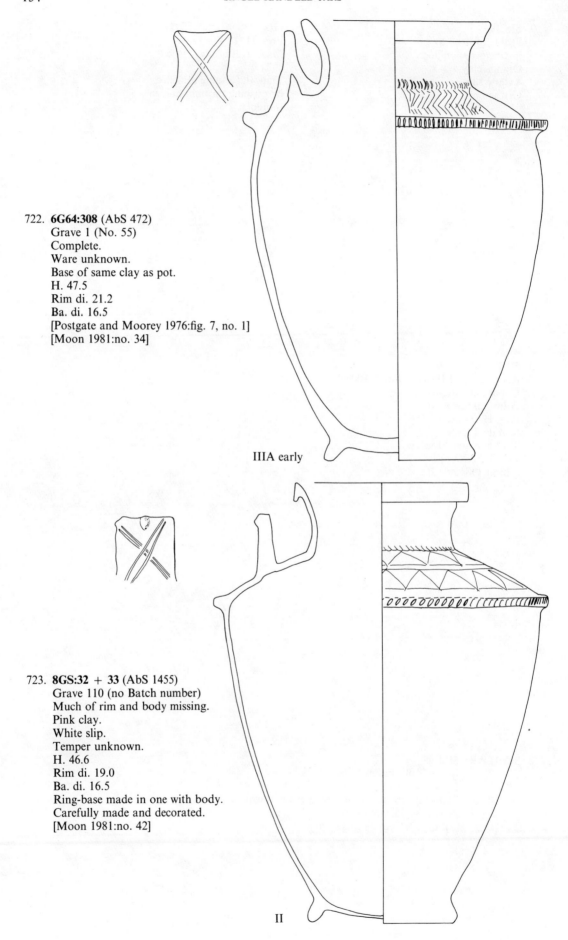

722. **6G64:308** (AbS 472)
     Grave 1 (No. 55)
     Complete.
     Ware unknown.
     Base of same clay as pot.
     H. 47.5
     Rim di. 21.2
     Ba. di. 16.5
     [Postgate and Moorey 1976:fig. 7, no. 1]
     [Moon 1981:no. 34]

IIIA early

723. **8GS:32 + 33** (AbS 1455)
     Grave 110 (no Batch number)
     Much of rim and body missing.
     Pink clay.
     White slip.
     Temper unknown.
     H. 46.6
     Rim di. 19.0
     Ba. di. 16.5
     Ring-base made in one with body.
     Carefully made and decorated.
     [Moon 1981:no. 42]

II

724. **6G85:41** (AbS 1857)
Grave 165 (Batch 1805)
Fragmentary: rim
and handle intact,
part of shoulder and
upper body preserved.
Pink clay.
Cream slip out.
Sandy temper.
Pres. H. 32.3
Rim di. 15.8-16.2

725. SIMILAR: **6G52:3**
Grave 17 (No. 3)
Rim and base missing.
Red clay, temper unknown.
Prcs. H. 24.3, max. width c. 34.0
Handle hollow.
[Moon 1981:no. 41]    IIIA

IIIA

726.          **6G36:171** (AbS 1750)
Grave 127 (Batch 2463)
Fragmentary.
Pink clay, cream slip, temper unknown.
H. 39.5, rim di. 16.5, ba. di. 17.5
Ring-base added.    IIIA-B

727.          **6G36:42** (AbS 1749)
Grave 115 (Batch 2411)
Gaps in body.
Pink clay, cream slip, temper unknown.
H. 39.3, rim di. 17.0, ba. di. 17.0
Handle has rows of vertical, not slanting marks.    III

728. **4I09:160 + 224** (AbS 1397)
Grave 94 (No. 6)
Complete but for chips.
Red clay.
Temper unknown.
H. 50.3
Rim di. 16.3
Ba. di. 16.8
Ring-base added
in veg.-tempered clay.
Contained bone
4I09:225, and bone and
reed impression 4I09:234
[Moon 1981:no. 33]

IIIA

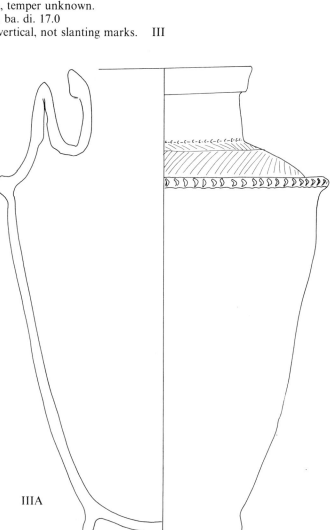

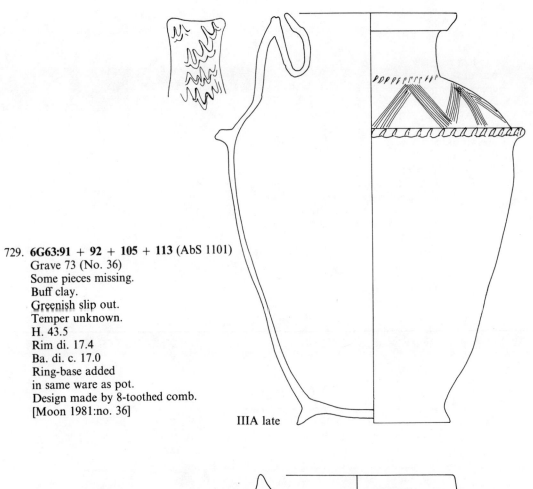

729. **6G63:91 + 92 + 105 + 113** (AbS 1101)
    Grave 73 (No. 36)
    Some pieces missing.
    Buff clay.
    Greenish slip out.
    Temper unknown.
    H. 43.5
    Rim di. 17.4
    Ba. di. c. 17.0
    Ring-base added
    in same ware as pot.
    Design made by 8-toothed comb.
    [Moon 1981:no. 36]

IIIA late

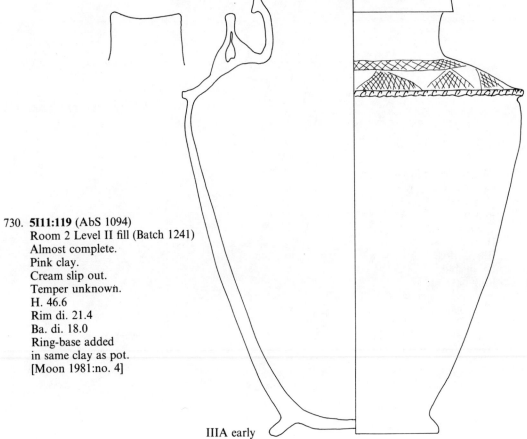

730. **5I11:119** (AbS 1094)
    Room 2 Level II fill (Batch 1241)
    Almost complete.
    Pink clay.
    Cream slip out.
    Temper unknown.
    H. 46.6
    Rim di. 21.4
    Ba. di. 18.0
    Ring-base added
    in same clay as pot.
    [Moon 1981:no. 4]

IIIA early

731. **6G85:61 + 64** (AbS 1913)
Grave 171 (Batch 1809)
Two thirds of rim missing, parts
of rib and some of base gone.
Badly cracked and salted.
Red clay.
Sparse sandy temper, veg. in base.
H. c. 29.2
Rim di. c. 15.0
Ba. di. c. 8.4
(Measurements approxi-
mate as very fragile)
Base and rib added
in veg.-tempered clay.

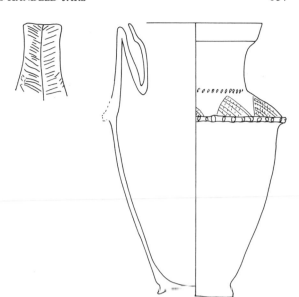

IIIA

732. **6F05:17** (AbS 1930)
Grave 168 (Batch 6000)
Most of lower part and
some of shoulder missing.
Two bits of added
ring-base may belong.
Pink clay.
Yellow slip out.
Fine grit
and veg. temper.
Pres. H. 19.8
Rim di. 16.6-17.0
Max. width 31.2
Rib added in
straw-tempered clay.

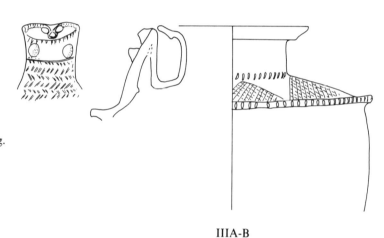

IIIA-B

733. SIMILAR: **6F05:67** (AbS 1972)
Grave 176 (Batch 6008)
Complete but for chips.
Orangey red clay, yellowish slip, grit temper.
H. 40.6, rim di. 16.8, ba. di. 16.6
Base and rib added in straw-tempered clay.
Handle constructed from cylinder
of clay pinched together at top, and fitted
to body over short spout pulled out from shoulder.
Herringbone pattern like no. 724   IIIB

734.            **6G38:83** (AbS 903)
North-west of north wall of Room 115 (Batch 808)
Rim and neck only.
Pink clay, temper unknown.
Pres. H. 8.8, rim di. 16.4
[Moon 1981:no. 9]   III

735. **6G75:158**
      Grave 162 (Batch 3618)
      Most of neck
      and shoulder extant,
      and a little of body.
      Pink clay.
      Yellowish slip out.
      Grit temper.
      Pres. H. 21.0
      Max. width 28.8

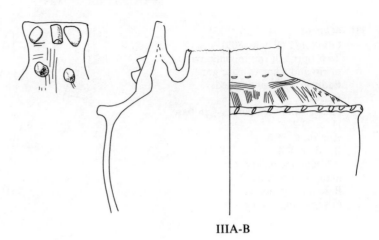

IIIA-B

736. VERY SIMILAR: **6G45:66** (AbS 1794)
                    Grave 143 (Batch 2919)
                    Part of rim and handle and shoulder frags. extant.
                    Pink clay, cream slip, fine grit and veg. temper.
                    Rim di. 14.0, handle 6.0 x 6.0
                    Handle hollow, shoulder random-combed.   IIIA-B

737.                **6G38:189** (AbS 1419)
                    Room 110, cut below Grave 51 (Batch 832)
                    Handle only, chipped.
                    Red clay, greenish slip, temper unknown.
                    6.3 x 5.1
                    Hollow.
                    [Moon 1981:no. 47]   IIIA-B

738. **6G76:551 + 552 + 697** (handle AbS 1793)
      Surface, perhaps part of
      Grave 146 (Batch 2629 + 2630)
      Fragmentary: nothing of lower body.
      Red clay.
      Cream slip.
      Grit temper.
      Solid disc-shaped peg at base of handle.
      Pres. H. 20.2
      Rim di. 13.6
      Bitumen has been used to fix top of
      handle to rim of jar.

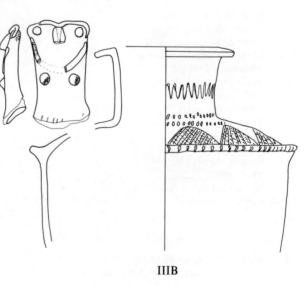

739. SIMILAR: **6G54:94**
               Ash Pit (Batch 106 + 107)
               Handle and base missing.
               Red clay, temper unknown.
               Pres. H. 36.5, rim di. 11.6
               [Moon 1981:no. 8]   IIIB

IIIB

740.                **6G63:36** (AbS 1140)
                    Room 62, upper fill (Batch 911)
                    Part of handle only.
                    Red clay, temper unknown.
                    Solid.
                    5.1 x 5.3
                    [Moon 1981:no. 23]   IIIB

741. FAIRLY SIMILAR: **6G54:93**
                     Ash Pit (Batch 102 + 106)
                     Part of upper body only.
                     Ware unknown (except surface cream)
                     Pres. H. 24.4, rim di. 11.6
                     [Moon 1981:no. 7]   IIIB

742. **6G75:261 + 264**
Grave 195 (Batch 3643)
Profile rim to lower
body; second piece
gives profile lower
body to base.
Handle broken off.
Hard red clay.
Sandy grit temper.
H. 39.7
Rim di. (reconstruc.) 9.2
Ba. di. 10.2
Base added in veg. tempered clay.

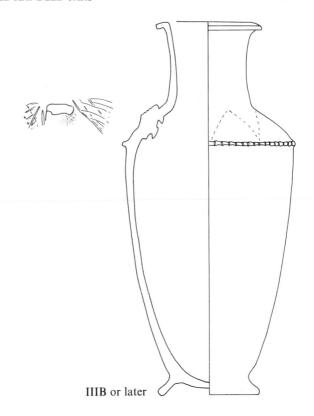

IIIB or later

743. **6FS:24** (AbS 1933)
Grave 173 (Batch 5212)
Intact but cracked.
Pink clay varying to buff.
Yellowish slip.
Temper of fine grit
and a little fine veg.
H. 38.4
Rim di. 10.7-10.9
Ba. di. 12.5
Base added in
straw-tempered clay.

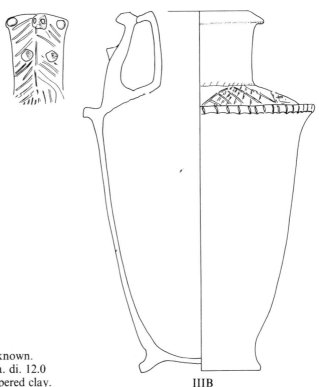

744. SIMILAR: **6G66:24** (AbS 418)
Grave 5 (No. 6)
Almost complete.
Cream clay, temper unknown.
H. 41.6, rim di. 11.0, ba. di. 12.0
Base added in veg.-tempered clay.
[Moon 1981:no. 37]   IIIB

IIIB

745.            **6G38:130** (AbS 1035)
Surface (Batch 803)
Rim missing, base does not join.
Pink clay, cream surface out, temper unknown.
Pres. H. top 11.7, pres. H. bottom 8.0, ba. di. c. 18.0
Base added, presumably in veg.-tempered clay.
[Moon 1981:no. 10]   IIIB

746. SIMILAR: **6G63:124** (AbS 1424)
Pit in Room 61 (Batch 923)
Handle and some small fragments only.
Red clay, temper unknown.
7.9 x 5.4
Hollow.
[Moon 1981:no. 29]   III

747.          **6G45:16** (AbS 1751)
Grave 136 (Batch 2902)
Rim, ring-base, and parts of body missing.
Pink clay.
Cream slip.
Temper unknown.
Max. width 27.0   III

748. **6G75:522**
Grave 162 (S)
(Batch 3673)
Fragmentary, but
much of neck and
shoulder extant.
Pink clay.
Cream slip.
Grit temper.
Pres. H. upper
part 28.8
Pres. H. lower
part 20.4 (H. perhaps 40)
Rim di. (reconstruc.) 14.0
Ba. di. c. 15.0
Base added in
veg.-tempered clay.

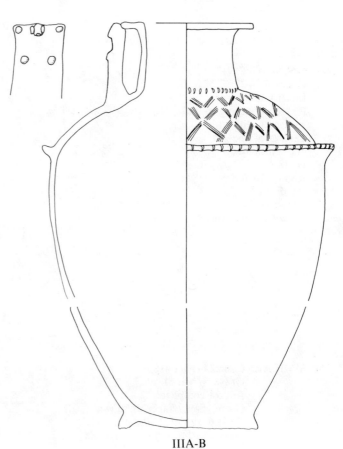

IIIA-B

749. SIMILAR: **4I09:207** (AbS 1412)
Grave 95 (No. 1)
Part of base mising.
Buff clay, cream slip, temper unknown.
H. 38.3, rim di. 13.3, ba. di. 15.5
Base added in coarse veg.-tempered clay.
[Moon 1981:no. 31. In the illustration
(fig. 5 no. 31) the view with the profile
has been accidentally changed with that
of no. 32. The left breast, not the right, is missing.]   IIIB

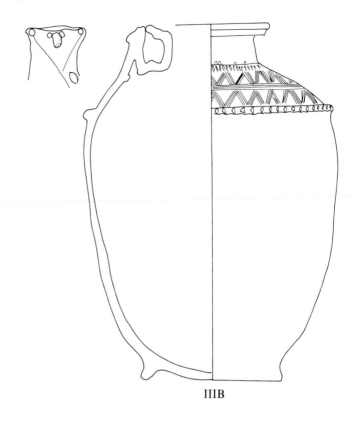

IIIB

750. **4I08:21** (AbS 1216)
Grave 84 (No. 2)
Some pieces missing.
Red clay.
Cream slip out.
Temper unknown.
H. 37.2
Rim di. 13.7
Ba. di. 15.1
[Moon 1981:32;
In the illustration
the view with the
profile has been
accidentally changed
with that of no. 31]

751. **6G37:110** (AbS 626)
Grave 32 (No. 11)
Complete.
Ware unknown.
H. 41.5
Rim di. 18.1
Ba. di. 18.5
[Postgate and Moorey 1976:
fig. 7, no. 2 and
Pl. XXIIId; Moon 1981:
no. 40 (number
erroneously omitted)]

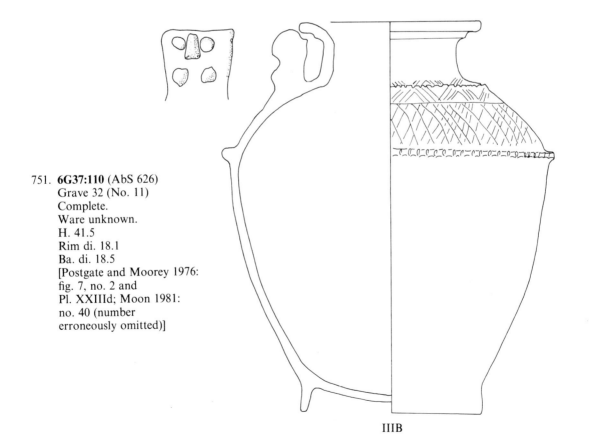

IIIB

752. **6G63:384** (AbS 1420)
Grave 100 (Batch 977)
Rim and about
half body complete,
base damaged.
Buff clay.
Cream slip.
Temper unknown.
H. 31.0
Rim di. 17.2
Ba. di. c. 17.0
[Moon 1981:no. 35]

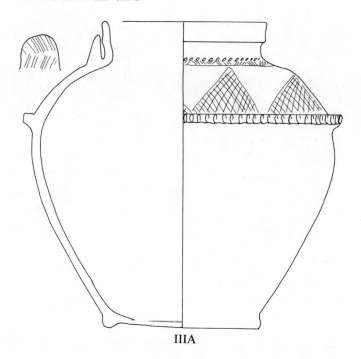

IIIA

753. **6G47:211** (AbS 1787)
Grave 124 (Batch 2596)
Pink clay.
Buff slip out.
Grit temper.
11.7 x 6.0
Lower end moulded into hollow,
perhaps to fit over peg on jar-shoulder.

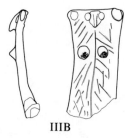

IIIB

754. **6G47:220** (AbS 1788)
Pit in Room 120 (Batch 2507)
Pink clay.
Cream slip out.
Grit temper.
6.3 x 4.8
Solid, but attached in same way as spout handle.

II?

755. **6G76:454** (AbS 1792)
Pit into Ash Tip (Batch 2609)
Pink clay.
Cream slip out.
Grit temper.
7.6 x 5.2

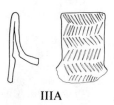

IIIA

756. SIMILAR: **6G56:85** (AbS 1436)
Room 49 fill (Batch 2017)
Handle only.
Greenish clay, temper unknown.
8.0 x 6.8
Solid.
[Moon 1981:no. 22]   I?

757. **6G35:82** (AbS 1784)
Rubbish stratum in Room 121 (Batch 2813)
Pale pink clay.
White slip.
Fine grit temper.
5.9 x 5.6
Fixed by means of plug
passed through shoulder of jar.

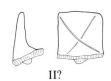

II?

758. SIMILAR: **6G66:162** (AbS 938)
West edge of Ash Tip (Batch 431)
Condition and ware unknown.
6.5 x 6.7
Hollow.
[Moon 1981:no. 25]   I

759. **6G45:118** (AbS 1786)
Grave 156 (Batch 2942, disturbed)
Pink clay.
Yellowy slip.
Grit temper.
8.6 x 7.2
Smoothed onto shoulder.

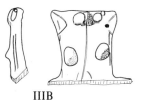

IIIB

760. SIMILAR: **5I21:273**
Room 4 Level I fill (Batch 1121)
Shoulder fragment and handle only.
Buff clay, cream surface, temper includes much straw.
7.5 x 7.6
Solid.
Shoulder has horizontal rows of herringbone hatching.
[Moon 1981:no. 11 – context corrected here]   IIIA

761. **6G64:1089** (AbS 1790)
Sounding Level II (Batch 2718)
Pink clay.
White slip.
Grit temper.
Solid. Fixed by plug passed through shoulder.
8.6 x 7.2
Rocker bands.

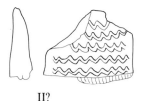

II?

762. **6G64:1041** (AbS 1789)
Sounding Level II (Batch 2733)
Buff clay.
Grit temper.
Solid. Fixed by means of plug passed
through vessel and stuck onto spout.
6.8 x 6.5
Sewage stained.
Decoration effected with stick or blunt comb.

II?

763. SIMILAR: **5I21:369**
                  Pit west of Room 4 (Batch 1132)
                  Red clay, cream surface, temper unknown.
                  4.0 x 3.9
                  Solid.
                  [Moon 1981:no. 12]   II?

764.
                  **5I10:223** (AbS 1308)
                  Pit in Room 1 (Batch 1046)
                  Red clay, cream slip, temper unknown.
                  6.0 x 5.9
                  Solid.
                  [Moon 1981:no. 13]   II?

765.
                  **6G55:163** (AbS 710)
                  Floors east of Room 47 (Batch 352)
                  Red clay, buff surface, temper unknown.
                  6.0 x 7.0
                  Solid.
                  [Moon 1981:no. 24]   II?

766. **6G64:1090** (AbS 1791)
Ash Pit cutting Room 44 (Batch 86)
Pink clay.
Buff slip.
7.6 x 8.2
Grit and coarse veg. temper, including grains!
Very rough.

II?

767. **6G66:161** (AbS 940)
Western edge of Ash Tip (Batch 431)
Pink clay.
Paler surface out.
Grit temper.
7.0 x 7.5
Fixed by well-concealed hole in shoulder.

II?

JARS NOT ILLUSTRATED:

768. **6G47:103** (AbS 1752)
Grave 124 (Batch 2550)
Part of rim, most of handle
and much of body missing.
Pink core, cream slip, fine sparse grit.
H. 42.7, rim di. 15.0, ba. di. 13.0
Ring-base added in veg.-tempered clay.
Handle probably solid with pinnate motif.
Body shape probably similar to no. 744   IIIB

769. **6G63:179** (AbS 1299), Room 61 fill (Batch 925)
Fragment of unusual jar with representational incised decoration
including a human figure on the handle.
[Moon 1981:no. 5]   III

770. **6G74:85** (AbS 530), cut in Rooms 54-55 (Batch 606)
Miniature jar. [Moon 1981:no. 6]   III

771. **6G37:96** (AbS 1018), Grave 32 (No. 6)
Handle has circular emplacement.
[Moon 1981:no. 39 – shown at wrong scale]   IIIB

HANDLES NOT ILLUSTRATED:

772. **6G44:68** (AbS 1785)
Grave 140 (Batch 3104)
Fragmentary.
Ware unknown.
9.4 x 5.6
Two applied breasts, with two incised
diagonal lines crossing between them.     III

773. **6G56:82** (AbS 1421)
Room 49 fill (Batch 2012)
Reddish clay, cream slip, grit and coarse grit temper.
6.4 x 6.7
Solid.
Traces of perfunctory St. Andrew's cross.     II?

774. **5I21:260** (AbS 888), Grave 26 (No. 39)
Ladder-pattern St. Andrew's cross. [Moon 1981:no. 14]    II?

775. **No number** (AbS 1393), surface (no Batch number)
Diagonal incised lines. [Moon 1981:no. 15]    III

776. **5I21:261** (AbS 887), surface (Batch 1100)
Pinnate motif. [Moon 1981:no. 16]    II?

777. **5I21:259** (AbS 889), surface (Batch 1100)
Ladder-patterns. [Moon 1981:no. 17]    I?

778. **6G64:639** (AbS 717), Grave 1 fill (Batch 24)
Pinnate motif. [Moon 1981:no. 18;
not included in Postgate 1985]    I?

779. **No number** Grave 2 fill (Batch 15)
Pinnate motif. [Moon 1981:no. 19;
not included in Postgate 1985]    II?

780. **6G63.137** (AbS 1142), Room 61 fill (Batch 920)
Applied features. [Moon 1981:no. 20]    III

781. **6G63:242** (AbS 1309), Room 61 fill (Batch 920)
Undecorated. [Moon 1981:no. 21]    I?

782. **6G54:96** (AbS 718), Ash Pit cutting
Room 44 (Batch 104)
Inverted pinnate motif. [Moon 1981:no. 26]    II or III

783. **6G66:114** (AbS 709), Ash Tip (Batch 431)
Random comb marks. [Moon 1981:no. 27]    II?

784. **6G55:169** (AbS 934), Ash Pit (Batch 360)
Pinnate motif and applied features.
[Moon 1981:no. 28]    IIIB

785. **6G38:193** (AbS 1422), Grave 51 (No. 22)
Applied nose. [Moon 1981:no. 30]    II?

786. **5I21:217** (AbS 751), Grave 35 (No. 4)
Double pinnate motif. [Moon 1981:no. 43]    IIIA early

787. **5I21:214** (AbS 758), Grave 35 (No. 3)
Pinnate motif. [Moon 1981:no. 44]    IIIA early

788. **6G63:123** (AbS 1141), Grave 75 (No. 4)
Applied features. [Moon 1981:no. 45]    IIIB

789. **6G37:133** (AbS 1020), Grave 38 (No. 26)
Pinnate motif. [Moon 1981:no. 47]    IIIA

# MISCELLANEOUS JAR FORMS

No matter how broad the 'categories' one chooses to group pots, there are always some left over. Most of those presented here are missing their bases and cannot therefore be placed in the basic division into round, ring- or flat base used here. Perhaps more to the point, most are ED I or II, and their classification as 'miscellaneous' reflects the fact that this is a predominantly ED III corpus. The two criteria for banishment to this section are not unconnected: ED I and ED II jars more often have round or slightly convex bases, which are more easily lost.

The majority of the ED I jars here have some form of decoration on the shoulder, a practice which barely survives into ED II: nos. 793-794, 796, 798, 800. No. 791, made of coarse, hand-moulded, lightly baked clay, is unusual both in form and manufacture. Such vessels are, however, common at this period in northern Mesopotamia, as observed in recent excavations near Eski Mosul. The lugs take a variety of forms.

Of the ED II jars, No. 790 has the flattened rim mentioned above (p. 126), and 794 and 798 have the sharply bevelled rim more typical of early ED jars. No. 794 could well have had a single handle, but there is too little left to be sure. The double row of neck-incision is also an early ED feature: ED III jars usually have only one row, though in ED IIIB double rows re-appear on upright-handled jars, albeit in different forms (for instance on no. 738 above).

No. 799 is probably a much under-represented type. Band-rims like this and other ED III rim forms of the same size order are common enough among sherds. The rather vague reserve-slip on the shoulder occurs more often on large shoulder-sherds at this date than on fragments of smaller vessels.

790. **5I88:41**
Room 190 fill (Batch 7109 + 7111)
Base missing, rest fragmentary.
Pink clay.
Cream slip.
Grit and white grit temper.
Pres. H. 9.4
Rim di. (reconstruc.) 9.0
[Postgate 1984:fig. 7. no. 4]

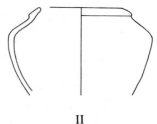

II

791. **2G36:81**
Large pit in West Mound
Level II (Batch 5608)
Pink clay.
Cream slip.
Rough grog temper.
Pres. H. 10.2
Rim di. c. 13.0
Two lugs preserved.
Hand-made.
[Postgate and Moon 1982:fig. 6 no. 6]

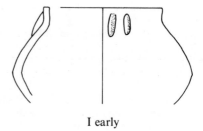

I early

792. **2G36:66** (AbS 2078)
Large pit in West Mound
Level II (Batch 5406)
Rim and shoulder only,
tiny piece of lower body.
Pinkish clay.
Cream slip out.
Grit and white grit temper.
Pres. H. 11.4
Rim di. c. 8.8
Combed decoration.

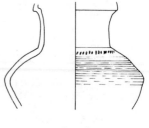

I early

793. **2G36:193** (Batch 5447)
Large Pit, West Mound Level II
Fragmentary: profile
of upper part only.
Pink clay.
Buff surface.
Temper of fine grit
including white grit.
Pres. H. c. 11.0
Rim di. c. 11.0
Horizontal reserve-
slip on shoulder.

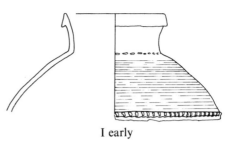

I early

794. **5IS:289**
Grave 193 (Batch 5385)
Very fragile and corroded: good
profile of rim and neck, non-
joining fragment provides
profile to below shoulder.
Red clay.
Sparse grit temper.
Proo. II. 9.3
Rim di. 12.0
Max. width (reconstruc.) 10.6

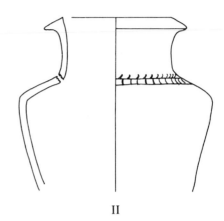

II

795. **2G36:192**
Large pit in West Mound
Level II (Batch 5408)
About a third of
neck and shoulder only.
Rim abraded.
Pink clay.
Yellowy surface out.
Grit and mica temper.
Pres. H. 15.0
Rim di. c. 17.0

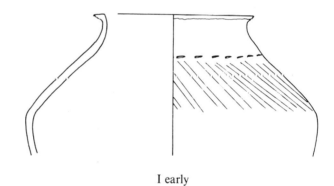

I early

796. **2G03:2**
West Mound
Room 8
(Batch 5803)
Base and
half rest
missing.
Pink clay.
Grit temper
including mica.
Pres. H. 21.0
Rim di. 14.0
Scraped down
inside and out.

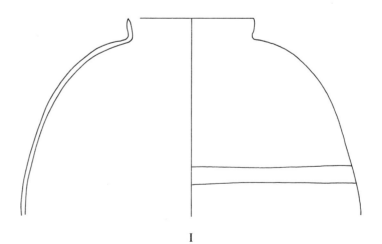

I

797. **5I31:31**
     Grave 81 (No. 18)
     Rim and part of shoulder only.
     Greenish clay.
     Grit temper.
     Pres. H. 15.3
     Rim di. 18.8
     Max. width 47.6

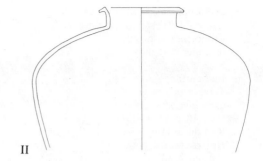

II

The recorded dimensions do not make sense and probably derive from trying to measure from the drawing instead of the pot, without knowing what scale it was drawn at. Unfortunately the pot is no longer extant and the scale of drawing not recorded. The probable dimensions are:
Pres. H. 15.3, rim di. 9.4, max. width 23.8, but they could be twice as great.

798. **2G36:41** (AbS 2077)
     Large pit in West Mound
     Level II (Batch 5403)
     Most of lower body and
     some of shoulder missing.
     Pink clay.
     Cream slip out.
     Fine mixed temper.
     Pres. H. 16.8
     Rim di. 11.4-11.6
     [Postgate and Moon
     1982:fig. 6 no. 6]        I early

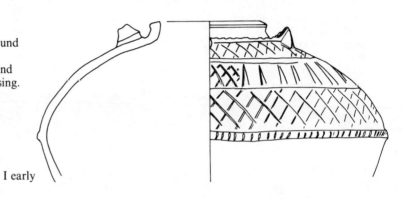

799. **No number**
     Room 50, below Level
     IB floor (Batch 257)
     Condition and
     ware unknown.
     Pres. H. 29.6
     Rim di. 16.0
     Max. width 43.2
     Scored slip on
     shoulder.

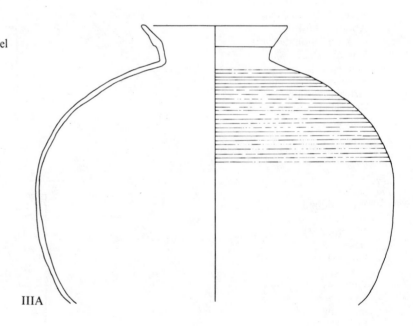

IIIA

800. **2G46:115** (AbS 2079)
Fill below ED I enclosure wall (5531)
Most of base, much of lower
body and some of rim missing.
Red clay.
Traces of cream slip.
Temper of grit and white grit.
Pres. H. 21.6
Rim di. 13.0
Max. width 25.0
Base smoke-blackened underneath.
Combed design with scraped line.
[Postgate and Moon 1982 fig. 6 no. 10]

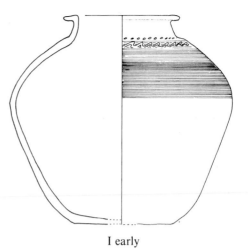

I early

# MINIATURE VESSELS

This section is not meant to be a collection of all pots under a certain size, but of those small vessels which seem to be a deliberate miniature version of a larger form. It must be admitted that larger forms are not in fact known for all of them.

Most miniatures are hand-made. Nos. 804 and 807 are the crudest, and are of the type found in such quantity in the Ash Tip (to be published separately, see p. 1), often no more than a piece of clay rolled into a ball and a finger stuck in to form a rough hollow. The size of the finger often indicates a very junior craftsman. Sometimes they do take more elaborate forms, including miniature upright-handled jars such as no. 809. These tiny vessels are frequently sun-dried rather than fired.

Nos. 805 and 806 are recognizable miniature forms of shapes familiar in larger sizes. No. 806 has the grooved shoulder and fine manufacture often associated with red paint bands on full-scale jars of this shape (see p. 89 above).

Nos. 802 and 803 could be clumsy attempts to represent jars with high ring-base (nos. 588-618 above), or they could be seen as specialised miniature form. Similar tiny jars occur at Ur (Woolley 1934 Pl. 266 no. 241).

Nos. 810 and 811 conform least well to the criteria outlined in the first paragraph, and perhaps such pots were always made in small sizes, as they were clearly intended to be hung up. Fragments like these are very rare on the site. The double tubular lug is common at Chuera (e.g. Kühne 1976 Pl. 40 no. 1).

As typified by these last two, miniature vessels occur throughout the Early Dynastic period, indeed at most periods, and seem to be ubiquitous. It would be naive to look for a single use for them all. No doubt some were merely children's toys, while others had a more serious purpose. Certainly the quantities found in the Ash Tip suggest a special reason for their being there.

801. **6G63:433**
 Pit in Room 61 (Batch 904)
 Rim and some of body missing.
 Reddish clay.
 Cream surface.
 Grit temper.
 Pres. H. 6.2
 Ba. di. 3.4
 Hand-made.

III

802. **6G76:77** (AbS 1583)
 Grave 130 (Batch 2606)
 Base missing.
 Red clay.
 Fine grit temper.
 Pres. H. 9.3
 Rim di. 3.5
 Max. width 6.2
 Hand-made or hand-finished.

III

803. **6G38:106** (AbS 760)
 Grave 51 (No. 6)
 Base missing.
 Ware unknown.
 H. 9.0
 Rim di. 5.2
 Hand-made.
 Shaved down near base.
 Hole either side of neck.
 [Postgate and Moorey 1976:fig. 8 no. 21]

IIIB

804. **6F05:144**
   Grave 183 fill (Batch 6012)
   Intact.
   Reddish buff clay.
   No obvious inclusions.
   H. 4.2
   Rim di. 1.5
   Max. width 3.3

IIIA

805. **6G75:196** (AbS 2024)
   Grave 162 upper fill (Batch 3627)
   Intact.
   Buff slip with red and grey patches.
   Grit temper.
   H. 6.6
   Rim di. 5.2-5.6
   Lower body scraped down.

IIIA-B

806. **6G37:198** (AbS 1174)
   Grave 80 (No. 2)
   Parts of rim
   and body missing.
   Pink clay.
   Cream slip.
   Very fine grit temper.
   H. 7.1
   Rim di. 3.9
   Lightly burnished out.
   Hand-made but very neat.

II

807. **2GS:281** (AbS 1757)
   2G98 subsurface (Batch 5181)
   Intact.
   Pinkish clay.
   Buff slip.
   Grit temper.
   H. 3.9
   Rim di. c. 3.0
   Difficult to say if wheel- or hand-made.
   [Postgate 1983:p. 85, fig. 292 and Pl. VIIf]

I

808. **6G47:130** (AbS 1625)
   Grave 129 (Batch 2563)
   Parts of rim and base missing.
   Pink clay.
   Surface shows differential firing.
   No temper.
   H. 6.5
   Rim di. 3.5
   Ba. di. 3.0
   Hand-made.
   Lightly fired if at all.

III

809. **6G64:225**
Grave 1 upper fill (Batch 24)
Handle only.
Buff clay.
Temper unknown.
H. 1.8
Width 2.1
Hand-made.
Lightly baked.
[Not included in Postgate 1985]

IIIA early

810. **6G54:350** (AbS 1274)
Sounding Level II floor (Batch 183)
Parts of rim and body missing.
Reddish clay.
Cream slip out.
Temper unknown.
H. 4.9
Rim di. 5.5
Max. width 9.7
Only one lug extant.
[Postgate 1977:fig. 5 no. 5]

I

811. **6G64:218** (AbS 396)
Grave 1 (No. 9)
Rim chipped, surface cracked.
Fine overfired clay.
Temper unknown.
H. 7.7
Rim di. 6.8
Two pairs of tubular lugs.
[Postgate and Moorey 1976:fig. 8 no. 20]

IIIA early

# STONE IMITATIONS

To consider a pottery vessel to be an imitation of stone is only a guess at the intention of its creator, but in the case of a pot like no. 812, with its many stone parallels, it is a reasonable probability (compare Delougaz 1952 Pl. 48 c and d). When jar no. 812 was found, members of the excavation team laid quite heavy bets on its being stone rather than clay as subsequently confirmed. It is unfortunate that our enthusiasm did not extend to recording the ware in more detail, but perhaps the anecdote serves the same end. Like stone vessels, the imitations undergo little change in shape during the ED period, at least at other sites. It happens that all our examples here were found in ED III contexts, but the smaller fragments could easily be derived.

The impressed decoration on nos. 814-820, apparently intended for inlaid fill, is found elsewhere, and the concentric circle pattern seems to have been popular (e.g. McCown et al 1978 Pl.47 no. 3). The fragments nos. 817 and 818 must have belonged to an elongated shape, perhaps like an example known from Kish (Mackay 1929 Pl. XLV no. 5).

812. **4I09:100** (AbS 1207)
Grave 82 (No. 2)
Intact but salted.
Green clay.
Perhaps originally burnished.
Temper unknown.
H. 9.1
Rim di. 7.8
Contained bone 4I09:191

III

813. **6G37:197** (AbS 1175)
Room 104, cut in south-
east corner (Batch 529)
Part of rim and body missing.
Buff clay.
Cream slip out.
Very fine grit temper.
H. 7.4
Rim di. 6.0
Ba. di. 3.8-4.3

III

814. **6G36:172** (AbS 1796)
Grave 127 (Batch 2463)
About one third pre-
served, including base.
Pink clay.
Cream slip.
Grit temper.
Pres. H. 4.8
Single vertically pierced lug, perhaps four
originally as undecorated area near lug is repeated
about a quarter of the way round near break.

IIIA-B

815. **6G37:56** (AbS 692)
Grave 37 (No. 7)
About a quarter preserved, no base.
Greyish brown clay.
Sparse grit temper.
Pres. H. 7.9
White inlay in incisions.
Probably two lugs originally.

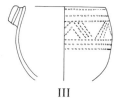

III

816. **6G46:10** (AbS 1426)
    Grave 62 (No. 5)
    Rim missing.
    Buff clay.
    Cream slip.
    Temper unknown.
    H. 8.0
    Max. width 9.5
    Hand-made.
    Finger-impressions on
    base give dimpled effect.

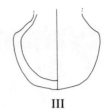

III

817. **6G65:320**
    Pit south of Room 49 (Batch 216)
    Fragment only, of upper part.
    Green clay.
    Veg. temper.
    Pres. H. 7.3
    Impressed circles and punched dots.
    Probably wheel-thrown.

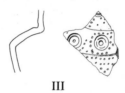

III

818. **6G76:850**
    Ash Tip (Batch 2667)
    Fragments only.
    Brown clay.
    Temper of sparse fine veg.
    Pres. H. 6.6
    Outer surface burnished.

IIIB

819. **6G74:92** (AbS 1021)
    Rooms 51 and 53 fill (Batch 609)
    Fragment only, surface eroded.
    Red clay.
    Vague cream slip out.
    Sandy grit temper.
    Pres. H. 3.5
    Rim di. c. 5.3
    Punched decoration in vertical
    rows, perhaps made with comb.

III

820. **6G62:30** (AbS 1247)
    Pit in Room 65 (Batch 2203)
    Grey clay.
    Temper unknown.
    3.0 x 2.8
    Impressed squares and circles.

III

# MISCELLANEOUS DECORATED FRAGMENTS

Notwithstanding our avowed intention to leave sherds for a future publication (p. 1), there are a few which merit special exemption.

Fragments of clay snake (like nos. 821-822) turn up occasionally on most parts of the site, none so far attached to their parent vessels.

Incised pieces like nos. 823 and 824, which do not belong to any of the standard decorated forms such as stemmed dishes or stone imitations are rare.

The polychrome sherd no. 825 is definitely Scarlet Ware, identical in colour and painting technique to specimens from the Lower Diyala and Hamrin regions. It is difficult to demonstrate this diagnosis without coloured illustration, but it is hoped that a sample will undergo neutron activation soon to try and determine whether the pot actually came from further north or in fact represents local production of a kind of pottery quite alien to the southern Sumerian assemblage.

821. **6G64:984** (AbS 1562)
Sounding Level II (Batch 2733)
Spout only.
Dark red clay.
Cream slip out.
Grit and veg. temper.
6.8 x 1.2 (mouth of spout)
Circles made with quill or
similar tubular implement.

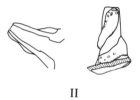

II

822. **5I10:48** (AbS 403)
Room 2 fill (Batch 1010)
Pink clay.
Cream slip out.
Fine grit including mica.
c. 15.2 x 9.2
Snake decorated with spots
incised with quill or similar.

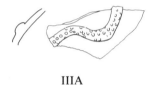

IIIA

823. **6G54:103**
Ash Pit cutting Room 44 (Batch 116)
Fragment only.
Fine hard red clay.
Temper unknown.
Pres. H. 4.4
Rim di. 8.0
One hole extant.

IIIB?

824. **6G63:106** (AbS 1117)
Room 61 fill (Batch 920)
Ware unknown.
9.8 x 3.5

III

825. **6G64:647** (AbS 759)
Grave 2 fill (Batch 17)
Sherds of near-horizontal
shoulder including edge of neck.
Buff clay.
White slip.
Fine grit and veg. temper including mica.
c. 15.2 x 9.3
Red and black paint; the red areas have been outlined
first then filled in – the usual Scarlet Ware technique.
Non-joining sherd from lower body shows this was red-washed.
[Not included in Postgate 1985]

I

# ENIGMATIC FORMS

826. **2GS:216** (AbS 1483)
2G27 sub-surface (Batch 5127)
Complete but for
?base, and perhaps spout.
Overfired hard green clay.
Grit temper.
Pres. H. 8.8
Di. at top c. 13.0
[Postgate 1978:fig. 3
no. 8, and 1983:fig. 290
and Pl. VIIc]

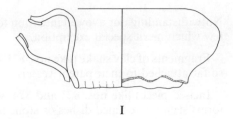

I

As the published illustrations of this unusual form vary somewhat it is worth a detailed description: it consists of a hollow circular tube with a single round opening on the outside. The opening is lined with a thin strip of clay as are the openings of spouted-jars where the spout fits on. The rough ridge around the vessel suggests it was once attached to something else, perhaps a base of some kind.

827. **6G37:547** (AbS 1756)
Room 102 floors
against north wall
(Batch 596)
About half extant.
Red clay.
Grit temper.
H. 20.8
Rim di. 25.5
Ba. di. 35.5
Probably four
lugs originally.

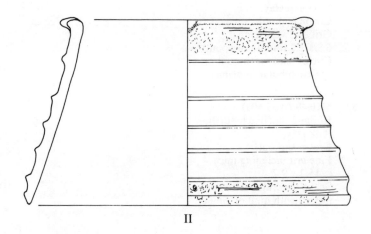

II

Both ends are coated in bitumen which bears what are either string-impressions or the imprints of hair pressed on by string i.e. perhaps hide. Could the vessel have been used as a drum?

# APPENDIX A

*Vessels not included*

The following specific vessels fall within the scope of this volume but are not included, mostly because they require further work which it has not yet been possible to do. For classes of vessels generally excluded see p. 1.

**1T:58** (AbS 1770), bowl, Grave 138.
**5I21:103** (AbS 693), bowl, Grave 26 (No. 38).
**5I21:124** (AbS 676), spouted jar, Grave 26 (No. 19).
**5I21:264** (AbS 906), spouted jar, Room 4 fill.
**6G36:241** (AbS 1769), spouted jar, Grave 116.
**6G38:104** (AbS 1031), jar, Grave 51 (No. 10).
**6G54:69**   spouted jar, Grave 48 (No. 15).
**6G55:66** (AbS 503), stemmed dish, surface.
**6G56:55** (AbS 1272), small jar, pit in Room 57.
**6G62:11** (AbS 1082), spouted jar, Grave 61 (No. 11).
**6G63:129** (AbS 1100), small jar with high ring-base, Grave 75 (No. 2).
**6G64:207** (AbS 905), cooking pot, Grave 2 (No. 22).
**6G64:527** (AbS 598), spouted jar, Grave 1 (No. 68).
**6G64:586** (AbS 700), spouted jar, (Grave 1 No. 85).
**6G64:593** (AbS 820), spouted jar, Grave 1 (No. 74).
**6G64:600** (AbS 815), spouted jar, Grave 1 (No. 78).
**6G64:606** (AbS 573), spouted jar, Grave 1 (No. 87).
**6G65:263** (AbS 1043), coarse vessel, cut in Rooms 47 and 49.
**6G74:54** (AbS 621), small jar with high ring-base, Grave 45 (not included in Postgate 1985).
**8GS:14** (AbS 1472), spouted jar, Grave 110.

# APPENDIX B

*A Summary of the Chronology of Abu Salabikh*
The excavations up to the end of the 1983 season suggest the following interpretation of the chronology of the site.

*The Outlying Mounds*
The West Mound has occupation of the ED I and Uruk periods, the latter including material we take to be contemporary with levels XIV to XI of the Innana sounding at Nippur, otherwise known as 'Jamdat Nasr'. Both Uruk and ED sherds are represented in surface work. Stratified deposits from actual excavation in 2G36 and 2G46 are termed 'Early ED I' from features such as the brick lays and the presence of cut-ware. Level I is the latest-preserved building level, of which little survives, Level II is the main excavated level, and Level III encompasses all pre-ED levels. There is an architectural gap between Levels II and III. These terms are not connected with Levels I, II and III anywhere else on the site.

Occupation on the North-East Mound is ED I as far as investigated, possibly running into ED II, and with a few ED III graves. Material from square OUS was exposed by machinery working on irrigation ditching and is isolated from controlled excavation.

*The Main Mound – Area E*
Three major building levels have been recognized during excavation of the large public building on Area E. Level I is ED III. Specifically, Level IC is taken as early ED IIIA, and Level IB is later IIIA. Little remains of 1A, but it could be ED IIIB, and some of the later graves and other intrusions into Area E are certainly IIIB, one or two perhaps later still (for instance Grave 198). The Ash Pit which destroyed the middle of the Level I Southern Unit building is IIIB. The Ash Tip, outside the building, was deposited during late ED III phases of its occupation, now eroded, but also contains a certain amount of derived earlier material.

Level III is known only from soundings and seems to be ED I. Level II, an earlier version of the main public building is little investigated so far, but must be at least partly ED II.

The Eastern Houses in 6G37 and 6G38 are ED II, their latest surviving phase perhaps ED IIIA.

*Main Mound – Area A*
The main building level on Area A is Level II, which is early ED IIIA. Level I is later ED IIIA. Trenches in 4I87 and 4I97 through the North-West Building made it possible to distinguish various phases of its north wall and Room 50: phase 4 is ED II, phase 3 is ED II-early IIIA, phases 2 and 1 are later IIIA.

Levels I, II, and III of Area A are not the same as I, II, and III of Area E.

The deep sounding in 5I31 goes back to ED I.

*Main Mound – Other Areas*
Surface work on the east slope of the mound between Areas A and E shows that the latest preserved levels there are mostly ED II. Excavation in 5I has produced material from houses and graves of this date. Work on the large enclosure walls in 5I78 and 5I79 penetrated ED I levels.

Grave 110 in 8G was found by a bulldozer and is not related to the rest of the excavation.

*Grave 38*
Grave 38 presents a dating enigma in that it contains some pottery of apparently conflicting dates, and a lot of pottery very difficult to date at all. The more glaring inconsistencies include a plain upright-handled jar unlikely to be later than ED II (no. 684 above); a spouted jar and a bottle that are also probably ED II (nos. 613 and 315); an upright handle with ED IIIA pinnate motif (no. 789); an ED III ring-based jar (no. 554); and remnants of a four-piece set presumably ED IIIA like others such. Some conical bowls (Grave 38 Nos. 34-39) are of proportions most common in ED II; Grave 38 No. 40 seems much later.

In the catalogue I have dated each vessel from this grave according to its individual merits. Perhaps the assemblage represents a unique meeting point of styles; or perhaps our understanding of the dating of ED pottery is more incomplete than we suspected; or perhaps the context is just confused. The grave was in fact thoroughly robbed, so anything is possible.

*Further Information*
More detailed information on stratigraphy and dating is divided among earlier reports as
follows.

Postgate and
Moorey 1976:     General description of the site and its location.
Area A, Rooms 1-9, 11-13, Levels I and II.
Area E, Rooms 30, 38-41, 44-51, Levels I and II.
Ash Tip and Ash Pit.

Postgate 1977:     Area A, as above plus Rooms 20-24, 26-33,
Deep sounding in 5I31.
Area E, Rooms 16, 23, 37, 39, 41, 47, 50-52, 56-
57, 60-62, 66-69. Also Eastern Houses (Rooms 101-106, 110-115).
Deep Sounding in 6G54.

Postgate 1978:     North-East Mound, rescue work.
Ash Tip.

Postgate 1980:     Area E, Rooms 32, 35, 36, 42, 47, 71, 73, 74, 75;
also Eastern Houses (Rooms 50-55, 102-104, 110,
119-120).
Deep Sounding in 6G64.
North-East Mound, controlled excavation.

Postgate
and Moon 1982:     West Mound, excavation.
Area E, Rooms 50, 53, 55, 58, 79-87,
90-96.
Surface clearance in 5I.

Postgate 1983:     West Mound, surface clearance, including pottery.

Postgate 1984:     Area E, Room 58 (stratigraphic link of Central
and South-East complexes).
Area A, Rooms 23, 24, 28, 29,
50, (stratigraphy of the North-West Building back
to ED II).
Excavation in 5I, Rooms 190, 192-193, 195.
Large Enclosure Walls in 5I78 and 79.
Surface clearance of 5H and 6H.

Postgate 1985:     Graves 1-99.

N.B. This volume is *not* consistently referred to in the catalogue, as so much repetition would be
involved. All further details of objects and provenance relating to these graves should be sought
there.

Preliminary information on Graves 100 onwards is currently distributed as follows:

Grave 100, Postgate 1977:295
      110,       1978:78-80
      116,       1980:95
      130,       1980:94
      149,       1980:95
      158,       1980:94
      162, Postgate and Moon 1982:133-136, and Postgate 1984:95-97
      176, Postgate and Moon 1982:130-131
      183,          1982:131
      185,          1982:124-125
      193,          1982:123-124, and Postgate 1984:101
      196, 201, 203, 205, 207, 210, Postgate 1984:103

# APPENDIX C

*Explanation of the catalogue entries*

All vessels are wheel-thrown unless otherwise stated.

*The Numbers*
The numbering system is fully explained in Postgate 1985 (p. 18), briefly summarized here.

The number in bold type is the object number given on site, unique to that particular vessel. These mostly take the form e.g. **6G64:90**. That would be the 90th object recovered from the 10 metre square 6G64 on the site grid. (As so much surface-stripping takes place at Abu Salabikh it is sometime impractical to record in 10 metre squares, so numbers take the form e.g. **5IS:60**. That would be the 60th object recovered from the 100 metre square 5I, usually from the surface.)

Some pots have an additional number with the form e.g. AbS 788. These have been deposited in the Iraq Museum and given a running number as required by the Iraqi authorities. The example would be the 788th object from Abu Salabikh placed in the Iraq Museum, as opposed to temporary storage on site.

The Batch number refers to the particular unit of excavated earth from which the vessel came, ideally a real archaeological feature such as a pit or hearth or floor. In practice such features are often excavated as several batches, and sometimes a batch accidentally includes elements of more than one feature. The Batch number is given here simply for reference, and the context it refers to is explained separately. In the case of pots from Grave 1-99 the Batch number is omitted as superfluous and instead the number in brackets following the grave number is that used in Postgate 1985, where all further details of provenance can be found.

One or two pots have no number or no Batch number. This is simply an oversight which it is too late to rectify.

*The Drawings and the Condition*
A number of draughtsmen of differing skills and opinions have worked on Abu Salabikh pottery, and for the sake of maximum accuracy inconsistencies of style have generally been retained if the vessel in question has not been re-examined. It is important to state the condition so that the reader can judge the likelihood of reconstructions. Any elements of doubt should be apparent from the description.

'Intact' means the vessel was found that way. 'Complete' means it was found in pieces and restored. These terms refer to the original condition, not that in which the pot may be found now. Most objects from Abu Salabikh have suffered to some extent from salt action, so this is not mentioned unless it has affected the reconstruction.

*The Ware*
The fabric of Abu Salabikh pottery is perhaps its most neglected aspect so far. It has not been possible to carry out systematic informed observation of each vessel. Indeed, until Siriol Mynors began a petrological study of some of the material in 1981, hardly any attempt had been made to record the tempering material, hence the large number of entries 'temper unknown'. In mitigation it might be said that the ED wares were certainly very uniform (many more differences were noticed among the Uruk pottery) and their description deemed a low priority. Further detail must await the publication of Ms. Mynors' report.

'Vegetable' temper is chopped straw or chaff – it is not usually possible to distinguish.

Unless otherwise stated the surface of the vessel is the same colour as the core. The term 'slip' is used only when it was obvious to the naked eye that a separate layer had been applied, otherwise 'surface' is not further elaborated. Whether in such cases the colour differences between core and surface are caused by self-slip (wet-smoothing), true slip, or just firing conditions is not known.

*Measurements*
These are to the nearest millimetre, and no more accurate than it is possible to be with a plastic ruler. Different people often come up with slightly different versions of the dimensions of a pot.

The height is taken as a single measurement at the topmost surviving point of the vessel.

Rim diameter is measured across the highest points of the rim. Many rims are in fact oval not round. In the case of incomplete vessels the diameter is obtained by placing the surviving section on a diameter chart, the result is prefixed with *circa* and is accurate to the nearest half centimetre at best. If too little survives even for that, the approximate measurement can sometimes be gained from a reconstructed drawing, in which case it is described here as 'reconstructed'.

The base diameter is taken as the distance across the lowest points of a ring-base, or the edges of the lowest carination in the case of a flat base.

*Cataloguing problems*
Ring-bases are normally made by attaching a separate ring of clay to the base of the vessel; they may subsequently be finger-pinched, producing a puckered effect. Occasionally they are made by pulling clay directly out of the bottom of the pot; this often, but not invariably, causes the same puckered effect. Sometimes the exact method of fixing has not been recorded, and from an entry in the field catalogue 'pinched ring-base' one cannot be sure whether the ring was first added or not.

An added ring often contains more vegetable temper than the fabric of the pot. I have translated the common entry in the field catalgoue 'coarse ring-base' as 'base added, presumably in vegetable-tempered clay', as this has turned out to be so in every case I have been able to check.

As with the drawing of the pots, many different hands contributed to the cataloguing of them. Some people, for example, have gone into detail with colour descriptions while others have been brief. Apart from the points mentioned above the differences have been left if I have not been able to see the pot again.

*Abbreviations used in the catalogue*

| | |
|---|---|
| approx. | approximately |
| ba. | base |
| c. | circa |
| di. | diameter |
| ED | Early Dynastic |
| FI | Fire Installation (hearth, kiln, etc.) |
| frag. | fragment |
| h. | height |
| incl. | including |
| max. | maximum |
| N. | north |
| no. | number |
| p. | page |
| pres. | preserved |
| prob. | probably |
| reconstruc. | reconstructed |
| S. | south |
| veg. | vegetable |

# APPENDIX D

*Group of associated vessels*

*Four piece sets from graves*

*Grave 1*
No. 168  Large bowl
No. 123  Sieve bowl
No. 134  Tiny open vessel
No. 305  Sieve stand

*Grave 26*
No. 155  Large bowl
No. 66    Conical bowl with hole in base
No. 129  Tiny open vessel
No. 304  Sieve stand

*Grave 28*
No. 167  Large bowl
No. 120  Sieve bowl
No. 128  Tiny open vessel
No. 296  Sieve stand

*Grave 42*
No. 159  Large bowl
No. 127  Sieve bowl
No. 130  Tiny open vessel
No. 295  Sieve stand

*Grave 48*
No. 164  Large bowl
No. 124  Sieve bowl
No. 131  Tiny open vessel
No. 301  Sieve stand

*Grave 96*
No. 157  Large bowl
No. 119  Sieve bowl
No. 135  Tiny open vessel
No. 298  Sieve stand

*Grave 182*
No. 163  Large bowl
No. 125  Sieve bowl
No. 136  Tiny open vessel
No. 297  Sieve stand

The following disturbed graves contained either one or two members of what may well have been a complete set: 2, 38, 49, 54, 73, 95, 118, 143, 162, 171.

*Other associated groups*

*Room 111, late floors*
No. 634        Spouted jar
No. 481        Flat-based jar
Not included  Large jar, perhaps upright-handled (6G38:151)

*West Mound Room 8*
No. 715        Single-lugged jar
No. 716        Single-lugged jar
No. 611        Ring-base jar

*Inside storage jar No. 443*
No. 56        Conical bowl
No. 69        Conical bowl
No. 679        Spouted jar

# BIBLIOGRAPHY

Delougaz, P.
1952

*Pottery from the Diyala Region* (Chicago, Oriental Institute Publications, Vol. 63).

Finkbeiner, U.
1985

'Uruk – Warka XXXVII. Survey des Stadtgebietes von Uruk. Vorläufiger Bericht über die 3.Kampagne 1984', *Bagdader Mitteilungen* 16, 17-58.

Fujii, H. (ed.)
1981

Preliminary report of excavations at Gubba and Songor (*al Rafidān* Vol. II).

Gibson, M. (ed.)
1981

*Uch Tepe I: Tell Razuk, Tell Ahmed al-Mughir, Tell Ajamat* (Chicago and Copenhagen).

Kühne, H.
1976

*Die Keramik vom Tell Chuēra und ihre Beziehungen zu Funden aus Syrien-Palästina, der Türkei und dem Iraq* (Berlin, Vorderasiatische Forschungen der Max Freiherr von Oppenheim Stiftung, 1).

Lebeau, M.
1985

Rapport préliminaire sur la séquence céramique du chantier B de Mari (IIIè millénaire), *Mari, Annales de Recherches Interdisciplinaires* 4, 93-126 (Paris).

Mackay, E.
1925

*Report on the Excavation of the 'A' Cemetery at Kish, Mesopotamia* (Chicago, Field Museum of Natural History, Anthropology Memoirs Vol. 1 No. 1).

1929

*A Sumerian Palace and the 'A' Cemetery at Kish, Mesopotamia* (Chicago, Field Museum of Natural History, Anthropology Memoirs Vol. 1 No. 2).

McCown, D. et al
1978

*Nippur II: The North Temple and Sounding E* (Chicago, Oriental Institute Publications 97).

Moon, J.A.
1981

'Some new Early Dynastic Pottery from Abu Salabikh', *Iraq* 43, 47-75.

1982

'The distribution of upright-handled jars and stemmed dishes in the Early Dynastic period', *Iraq* 44, 36-69.

1985

Some Introductory Remarks on the Pottery (Postgate 1985, 6-10).

Parrot, A.
1956

*Mission archéologique de Mari, I: Le Temple d'Ishtar* (Paris, Institut Français d'Archéologie de Beyrouth, Bibliotheque archéologique et historique, tome 65).

1967

*Mission archéologique de Mari, III: Les Temples d'Ishtarat et de Ninni-Zaza* (Paris, Institut Français d'Archéologie de Beyrouth, Bibliotheque archéologique et historique, tome 86).

Postgate, J.N.
1977

'Excavations at Abu Salabikh, 1976', *Iraq* 39, 269-299.

1978

'Excavations at Abu Salabikh, 1977', *Iraq* 40, 77-86.

1980

'Excavations at Abu Salabikh, 1978-79', *Iraq* 43, 87-104.

1983

*Abu Salabikh Excavations Volume 1: The West Mound Surface Clearance* (London).

1984

'Excavations at Abu Salabikh, 1983', *Iraq* 46, 95-113.

Postgate, J.N. (ed.)
    1985                    *Abu Salabikh Excavations Volume 2: Graves 1 to 99* (London).

Postgate, J.N. &
Moon, J.A.
    1982                    'Excavations at Abu Salabikh, 1981,' *Iraq* 44, 103-136.

Postgate, J.N. &
Moorey, P.R.S.
    1976                    'Excavations at Abu Salabikh, 1975', *Iraq* 38, 133-169.

Rumayidh, S.
    1981                    'Initial results of the excavations at Tell Chawkhah' (Jokha), *Sumer* Vol. 37,
                            112-131 (Arabic section).

Woolley, C.L.
    1934                    *The Royal Cemetery: A Report on the Pre-dynastic and Sargonid Graves
                            Excavated Between 1926 and 1931* (London and Philadelphia, Ur Excavations
                            Vol. 2).

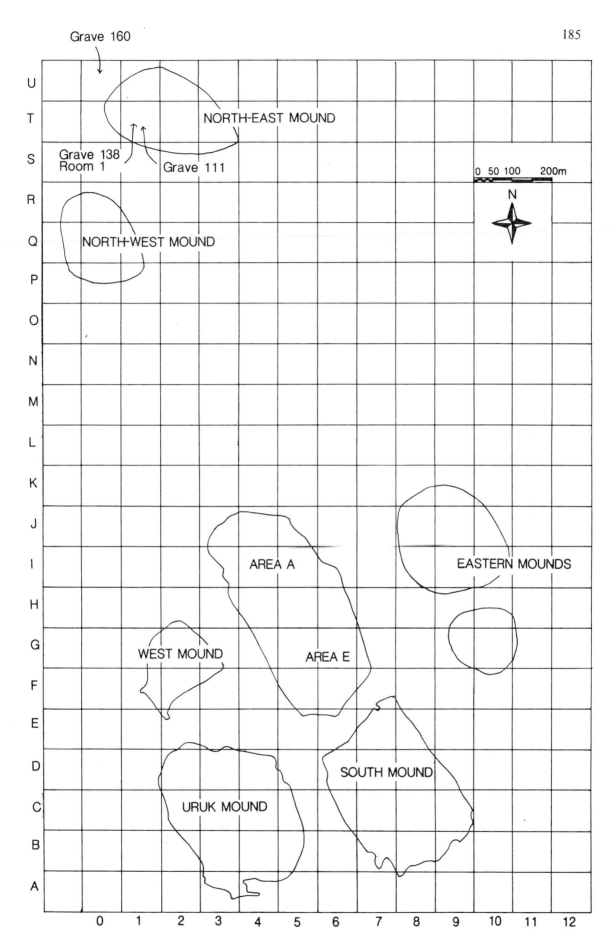

Fig. 1.   The site of Abu Salabikh showing outlying mounds.

*N.B.*   Figures 1–5 are intended as a guide to the locations and provenances mentioned in the text, and are subject to revision. Architectural details in particular are not necessarily complete.

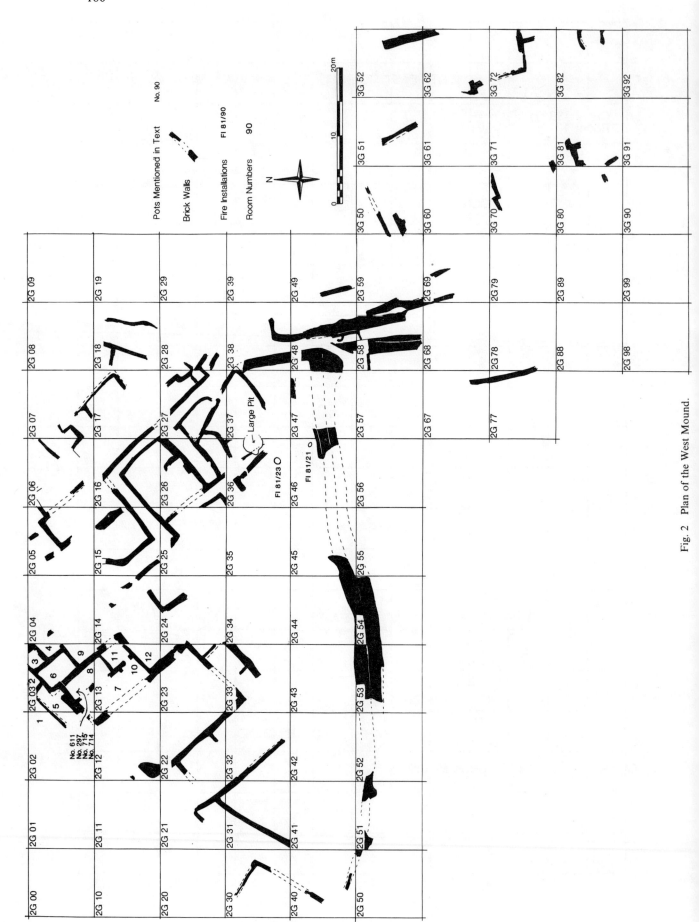

Fig. 2  Plan of the West Mound.

Fig.3. Main Mound: plan of Area A.

188

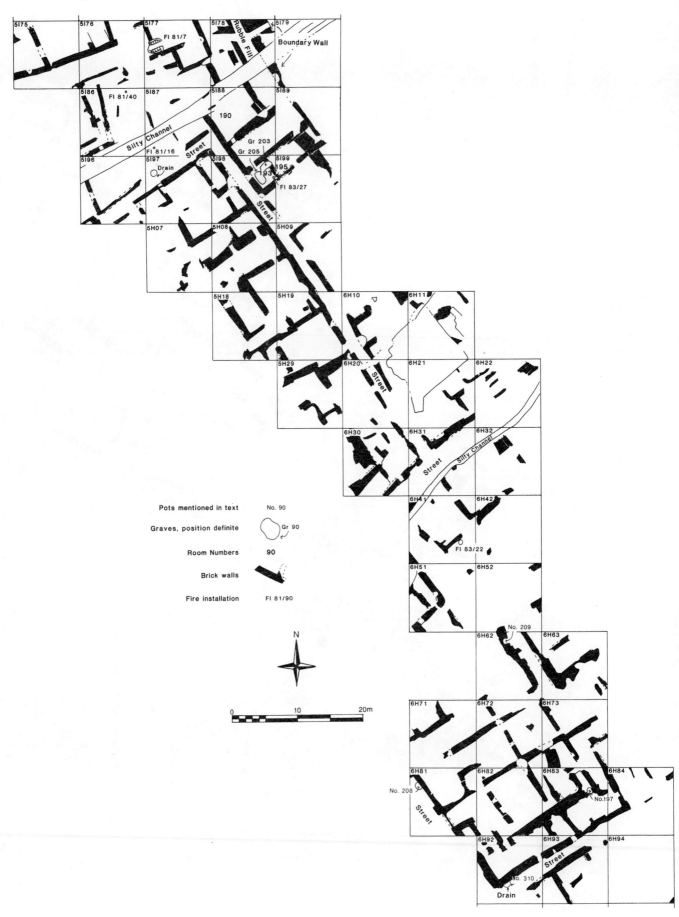

Fig. 4.   Main Mound: plan of the east side between Areas A and E.

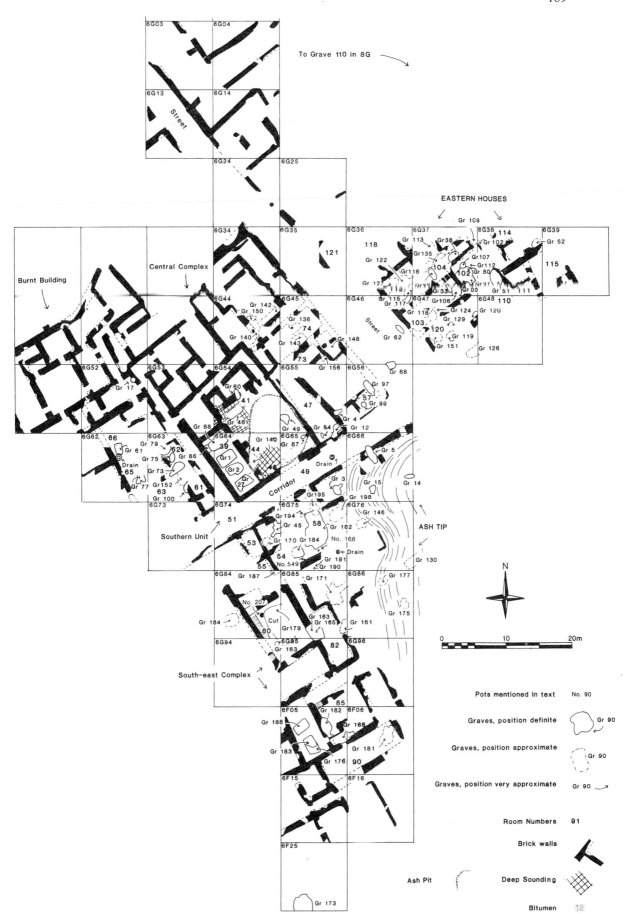

Fig. 5  Main Mound: plan of Area E.

*PLATE* I

*a.* Moulded bowl No. 142.

*b.* Small painted jar No. 363.

*PLATE* II

b. Spouted jar No. 706.

a. Spouted jar No. 696.

*PLATE* III

*a.* Jar with four rim tabs No. 332.

*b.* Nos. 444 and 443 *in situ*.

*PLATE* IV

*b.* Coarse bowl No. 197.

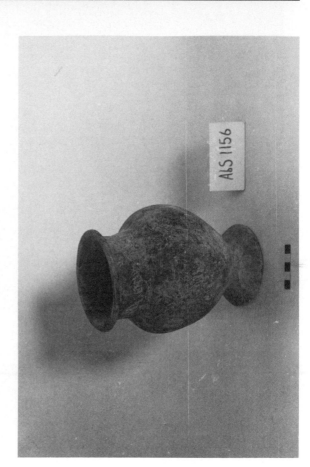

*d.* Ring-based jar No. 573.

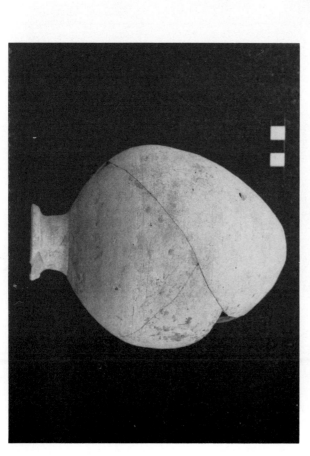

*a.* Large bottle No. 324.

*c.* Footed jar No. 600.